Our God is a co

Be
HOLY
AND
Come Near

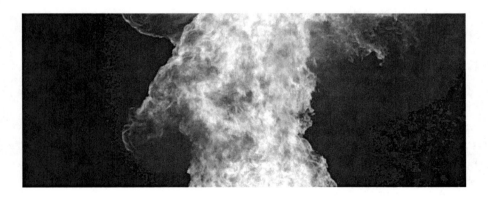

◈ A Devotional Study of Leviticus ◈

Warren Henderson

All Scripture quotations are from the New King James Version of the Bible, unless otherwise noted. Copyright © 1982 by Thomas Nelson, Inc. Nashville, TN

Be Holy and Come Near
– A Devotional Study of Leviticus
By Warren Henderson
Copyright © 2015

Cover Design: Ben Bredaweg
Cover Photo: © Pancaketom/Dreamstime.com:
    Pillar of Fire
Editing/Proofreading: Randy Amos,
    Kathleen Henderson, David Lindstrom,
    and Dan Macy

Published by Warren A. Henderson
3769 Indiana Road
Pomona, KS 66076

Perfect Bound ISBN 978-1-939770-28-8
eBook ISBN 978-1-939770-29-5

ORDERING INFORMATION:
Gospel Folio Press
Phone 1-905-835-9166
E-mail: order@gospelfolio.com
Also available in many online retail stores

Other Books by the Author

Afterlife – What Will It Be Like?
Answer the Call – Finding Life's Purpose
Behold the Saviour
Be Angry and Sin Not
Conquest and the Life of Rest – A Devotional Study of Joshua
Exploring the Pauline Epistles
Forsaken, Forgotten, and Forgiven – A Devotional Study of Jeremiah
Glories Seen & Unseen
Hallowed Be Thy Name – Revering Christ in a Casual World
Hiding God – The Ambition of World Religion
In Search of God – A Quest for Truth
Knowing the All-Knowing
Managing Anger God's Way
Mind Frames – Where Life's Battle Is Won or Lost
Out of Egypt – A Devotional Study of Exodus
Overcoming Your Bully
Passing the Torch – Mentoring the Next Generation
Revive Us Again – A Devotional Study of Ezra and Nehemiah
Seeds of Destiny – A Devotional Study of Genesis
The Bible: Myth or Divine Truth?
The Evil Nexus – Are You Aiding the Enemy?
The Fruitful Bough – Affirming Biblical Manhood
The Fruitful Vine – Celebrating Biblical Womanhood
The Hope of Glory – A Preview of Things to Come
The Olive Plants – Raising Spiritual Children
Your Home the Birthing Place of Heaven

Preface

The Pentateuch is one continuing storyline which ultimately reaches its typological climax in the subsequent book of Joshua. Notice how the following prepositions form a mini-outline of these six books. In Genesis, sin brought man *down*. In Exodus, he is redeemed by blood and brought *out* of the world. In Leviticus, man is permitted to come *near* (but not too close) to God in worship by substitutional sacrifices. In Numbers, man is guided *through* trials and is refined for service. In Deuteronomy, which means "Second Law," man is brought *back* to remember his responsibility to the Lord and the consequences of rebellion. In Joshua, the redeemed people are led by Joshua through the Jordan River *into* victorious living as they seize their inheritance.

In Exodus, God's covenant people had been redeemed by the blood of the Passover lamb and delivered from both bondage and Egypt. The book of Leviticus then reveals two central truths concerning Jehovah's new beginning with His people: they were permitted to come near to worship Him through blood atonement and they must be a holy people, for their God is holy. To this end, the book can be divided into two thematic sections: The Way to Approach God (chps. 1-16), and The Walk of Holiness Before God (chps. 17-27). The first division contains four major sections: The Sacrifices (chps. 1-7), The Cleansing and Institution of the Priesthood (chps. 8-10), The Laws of Cleanliness (chps. 11-15), and The Day of Atonement (chp. 16). The second division is also composed of four major sections: The Law of the Sacrifice (chp. 17), The Laws of Personal Holiness (chps. 18-22), The Feasts of Jehovah (chp. 23), Miscellaneous Laws, Warnings, and Promises (chps. 24-27).

The first Hebrew word of the Leviticus text, *qara'*, which means "to call out" (1:1), introduces us to the theme of the book. Jehovah is calling His people to come near to Him, but they must be cleansed from defilement to do so – they must be holy. Other key words or phrases in Leviticus include: "holy/holiness," "blood," "atone/atonement," "offering," "sacrifice," "clean/unclean," "sin," "priest(s)," "before the Lord," and "eighth." The suggested key verse is Leviticus 20:26: *"You shall be holy to Me, for I the Lord am holy, and have separated you from the peoples, that you should be Mine."* Leviticus shows us that holiness has two main components: our separation from sin and our commitment to the glory of God. God is holy and He wants His people to come near Him in holiness but only through His means of purification.

The writer of Hebrew confirms this same reality in the Church Age:

Let us have grace, by which we may serve God acceptably with reverence and godly fear. For our God is a consuming fire (Heb. 12:28-29).

Let us therefore come boldly to the throne of grace, that we may obtain mercy and find grace to help in time of need (Heb. 4:16).

Brethren, having boldness to enter the Holiest by the blood of Jesus, by a new and living way which He consecrated for us ... let us draw near with a true heart in full assurance of faith, having our hearts sprinkled from an evil conscience and our bodies washed with pure water (Heb. 10:19-23)

There is a danger of forgetting that the Bible reveals, not first the love of God, but the intense, blazing holiness of God, with His love as the center of that holiness.

— Oswald Chambers

God invites believers in the Church Age to come near Him, but only as redeemed and cleansed by the blood of the Lord Jesus Christ; this is what is symbolized by the various offerings in Leviticus.

Be Holy and *Come Near* is a "commentary style" devotional which upholds the glories of Christ while exploring the book of Leviticus within the context of the whole of Scripture. I have endeavored to include in this book some of the principal gleanings from other writers. *Be Holy* and *Come Near* contains dozens of brief devotions. This format allows the reader to use the book either as a daily devotional or as a reference source for deeper study.

— Warren Henderson

Understanding the Levitical Types

God understands our natural limitations to comprehend spiritual and eternal matters. As a declaration of grace to us, He exercised various literary forms in the Old Testament, including word pictures, prophecies, shadows, types, allegories, symbols, and plain language, to anticipate the revelation of His supreme gift of love to the world – His own Son. These word pictures prepared humanity to both recognize Christ and freely accept His offer of salvation when He arrived. Consequently, a thorough study of Leviticus, which has a central theme of divine communion with man through blood atonement, cannot fail to display these literary forms of revelation. Of particular interest throughout the book is the Holy Spirit's usage of *types*.

By the word *type*, we simply mean a picture, figure, or pattern that reflects something or someone in reality (which is the antitype). The word "type" or "print" comes from the Greek word *tupos*. It is used to speak of the nail "print" in the Lord's hand (John 20:25) and of the tabernacle furniture which was to be fashioned according to the "pattern" given Moses in the mount (Heb. 8:5). Thomas said he would not believe that the Lord had been raised up unless he saw and felt the print of the nails in the Lord's hands. In other words, the pattern left in the Lord's hand would match the nail, yet it was not the nail. However, the print furnished evidence of what the nail was like (size and shape). Likewise, Scripture is saturated with "types" of Christ. These offer evidence of Christ, but are not Christ. There is no perfect "type" or "pattern," or it would be the real thing. Therefore, all types, foreshadowings, symbols, analogies, and patterns are inadequate to express fully and completely every aspect of His person and work.

Biblical typology has perhaps suffered more at the hands of overzealous theologians than by those who would undermine its proper use. Though a hermeneutical defense of this interpretative method is beyond the scope of this book, a fundamental understanding of its proper use in Scripture is important. John Walvoord offers this concise definition of *typology*:

> A *type* may be defined as an exceptional Old Testament reality which was specially ordained by God effectively to prefigure a single New Testament redemptive truth.[1]
>
> Typology is thus a form of prophetic statement. It differs from prophecy in that it may be discerned as typological only after its fulfillment is known. Once this antitype is revealed, one may look back and see that certain expressions and images have meanings besides the historical experience.[2]

F. W. Grant acknowledges the proper use of and, indeed, need for typology to understand the fullness of what God has revealed to mankind through Scripture:

> Some would have us stop where the inspired explanation stops. But in that case, how large a part of what is plainly symbolical would be lost to us! – the larger part of the Levitical ordinances, not a few of the parables of the Lord Himself, and almost the whole of the book of Revelation. Surely none could deliberately accept a principle which would lock up from us so large a part of the inspired Word.
>
> Still many have the thought that it would be safer to refrain from typical applications of the historical portions where no inspired statement authenticates them as types at all. Take, however, such a history as that of Joseph, which no direct Scripture speaks of as a type, yet the common consent of almost all receive it as such; or Isaac's sacrifice, of the significance of which we have the merest hint. The more we consider it, the more we find it impossible to stop short here. Fancy, no doubt, is to be dreaded. Sobriety and reverent caution are abundantly needful. But so are they everywhere. If we profess wisdom, we become fools: subjection to the blessed Spirit of God, and to the Word inspired of Him, are our only safeguards here and elsewhere.
>
> When we look a little closer, we find that the types are not scattered haphazardly in the Old Testament books. On the contrary, they are connected together and arranged in an order and with a symmetry which bear witness to the divine hand which has been at work throughout. We find Exodus thus to be the book of redemption; Leviticus, to speak of

what suits God with us in the sanctuary of sanctification, then Numbers, to give the wilderness history – our walk with God (after redemption and being brought to Him where He is) through the world. Each individual type in these different books will be found to have most intimate and significant relation to the great central thought pervading the book. This, when laid hold of, confirms immensely our apprehension of the general and particular meaning, and gives it a force little if at all short of absolute demonstration.[3]

It is God's uniform figurative repetition of over a hundred numbers, colors, metals, materials, objects, creatures, people, and people groups throughout the Bible which is one of the many evidences demonstrating that all Scripture comes from one Mind – it is God-breathed (2 Tim. 3:16). Through the observed consistency of symbolic meanings applied in Scripture and the revelation of the New Testament, we are able to understand Old Testament types with a high degree of accuracy– these, generally speaking, have their center and fulfillment in the Lord Jesus Christ.

The "Eighth" Day

In biblical study, numerology forms a portion of the broader study called typology. In Scripture, most numbers have a literal meaning (e.g., Christ arose from the grave on the *third* day), but some numbers serve a figurative purpose. We understand that the Lamb with *seven* horns in Revelation 5:6 symbolically represents the Lamb of God's omnipotence, because in Scripture seven is the number of perfection, and a horn represents power. Sometimes both a figurative and a literal meaning may be intended, especially when the obvious literal sense is within a personal narrative and the figurative sense conveys a future meaning verified elsewhere in Scripture. For example, the seven-year famine in Joseph's day was both an actual devastating famine that affected the whole land and also a forewarning of a yet future seven-year Tribulation Period that will devastate the entire planet.

The numbers one through forty, as well as many numbers above forty, are each used in a specific, figurative manner throughout the Bible to show a particular meaning. The number *eight*, for example, is repeatedly used in the Bible to speak of "new beginnings" such as new life or a new order. In actuality, we are already familiar with this concept: the eighth day begins a new week in our calendars and the eighth note in a musical scale begins a new octave. Seven is God's number of completeness (Gen. 2:3), which means eight is the start of a new series, just as the seventh day, Saturday, yields to the eighth, Sunday, to begin a new week. Accordingly, the Lord rose from the dead on Sunday to demonstrate the newness of His resurrection life.

This symbolism can be seen throughout both the Pentateuch and the history books of the Old Testament. In Noah's day, eight souls entered an ark (a picture of Christ), to escape God's judgment upon the wicked through a flood (1 Pet. 3:20). The ark protected its occupants from God's wrath, lifted them off the earth to be alone with God, and safely carried them to a new life in a new world. The prophet Samuel was to anoint a new king of Israel, a man after God's own heart – that man was David, the eighth son of Jesse (1 Sam. 17:12). Through David a new and everlasting dynasty would be established: the Lord Jesus Christ will rule from the throne of David forever.

As Leviticus introduces a new era of opportunity for the Jewish nation to *come near* to Jehovah, the word "eighth" appears ten times, significantly more than any other book in the Bible. It fact, one-fourth of all occurrences of the word "eighth" in the Bible are found in Leviticus. While Genesis is a book of initial "beginnings," Leviticus (which institutes blood atonement and blood cleansing) is a continuing story of "new beginnings" after the fall of mankind.

Animal and Bird Symbolism

Besides the symbolic representation of numbers, various animals and birds are also employed to represent important aspects of Christ's character and attributes, and His redemptive ministry in Scripture. What is fascinating is that some spiritual beings were created with the faces of earthly animals and birds to convey the same meanings. For this reason, God describes to us what some of these spiritual beings (e.g., cherubim and seraphim) do and how they appear before God's throne in heaven. God has clearly shown Himself to all men through creation (Rom. 1:20). Accordingly, all creation, visible or invisible, provides a wonderful testimony of God's greatness: *"Bless the Lord, all His works, in all places of His dominion. Bless the Lord, O my soul!"* (Ps. 103:22). Included in *"all places of His dominion"* are spiritual beings in heavenly realms, which continually declare the glory of God and praise His name (Ps. 103:20).

The Testimony of Faces
The scriptural accounts of the cherubim in Ezekiel 1 and 10, and of the four living creatures in Revelation 4 (which may be the seraphim in Isaiah 6) disclose that these beings have the same faces – four kinds of faces to be more exact. Each of the seraphim and each of the four living creatures has one of these faces, while, apparently, the cherubim each have all four: that is, the face of a lion, the face of an ox, the face of a man, and the face of an eagle. The faces of these beings reflect the same glories of the Lord Jesus that are presented in the main themes of each Gospel. The *lion* is the king of the beasts, which reflects Matthew's perspective of Christ the King. The *ox*, as a beast of burden, is harnessed for the rigors of serving, and pictures Mark's presentation of Christ the Servant. The face of the *man* clearly agrees with Luke's prevalent theme of the Lord's humanity. Lastly, the *eagle* flies high above all the other creatures; the divine essence of the Savior is in view here as it is in John's gospel.

So why does the Spirit of God employ so many depictions of Christ in typological form throughout the Old Testament and why are these often in a plural presentation? Ultimately, as Andrew Jukes explains, this multiplicity of expression is for the fuller exaltation of the Son of God:

> The fact is that our perceptions do not grasp realities, but their form. If therefore what is seen is to be described, we must have many representations even of the same object; and this not only because the same object may be viewed on different sides, but because the amount of what is seen even on the same side will depend on the light and capacity of the beholder. He who made us knew this and provided for it. Hence of old, in type and figure, we have view after view of Him who was to come; not only because His offices and perfections were many, but also because we were weak and needed such a revelation.

> Thus in the single relationship of offering, Christ is seen a Burnt offering, Peace offering, and Sin offering [also a Meal offering and Trespass offering], each but a different view of the same one offering; each of which again may be seen in various measures, and yet the offering itself is only one. And just as the selfsame act of dying on the

cross, our Lord was at the same moment a sweet savor offering, willingly offering to God a perfect obedience, and also a sin offering, bearing the judgment due to sin, and as such made a curse for us; so in the selfsame acts of His life, each act may be seen in different aspects, for each act has a Divine fullness.[4]

With this understanding we now turn our attention to the Levitical sacrifices. We see that only four animals and two kinds of birds were to be offered: oxen and cattle were taken from the herd, sheep and goats from the flock, while turtle doves and pigeons represented the fowls. Each of these has a particular and unique representation of Christ's personage, attributes, or ministry.

Oxen or Cattle

The offering of the herd would include oxen or cattle. Only a male, a bull, was permitted for the burnt offering and some sin offerings. Oxen and cattle were yoked to pull farm implements, sleds, carts, wagons, etc. Oxen, especially, were beasts of burden and thus represent Christ as the lowly servant of Jehovah. This vantage point is further brought to light in Mark's gospel, which shows the Lord quickly traveling from one place to another to provide continuous service to others without thought of Himself:

> *Yet it shall not be so among you; but whoever desires to become great among you shall be your servant. And whoever of you desires to be first shall be slave of all. For even the Son of Man did not come to be served, but to serve, and to give His life a ransom for many* (Mark 10:43-45).

The Lord's meek and humble character, His compassion for the suffering, and His resolute spirit in the face of opposition invite us to follow His example – He was a true Servant of God. Mark's perspective of Christ's selfless ministry shows us that true love needs no title to serve, just the power to do so, which is supplied by Him alone.

Sheep

In Scripture, sheep are known for their tendency to go their own way and to become lost (Luke 15:4). Isaiah compares this propensity to the nature of fallen humanity; each of us proves our inherent depravity by going our own way and not following after God (Isa. 53:6; 1 Pet. 2:25). Yet, this natural tendency is contrasted with the Lord's perfect sinless behavior, who as the Lamb of God always did the Father's will (John 5:30). Sheep are defenseless creatures; it is likely this disposition of meekness and lowliness that the Spirit of God desires us to appreciate about the Lord Jesus:

> *He was oppressed and He was afflicted, yet He opened not His mouth; He was led as a lamb to the slaughter, and as a sheep before its shearers is silent, so He opened not His mouth* (Isa. 53:7).

> *Who, when He was reviled, did not revile in return; when He suffered, He did not threaten, but committed Himself to Him who judges righteously* (1 Pet. 2:23).

The Lord Jesus did not try to defend Himself when arrested. He did not resist His accusers, but rather submitted to and endured their mockery and cruelty, though He had the wherewithal to deliver Himself from it.

The Goat

Goats are used to symbolize evil in the Bible. For example, those who align with the Antichrist during the Tribulation Period are referred to as goats when the Lord judges the nations; unlike His "sheep," these individuals are condemned and not permitted to enjoy Christ's millennial kingdom (Matt. 25:33,41). At Calvary, the Lord Jesus Christ, who knew no sin, took our sin upon Himself; He became sin for us:

> *For He made Him who knew no sin to be sin for us, that we might become the righteousness of God in Him* (2 Cor. 5:21).

> *Who Himself bore our sins in His own body on the tree, that we, having died to sins, might live for righteousness – by whose stripes you were healed* (1 Pet. 2:24).

On the Day of Atonement, the High Priest, with his hands on the head of a goat, confessed the sins of the people. This goat, identified as the scapegoat, was then taken out into the wilderness and released; however, a second goat was sacrificed and its blood sprinkled on the mercy seat before God. This symbolized how Christ would suffer and die in the place of the sinner, so that God could righteously remove the judicial penalty of sin from his or her account and impute to him or her a righteous standing. As God has already judged His Son, those who take advantage of Christ's offering by trusting Him as Savior will never experience God's wrath for their sins. Their sin was completely judged once and for all in Christ (Heb. 9:26, 10:10, 12). Thus, on the Day of Atonement, Christ is pictured in both the goat that suffered death for sin, and in the goat which effectively carried away their sins from God's presence.

The Turtledove
The turtledove may represent mourning in Scripture (Isa. 38:14, 59:11). The Lord Jesus was grieved over Israel's rejection of Himself as their Messiah and this is symbolized by the turtledove.

> *O Jerusalem, Jerusalem, the one who kills the prophets and stones those who are sent to her! How often I wanted to gather your children together, as a hen gathers her chicks under her wings, but you were not willing! See! Your house is left to you desolate* (Matt. 23:37-38).

> *He came to His own, and His own did not receive Him* (John 1:11).

When the Son withdrew from the dimensionless and timeless realm of majesty on high to descend to the earth, He willingly placed Himself under creation order and the rule of fallen humanity. It is one thing to suffer for your own bad behavior; it is quite another to suffer and die in the place of another when you have not done anything wrong. And a grander mystery yet is what compelled the Lord to willingly die for those who did not in the slightest degree appreciate His sacrifice.

The Pigeon
The pigeon may symbolize the innocence and gentleness of the Lord Jesus (Matt. 10:16). He blessed little children, healed the sick, freed those who were demonically possessed, and tirelessly taught the masses the way of life. It is also worth noting that birds were primarily a poor man's offering, and this corresponds to the poverty Christ took upon Himself when He entered this world:

And Jesus said to him, "Foxes have holes and birds of the air have nests, but the Son of Man has nowhere to lay His head" (Matt. 8:20).

For you know the grace of our Lord Jesus Christ, that though He was rich, yet for your sakes He became poor, that you through His poverty might become rich (2 Cor. 8:9).

The Lord Jesus ventured from the glories of heaven to be incarnated in the womb of a virgin and then to be born into a poor family (Luke 1:34, 2:24). He then lived as a lowly stranger, the Messenger of God among the very hostile creatures He had created and was laboring to save.

Summary

Each type of animal or fowl sacrificed to Jehovah in the Levitical offerings had symbolic meaning pertaining to the person and character of Christ. This imagery is held consistent throughout Scripture, for even before the days of the Law, Abraham offered all of the animals and fowls mentioned in Leviticus in one great sacrifice of the covenant (Gen. 15:9). Furthermore, the specific procedures and portions of the various sacrifices spoke of His Father's adoration and of His various ministries to humanity.

Whatever creature was presented in blood sacrifice to the Lord had to be inspected and found without blemish (1:3). This practice typifies the Lord's impeccable nature as demonstrated during His earthly sojourn in His spotless, sinless, and blameless life (Heb. 9:14; 1 Pet. 1:19). Additionally, whatever offering was presented to the Lord had to be performed in the exact manner specified, or it would not be accepted. This stipulation would not only test the hearts of men, but also preserve the distinct meaning of each offering so there would be no confusion as to what God wanted us to understand and appreciate about His Son.

Overview of the Levitical Offerings

A Gentile believer living in the Church Age might well ask, "What practical value is there in studying the five Jewish offerings recorded in the first seven chapters of Leviticus?" The Gentiles were never put under the Law and certainly are not judicially constrained by it as Christians (Rom. 7:4; Gal. 2:16). The real benefit of studying the five sacrifices mentioned in the opening chapters of Leviticus is to grow in our appreciation of Christ whose person and work are symbolized in the offerings. This knowledge should then prompt believers to desire to live a holy and consecrated life for God.

It is crucial that we understand the change in the tenor between the latter portion of Exodus and Leviticus 1. The revelation of the Levitical offerings was not provided on Mount Sinai, but rather *"the Lord called to Moses, and spoke to him from the tabernacle of meeting"* (Lev. 1:1). This contrasts the ominous judicial position that Jehovah exhibited on a fiery and quaking Sinai with that of a gracious God, dwelling in peace with and among His people. In Exodus, except for His personal conversations with Moses, God was distant and unapproachable. In Leviticus, God resides in the tabernacle which Moses had just erected in the center of their camp. In Exodus, the Israelites were delivered from bondage and *came out* of Egypt, but they could not *come near* to God, as the Law, which reflected God's holy character, had made them conscious of their own depraved conduct and nature. However, in Leviticus, God invites man to *come near* and to have fellowship with Him through the substitutional provision of shed blood.

As a result of blood-atoning sacrifices first introduced in Exodus and further explained and specified in Leviticus, Jehovah's previously horrifying presence has been tempered by grace and mercy. His abiding holy being was shown in a visible display of glory above the tabernacle during the day and a pillar of fire rising above it at night (Ex. 40:33-38). Thus, in Leviticus we see Jehovah, the immutable, holy God, speaking to

Moses from above the mercy seat in the tabernacle which is pitched among His people, instead of from the verboten Sinai.

The blood sacrifices and meal offerings of Leviticus righteously accommodated the inflexible holiness of God, as declared in the Law, such that grace in its purest form could co-exist together with holiness in peaceful bliss. This is the theme of Leviticus and foreshadows what the Lord Jesus Christ has now accomplished for all believers! To this end, each of the offerings mentioned in the first seven chapters of Leviticus have special significance to every child of God. These are:

The burnt offering (Lev. 1:1-17, 6:8-13)
The meal offering (Lev. 2:1-16, 6:14-23)
The peace offering (Lev. 3:1-17, 7:11-34)
The sin offering (Lev. 4:1-35, 6:24-30)
The trespass offering (Lev. 5:1-6:7, 7:1-10)

David writes of the One who would willingly come in faithful obedience to God to fulfill what is typified in each of these Levitical offerings:

Sacrifice [zebach] and offering [minchad] You did not desire; My ears You have opened. Burnt offering [olah] and sin offering [chataah] You did not require. Then I said, "Behold, I come; in the scroll of the book it is written of me. I delight to do Your will, O my God, and Your law is within my heart" (Ps. 40:6-7).

The writer of Hebrews quotes from Psalm 40 to confirm that Christ's sacrifice at Calvary on behalf of humanity was a direct fulfillment of David's prophecy. God the Father did not want us to miss the link between the willing Servant and the suffering Son of God:

For the law, having a shadow of the good things to come, and not the very image of the things, can never with these same sacrifices, which they offer continually year by year, make those who approach perfect. For then would they not have ceased to be offered? For the worshipers, once purified, would have had no more consciousness of sins. But in those sacrifices there is a reminder of sins every year. For it is not possible that the blood of bulls and goats could take away sins. Therefore, when He came into the world, He said: "Sacrifice and offering You did not desire, but a body You have prepared for Me. In burnt offerings and sacrifices for sin You had no pleasure. Then I said, 'Behold, I have come – in the volume of the book it is written of Me – to do Your will, O God'" (Heb. 10:1-7).

A comparison of Psalm 40 and Hebrews 10 clearly reveals that the One who had His ear opened to be marked as a servant in Psalm 40:6 is the same One who offered His entire body, indeed His life (John 10:11), to God and fulfilled the complete meaning of all five Levitical sacrifices. C. H. Mackintosh, commenting on the faithful bondservant being a wonderful type of Christ, writes:

> The application of this to the Lord Jesus Christ will be obvious to the intelligent reader. In Him we behold the One who dwelt in the bosom of the Father before all worlds — the object of His eternal delight — who might have occupied, throughout eternity, this His personal and entirely peculiar place, inasmuch as there lay upon Him no obligation (save that which ineffable love created and ineffable love incurred) to abandon that place. Such, however, was His love to the Father whose counsels were involved, and for the Church collectively, and each individual member thereof, whose salvation was involved, that He, voluntarily, came down to earth, emptied Himself, and made Himself of no reputation, took upon Him the form of a servant and the marks of perpetual service. ...Thus we have, in the Hebrew servant, a type of Christ in His pure devotedness to the Father.[1]

The Hebrew words employed in Psalm 40 directly relate to all the Levitical offerings: *zebach* pertains to the *peace* offering, *minchad* the *meal* offering, *olah* the *burnt* offering, and *chataah* the *sin* offering. Although distinct, the sin and trespass (*'asham*) offering were often connected together: *"The trespass offering is like the sin offering; there is one law for them both"* (Lev. 7:7). The same practice was also true of the Passover, Unleavened Bread, and Firstfruits Feasts; though each was distinct, these feasts were often referred to in the singular as, *"the Feast of Unleavened Bread"* (Deut. 16:16).

Portions of the New Testament also refer to the Lord Jesus in the language of the Levitical offerings.

> *And walk in love, as Christ also has loved us and given Himself for us, an offering and a sacrifice to God for a sweet-smelling aroma* (Eph. 5:2).

> *But this Man, after He had offered one sacrifice for sins forever, sat down at the right hand of God, from that time waiting till His enemies are made His footstool. For by one offering He has perfected forever those who are being sanctified* (Heb. 10:12-14).

Before the foundations of the earth were laid, God had already predetermined the incarnation, death, resurrection, and exaltation of His Son, in order to rescue a fallen race, which as of yet He had not even created (1 Pet. 1:20). God foreordained that an innocent and perfect God-man would, as a substitute, suffer the death that you and I deserved in order that we might have an opportunity to escape death, be forgiven, and be restored to our Creator. Who but God could have devised such a plan? *"Oh, the depth of the riches both of the wisdom and knowledge of God! How unsearchable are His judgments and His ways past finding out!"* (Rom. 11:33).

The Levitical offerings presented by the Jewish priests did not provide propitiation for sin, but merely atoned for the sins of Jehovah's covenant people, thus permitting them to come near to Him for worship. Their relationship had been established by redemption through the Passover lamb in Egypt and would be maintained through a covenant that required the annual sprinkling of blood on the mercy seat of the Ark of the Covenant. This occurred on the Day of Atonement. As long as the Jewish nation continued by faith to show forth the merits of Christ's future substitutional death through the Levitical sacrifices, God would continue to dwell among them. God's presence with them ensured their blessing and protection. Paul explains this truth in his letter to the Romans:

> *But now the righteousness of God apart from the law is revealed, being witnessed by the Law and the Prophets, even the righteousness of God, through faith in Jesus Christ, to all and on all who believe. For there is no difference; for all have sinned and fall short of the glory of God, being justified freely by His grace through the redemption that is in Christ Jesus, whom God set forth as a propitiation by His blood, through faith, to demonstrate His righteousness, because in His*

forbearance God had passed over the sins that were previously committed, to demonstrate at the present time His righteousness, that He might be just and the justifier of the one who has faith in Jesus (Rom. 3:21-26).

The death of innocent animals, and the shedding and applying of their blood, could not remove the guilty stain of sin or its judicial penalty, but it did provide a temporary covering for sin. This permitted God to abide with His people in the tent of meeting and also allow His people to approach Him in worship. Christ's future sacrifice would properly satisfy God's righteous wrath for all human sin and negate the need for further blood sacrifices. Prior to Christ's first advent, it was only by animal blood, as C. H. Mackintosh explains, that a worshipper was made acceptable to God and then invited to *come near* to God in worship (though not into His intimate presence).

> In the first place, we would observe that *sacrifice is the basis of worship*. Acceptable worship to God must be based on a sacrifice acceptable to Him. Man being in himself guilty and unclean, he needs a sacrifice to remove his guilt, cleanse him from his defilements, and fit him for the holy presence of God. "Without shedding of blood is no remission." And without remission, and the *knowledge* of remission, there can be no happy worship; no real, hearty praise, adoration, and thanksgiving.[2]

The Levitical sacrifices accomplished this in the interim prior to Christ's death, resurrection, and exaltation. Until that time each offering would draw the offerer's attention to some aspect of Christ's personage or of His future sacrificial and priestly work, that is, to a specific way the Father wanted His Son to be appreciated. For this reason the sacrifices are mentioned and explained in a particular order: from what is most significant to God to what is most significant to man. That is, the order shows a holy God coming out to meet sinful man where he is at.

Three offerings (the burnt offering, the meal offering, and the peace offering) were called "sweet aroma" offerings because they were associated with one's choice to freely praise and thank God for His goodness. These present Christ's excellences and our access to God through Him. This is possible on the basis that sin has already been fully dealt with (i.e., in God's timeless view of the work of the cross). The final two offerings, the sin and trespass offerings, were demanded by God because of the offerer's sin, and thus were considered "non-sweet aroma" offerings; the only exception, the fat of the sin offering burnt on the Bronze Altar was considered a sweet savor to the Lord (4:31). In these offerings the perfections of Christ, though apparent and needful, are not the emphasis; rather, He is extolled as the suffering sin-bearer who identifies with the sinner to satisfy God's righteous demand for justice (Isa. 53:10).

Sweet Aroma Offerings (Freewill)

Burnt Offering – Literally, this was the ascending offering which was completely for God's pleasure. It was a freewill offering that was totally consumed, excluding the skins (7:8). The burnt offering pictures Christ's absolute devotion and submission to the Father's will in being a sacrifice for humanity's sin.

Grain Offering – This freewill offering speaks of who Christ is. His perfect character is symbolized in the fine meal, which had no leaven. The oil which saturated the offering indicates that Christ was born of and baptized by the Holy Spirit; olive oil is confirmed as a type of the Holy Spirit and His energizing power in Zechariah 4:3-6.

Peace Offering – God, the priests, and the common people all partook of this freewill offering to convey the sense of fellowship that God longs to enjoy with His people (Ex. 24:9-11; Mal. 1). The New Testament equivalent of this privileged place of communion and blessing with the Lord is referred to as the "Lord's Table" (1 Cor. 10:16-22).

Non-Sweet Aroma Offerings (Mandatory)

Sin Offering – At His death, Christ bore in His body our sin, taking the place of the sinner (1 Pet. 2:24). We are inherently fallen, sinful creatures deserving judgment. Christ as the sin offering satisfied God's righteous demand for justice concerning human sin.

Trespass Offering – In the trespass offering, we see that Christ made restitution for the damage our sin and trespasses cause. We are inherently fallen, and thus God demands punishment for our sin as shown in the sin offering. However, we also must realize that our sin hurts others and causes them to suffer loss, and thus recognize the necessity of the trespass offering.

The death and resurrection of our Lord Jesus Christ is presented to us in various ways throughout Scripture so that we might more fully understand what God has accomplished through Him. The sacrifices, first mentioned in Exodus 29 and further described in Leviticus 1 through 7, present different facets of Christ's life on earth and His sacrifice at Calvary: the burnt offering speaks of Christ's devotion to the Father as an offering totally consumed for God, the meal offering reflects the fine moral character of Christ and His sufferings prior to the cross, the peace offering acknowledges the communion of God with man through Christ, the sin offering pictures God's own payment for the offense of man's sin, and the trespass offering relates to restitution for the damage that sin causes. In all of these, the person and work of Christ are presented and appreciated.

The Order of the Offerings

The five offerings are presented twice in the first seven chapters of Leviticus, but in slightly different order. It is suggested that the first presentation follows the order of what is most significant from God's perspective to what is most important to man.

First Presentation to the People (Lev. 1:1-6:7)
The burnt offering
The meal offering
The peace offering
The sin offering
The trespass offering

The burnt offering was totally consumed by fire (except for the skin) and thus pictured the complete manifold sufferings of God's own Son at Calvary; this was most precious to God. In contrast, man is more concerned about how the sin of others affects him and how restitution should be made for such offenses. Yet, the spiritual man should seek to understand the proper progression of importance to God: God's full satisfaction in His Son, the moral excellence of Christ as shown in all that He did, the fellowship God desires with man through His Son, Christ suffering the penalty for humanity's sins, and the abundant restitution He provides for the damage sin causes to others (i.e., for He is *"bringing many sons to glory"*; Heb. 2:10).

The order of the five offerings as given to the priests, who would be performing the work associated with each sacrifice, was slightly different:

Second Presentation to the Priests (Lev. 6:8-7:38)
The burnt offering
The meal offering
The sin offering
The trespass offering
The peace offering

In this progression the offerings are in the same order, except the peace offering is mentioned last instead of third. The change in progression is not explained, so we can only surmise the reason. F. B. Hole suggests an explanation: "We suppose, that, while in the other cases the participators were only the priests, here the common person, who brought the offering was permitted to have a share."[3] Thus, the instruction manual for the priests began with the sacrifices for which they were solely responsible, before ending with the one that involved the participation of other Israelites. The distinction in order highlights an application for us: As God's priests in the Church age, we cannot offer acceptable sacrifices of praise, worship, and gifts unto the Lord until sin has been properly dealt with through confession (1 Jn. 1:9). Thus, the peace of God which a believer so desperately wants to maintain can only be achieved by keeping short accounts with the Lord. The peace of God that we desire to enjoy is unattainable until the stain of sin has been cleansed away by the blood of Christ.

Each offering pictures Christ giving His all in various aspects of the work of redemption and restoration. In the burnt offering all of the **sacrifice** was consumed, except for the hide (7:8), and in the case of a bird, its feathers and crop (1:16). In the meal offering, all of the

frankincense was burned on the Bronze Altar. In the peace offering, all of the **fat** and both the kidneys were burned. In the sin offering, all of the **blood** was poured out at the base of the altar. In the trespass offering, all of the **loss** resulting from sin was restored plus a fifth. Most certainly the Lord Jesus is our all in all and in a future day will completely repair all the damage that sin has caused, and a perfect creation will declare the glory of God, *"that God may be all in all"* (1 Cor. 15:28).

Summary

These five offerings are unique and each sets forth various aspects of the person and work of our Lord Jesus Christ. The burnt offering pictures Christ's absolute devotion to the Father and the Father's full appreciation of His Son. The meal offering pictures the Lord's moral perfection as linked with His deity. The peace offering presents Him as the One who made peace by the blood of His cross which permits us fellowship with God. The sin offering shows us how the sinless One was made sin for us that we might become the righteousness of God in Him. The trespass offering tells us that Christ made restitution for the damage that our sin causes.

Certainly, whatever meaning the sacrifices hold for us in application, we must realize that the offerings meant much more to God. Only He can fully appreciate the deep mystery of godliness pertaining to the Lord Jesus: *"Without controversy great is the mystery of godliness: God was manifested in the flesh, justified in the Spirit, seen by angels, preached among the Gentiles, believed on in the world, received up in glory"* (1 Tim. 3:16). As the various offerings were presented by the priests in the tabernacle, God the Father would breathe in that sweet reminder of His Son, the love of His heart, and would be refreshed in a way that no human can fully apprehend. Yet, when we labor in His Word, through the illumination of His Spirit, God permits us to breathe in that sweet portion which He supplies us.

Leviticus
Devotions

The Burnt Offering
Leviticus 1:1-17, 6:8-13, 7:8

The burnt offering did not originate in Leviticus; rather, it is first specifically mentioned in Genesis 8:20 after Noah and his family departed from the ark. A brief overview of burnt offerings in the Old Testament will confirm a consistent pattern and meaning. Abel's offering of the firstborn of his flock was likely a burnt offering, but the text does not explicitly state that detail (Gen. 4:4). However, Abel's action pleased the Lord and introduces a fundamental principle presented throughout Scripture: man cannot successfully approach God for worship and fellowship, except through a substitutional sacrifice, usually a lamb.

After caring for the ark-bound creatures for over a year, Noah built an altar and sacrificed several clean animals and fowl as a burnt offering to the Lord. There is nothing in the narrative which suggests that Noah was commanded to worship God in this way, but rather Noah chose to do so as an expression of his thankfulness to God for preserving his family through the cataclysmic flood. The next mention of the burnt offering is over four hundred years later when God commanded Abraham to offer up Isaac as a burnt offering (Gen. 22).

In obedience to God's command, Abraham went to the land of Moriah and upon the mount that God showed him built an altar to sacrifice his beloved son Isaac. During this trial of his faith, Abraham uttered two prophetic statements which preface both the events of the Passover Lamb sacrifice (Ex. 12) and the five Levitical offerings. First, *"God will provide Himself a Lamb for a burnt offering"* (Gen. 22:8). Second, *"In the mount of the Lord it shall be seen* [provided]*"* (Gen. 22:14). Both declarations speak of the future suffering and death of Christ; the Lord Himself declared this to the Pharisees, saying, *"Abraham rejoiced to see My day: and he saw it, and was glad"* (John 8:56). In the same way, all of these animal sacrifices have their ultimate fulfillment in the suffering and sacrifice of God's own Son at Calvary.

Some four hundred years after Abraham offered the ram as burnt offering in the place of Isaac, God formalized the specifics of the burnt offering with Moses (Ex. 29; Lev. 1-7). Accordingly, as we exercise faith in God's Word, we too can rejoice and be glad in the very day that Abraham foresaw. God did provide Himself a Lamb for the sacrifice on the same mountain where Abraham was commanded to sacrifice his only son of promise, Isaac. At the appropriate time to spare Isaac's life, God provided Abraham a ram to offer up instead of Isaac. In the same way, *"when the fullness of the time had come, God sent forth His Son, born of a woman, born under the law, to redeem those who were under the law that we might receive the adoption as sons"* (Gal. 4:4-5). God provided for us His only begotten Son (John 3:16) as *"the Lamb of God who takes away the sin of the world"* (John 1:29). To do the Father's will required Christ's all, His entire life – because it is a reflection of His Son's complete sacrifice for the glory of God; the burnt offering, which was to be fully consumed on the altar, was most precious to God and accordingly is mentioned first. Harry Ironside explains the mysterious nature of this offering:

> The burnt offering presents in some respects the view of the work of the cross that was more precious to God than all the rest [of the Levitical offerings] for it presents the Lord Jesus dying upon that cross primarily in order that He might glorify God His Father in the scene where He had been so terribly dishonored by man's sin. The remarkable fact about all the other offerings is this: parts of them were presented on the altar and went up to God; other parts were divided among the people and the priests. They were the food of the people of God. But the whole burnt offering was placed on the altar and it was all consumed; it all went up to God. He calls it "My offering, My food." There was something in the sacrifice of our Lord Jesus Christ that no one could understand but God Himself. There was something about it that you and I could never enter into, could never appreciate in its fullness, something that God alone could enter into, God alone could appreciate.[1]

How could man possibly comprehend how Christ completely offered Himself up to fully declare the glory of God? How can we fully understand how greatly the Father treasured the Son for doing so, or what the Son meant when He said, *"Therefore My Father loves Me, because I lay down My life"* (John 10:17)? We cannot. Reason dictates that we can recognize but a mere trifle of the significance that God affords to the burnt offering, which typifies Christ's life, fully expended for God.

In this sense, the burnt offering reminds us of the special incense that the priests were commanded to carefully formulate for God and place in the Most Holy Place of the tabernacle (Ex. 30:34-38). This incense was for God's enjoyment and His appreciation alone – man was not to duplicate it for himself. With that said, we can surmise from the whole of Scripture what is represented in the instructions for preparing and sacrificing the various burnt offerings. C. I. Scofield suggests that there are at least three aspects of the burnt offering that we can appreciate:

> The burnt offering (1) typifies Christ offering Himself without spot to God in delight to do His Father's will even in death; (2) it is atoning because the believer has not had this delight in the will of God; and (3) substitutionary (v. 4) because Christ did it in the sinner's stead. But the thought of penalty is not prominent (Heb. 9:11-14, 10:5-7). The emphatic words (Lev. 1:3-5) are "burnt sacrifice," "voluntary," "it shall be accepted for him," and "atonement."[2]

The burnt offering was a sweet savor sacrifice because it was not demanded by God; rather, as Noah demonstrated, it was a voluntary act of worship and appreciation. Jehovah appreciated the burnt offering more than the other sacrifices because it pictured the ultimate satisfaction He would enjoy because of His Son's full devotion to Himself; the Son's supreme loyalty would be demonstrated even unto death. The offering is substitutionary in the sense that the offerer's motives and behavior were not always purely devoted to serving God, but Christ's were. Accordingly, the smoke ascending from the burnt offering on the Bronze Altar symbolized that the Israelites were accepted by Jehovah in regards to their relationship with Him. This is in contrast to the rising smoke of burning incense on the Golden Altar, which declared that their worship and praise (as offered through a priest – picturing Christ) were esteemed acceptable.

This compound representation pictures the complete acceptance believers have in the Beloved and through the Beloved (Eph. 1:6). This positional acceptance in Christ then permits the value God places on the other four Levitical offerings to also be realized. As Arthur Pink further explains, the burnt offering became the basis of God's acceptance of the other offerings.

> The burnt offering was really the basis of all the other sacrifices, as may be seen not only from the fact that it is given precedence in Leviticus 1 to 5, but also because the altar itself took its name from this—"the altar of the burnt offering" (Ex. 40:10). It foreshadowed, therefore, the perfect devotedness of the Son to the Father, which was the basis or spring of the whole of His earthly life, ministry, and sacrificial death. He "glorified not Himself." When He spoke or acted, it was ever the Father's honor He sought. He could say, "I came not to do Mine own will, but the will of Him that sent Me." He could say, "I have set the Lord always before Me" (Ps. 16:8).[3]

How the sacrificial ashes were handled also confirms that the burnt offering was the basis of God's acceptance for the other sacrifices. The ashes of the burnt offering were temporarily placed on the east side of the Bronze Altar until a priest could change out of his priestly attire and carry the ashes out to a clean place (6:9-11). In this way the ashes from the burnt offering became the basis of acceptance for all the other offerings; ashes from the other sacrifices were piled upon the ashes of the burnt offering (4:12). Christ's sacrifice is the basis of man's acceptance with God; it is through Him that man is fitted to serve the Lord in an acceptable manner and that his service is acceptable. The ashes would also remind the Jews that God had a way of completely putting away the sting and the stain of their sins.

The Hebrew word for the burnt offering is *olah*, which means "to ascend." *Olah* conveys the picture of the entire burnt offering being consumed by fire on the Bronze Altar and the smoke rising up into God's presence as a sweet-smelling aroma. As the aroma reminds the Father of His Son's voluntary sacrifice, He is refreshed by its sweet fragrance.

Types of Burnt Offerings

If a Jewish man wanted to show his appreciation and gratefulness to God, he would choose one of three types of sacrifices for a burnt offering: an offering of the herd [cattle or oxen (1:3-9)], an offering of the flock [sheep or goats (1:10-13)], or an offering of the fowls [turtledoves or young pigeons (1:14-17)]. No matter what type of offering was selected the sacrifice had to meet strict qualifications. If taken from the herd or the flock the animal had to be a male and without blemish (1:3, 10). Likewise, God presented His best for the sacrifice at Calvary: Christ, a male in the prime of His life, demonstrated sinless perfection in every way – there was no physical or spiritual blemish in Him.

That the offerer was to follow God's example of sacrificing the best is further substantiated by the Hebrew words *ben baqar*, translated simply as "bull" or "bullock" in Leviticus 1:5. The compound construction of these words literally means "son of the herd." Hence, the best of the entire herd was to be offered; this would demonstrate the offerer's pure motives, that is, he was sacrificing something to the Lord that had substantial intrinsic value.

To offer a substandard sacrifice invited God's chastening judgment instead of His blessing. The prophet Malachi rebuked his fellow countrymen for offering inferior sacrifices to Jehovah and confirmed that they had prompted actions of His disapproval against them (Mal. 1:8, 13-14).

The Procedure

Once the offerer had chosen an acceptable sacrifice, he brought it to the entrance (i.e., gate) of the courtyard of the tabernacle. After the offerer explained the purpose of the sacrifice to a priest, who likely examined the animal to ensure its fitness, the priest, the offerer, and the sacrifice proceeded to the Bronze Altar. The sacrifice was then killed on "the north side of the altar" (1:11), which is more vaguely described as "before the Lord" (1:5, 3:7) or "in front of the tent of meeting" (3:8). The latter reference refers to the entrance into the Holy Place of the tabernacle, not to the entrance into the courtyard. The east side of the altar was for the ashes, and an elevated slope on the south side of the altar provided the priest access to the upper part of the altar. F. C. Cook describes the method of slaughter:

> The regular place for slaughtering the animals for Burnt offerings, Sin offerings, and Trespass offerings, was the north side of the Altar. Tradition tells us that before the sacrificer laid his hand upon the head of the victim, it was bound by a cord to one of the rings fixed for the

purpose on the north side of the Altar, and that at the very instant when the words of the prayer, or confession, were ended, the fatal stroke was given. The Peace offerings and the Paschal lambs might, it would seem, be slain in any part of the Court.

The mode of killing appears not to have differed from that of slaughtering the animals for food. The throat was cut while a priest or assistant held a bowl under the neck to receive the blood. The sacrificer, or his assistant, then flayed the victim and cut it into pieces, probably while the priest was engaged in disposing of the blood.[4]

The exact procedure, which involved both the offerer and a priest, is stated slightly differently for each type of sacrifice offered. It is the author's opinion that the procedures for offering from the flock and from the herd are the same, but the former is stated in less detail (i.e., the priests understood the procedure and it was not necessary to repeat every point). Concerning the fowls, it is noted that an age restriction is levied for pigeons; only young ones were acceptable (1:14). The pigeons sacrificed were likely the blue-rock pigeon, which is a considerably larger species than the other sacrificial bird, the turtle-dove; thus, only the younger, smaller pigeons were to be sacrificed.

The Procedure for an Animal

The offerer brought the sacrifice to the door of the tabernacle of the congregation (1:3).

The offerer at the north side of the altar put his hand on the head of the burnt offering (1:4, 11).

The offerer killed the animal before the Lord (1:5).

The priest brought the blood and sprinkled it all around on the Bronze Altar (1:5, 11).

The offerer removed the hide and cut the animal into its pieces with head and fat (1:6, 12).

The priest put fire on the altar and laid the wood in order on the fire (1:7, 12).

The priest laid the parts, the head, and the fat in order upon the wood (1:8, 12).

The priest salted the sacrifice (Num. 18:19; Ezek. 43:24).

The offerer washed the entrails and legs in water (1:9, 13).

The priest burned all on the altar (1:9, 13).

The Procedure for Fowl
    The offerer presented it to the priest (1:14-15).
    The priest brought it to the altar and wrung off its head (1:15).
    The priest pressed out the blood at the side of the altar (1:15).
    The priest plucked away the crop (gullet) with its feathers and put these on the east side of the altar (1:16).
    The priest cleaved open, but did not divide the body of the bird (1:17).
    The priest burned it upon the altar (1:17).

The explicit directions in Leviticus 1 chiefly pertain to the offerer. The priests were provided further instructions concerning the burnt offering in Leviticus 6:8-13. Specifically, if an offering burned on the altar all night, the next morning the priest was to put on his priestly linen garments and remove the ashes from the altar and put them beside the altar (6:9-10). The priest was then to put off his priestly attire and put on other garments and carry the ashes outside the camp and deposit them in a clean place (6:11-12). The priests were also to keep the fire burning on the Bronze Altar at all times; it was never to go out (6:13). This meant that daily and personal sacrifices could always be offered to and accepted by God at any time. Although not mentioned in Leviticus, Exodus 29:40-42 indicates that a meal offering and a drink offering were to accompany burnt offerings on the Bronze Altar.

Summary

The burnt offering pictures the complete devotion of the Lord Jesus Christ to do all that His Father asked of Him in providing the means of redemption and restoration for humanity. While we may use the whole of Scripture to surmise what is symbolized in the burnt offering, much of its meaning is beyond human comprehension – God the Father's appreciation of His Son surpasses any formation of mortal words or expression of human thought. Christ's life among sinners and His death at the hands of guilty sinners was of His own free will. Thus, His entire life is a sweet-smelling savor that ascended up into the far reaches of glory for His Father to appreciate. Just as the offerer personally identified himself with the sacrifice just before it was consumed on the altar, the believer is likewise identified with the sweetness of Christ's life and is thus made acceptable to God in the Beloved (Eph. 1:6).

Another exhibition of the freewill spirit of the burnt offering is Jethro's voluntary sacrifice after he was reunited with Moses and heard how Jehovah had wondrously delivered his son-in-law and the Jewish nation from Pharaoh and slavery in Egypt. The offering of Jethro, a Midianite, occurred after Moses had received the instructions recorded in Leviticus 1-7 (Ex. 18:16). This entire scene is a wonderful picture of the future day when Jew and Gentile, united together in Christ, will worship the Lord together in His earthly millennial kingdom. This will occur directly after Christ miraculously delivers His covenant people from the oppression of the Antichrist and draws to a close their suffering in the world. What God accomplished in Egypt centuries ago is strikingly similar to this future event, and the end result is the same: in Christ's kingdom all His subjects will voluntarily worship and praise the Savior to show their appreciation for Him.

Application

Thankfully, believers in the Church Age do not have to wait until the establishment of Christ's earthly kingdom to declare how we treasure Him; we have the grand and ever-present privilege of presenting ourselves as a living sacrifice to God. This is accomplished by renewing our minds and resisting conformity to the world and the impulses of our lusting flesh:

> *I beseech you therefore, brethren, by the mercies of God, that you present your bodies a living sacrifice, holy, acceptable to God, which is your reasonable service. And do not be conformed to this world, but be transformed by the renewing of your mind, that you may prove what is that good and acceptable and perfect will of God* (Rom. 12:1-2).

In this sense, every moment of every day can be a worship experience with the Lord. We should want what God wants, and saying "no" to what He disapproves is a pleasing sacrifice to Him. It is a sacrifice because it costs us something: our desires that are contrary to His will.

The Old Testament is full of portraits of God's substitutionary sacrifice of His Son for the sinner and the imputation of divine righteousness to his or her account. Christ is the believer's righteousness, in both the practical and positional sense of the word (1 Cor. 1:30, 2 Cor.

5:21). When the offerer put his hand on the head of his sacrifice, he was identifying himself with it and so was God. This identification is further extended to the offering priest who received the skin of the animal offered in a burnt sacrifice (7:8). The priest would likely fashion coverings for himself with the skin, such as shoes, clothes, or a hat. While the priest was in the tabernacle, his priestly service required him to be clothed with priestly garments. However, during his routine apart from the tabernacle, his clothing derived from the skins would be a constant reminder of the offering previously sacrificed. When observed by others, it would be the burnt offering sacrifice (the priest's covering) that would be noticed, not the priest himself.

What is the application for the believer today? *"Put on the Lord Jesus Christ, and make no provision for the flesh, to fulfill its lusts* (Rom. 13:14). The position of righteousness we have in Christ should cause us to "shine out" Christ practically during daily priestly service to Him. In our day to day life, others should not see us, but the "sacrifice" – the Lord Jesus. The inherent beauty of the bride of Christ in Revelation 19:7-9 is the glory of Christ seen in the bride. Not only does she have a position of righteousness, but the works of righteousness Christ has done through her are spectacular. C. H. Mackintosh reminds us that, in Christ, we have the opportunity to practically demonstrate the righteousness of God:

> The believer is, in himself, nothing at all; but in Christ, he is a purged worshiper, He does not stand in the sanctuary as a guilty sinner, but as a worshiping priest, clothed in "garments of glory and beauty." To be occupied with my guilt in the presence of God is not humility as regards myself, but unbelief as regards the sacrifice.[5]

When God looks at a believer, He sees the perfection of Christ. Thus, in Christ, there is nothing for the believer to fear, except to disappoint the One for whom he or she is to live. John put the matter this way: *"There is no fear in love; but perfect love casts out fear, because fear involves torment. But he who fears has not been made perfect in love. We love Him because He first loved us"* (1 Jn. 4:18-19). Just as the burnt offering was voluntary in Moses' day, so is our service to Christ today. Having understood our complete acceptance in Christ and our

Be Holy and Come Near

opportunity to declare His righteousness in word and deed, may we all wear the skin of His sacrifice with honor.

Meditation

>Done is the work that saves, once and forever done;
>Finished the righteousness that clothes the unrighteous one.
>The love that blesses us below is flowing freely to us now.
>The sacrifice is over, the veil is rent in twain,
>The mercy-seat is red, with blood of Victim slain.
>Why stand we then without, in fear?
>The blood of Christ invites us near.
>
>— Horatius Bonar

The Meal Offering
Leviticus 2:1-16, 6:14-23, 7:9-10

There are five types of meal offerings described in this chapter: dough (2:1-3), baked in an oven (2:4), baked or fried in a pan (2:5-6), cooked or boiled in a cauldron (2:7), and roasted by fire (2:13-16). With the exception of the grain offering that was to be roasted by fire, all the meal offerings were composed of fine flour. All five meal offerings included oil and salt. The dough and the grain offering, which were exposed directly to the flames of the altar, were also to include frankincense.

Besides the instances described in this chapter, there were other occasions in which a meal offering would be required: the rituals after the purification of a leper (Lev. 14:10, 20-21, 31), or the termination of a Nazirite vow (Num. 6:15-19), or as part of the "jealousy ritual" in which a husband suspected his wife's infidelity (Num. 5:15-16), or as the wave loaves at the Feast of Pentecost. It is further observed that there is no Scriptural record of a Jewish leper being cleansed after the giving of the Law and before the coming of Christ, so it is likely no meal offering was ever offered in this interim for that situation. This is discussed more fully in the Leviticus 14 commentary. The two leavened wave loaves presented to the Lord at Pentecost were a unique meal offering in that no part of the loaves was burned on the altar. The reason for this is contained within the typological discussion of Leviticus 23. Returning to the subject at hand, we will now examine the five meal offerings mentioned in Leviticus 2.

Types of Meal Offerings

The uncooked meal offering (dough) was brought to a priest, who was to take a memorial handful of the fine flour, oil, and salt mixture, along with all the incense provided by the offerer, and burn the combination on the altar. This symbolized that the entire offering was the

Lord's, but He was sharing the larger portion of it with the priest. So the memorial portion burned on the altar was a sweet aroma to the Lord, but the remaining portion belonged to Aaron and his sons who were to eat it in the Holy Place (6:16). There is a dual appreciation pictured in this procedure. What ascended up to God in the smoke of the offering speaks of God's regard for Christ's lowly and spotless humanity, as demonstrated during His earthly sojourn. However, what was eaten by the priests represents the regard that all God's people, every believer-priest, should have for the sinless and selfless personage of the Lord Jesus Christ.

The next three meal offerings were completely baked, cooked, or boiled through exposure to heat, but not direct flame. The process of baking or cooking suggests the idea of suffering. However, since the meal offering is a sweet-smelling offering to God, there is no suggestion that Christ was suffering for sin or, specifically, under the wrath of God as a substitute for sinners. So what suffering did Christ, as pictured in the meal offering, endure? C. H. Mackintosh answers this question:

> In contemplating the *life* of the Lord Jesus, ... as shadowed in the meal offering, we may notice three distinct kinds of suffering; namely, suffering for righteousness; suffering by the power of sympathy; and suffering in anticipation. As the righteous Servant of God, He suffered in the midst of a scene in which all was contrary to Him; but this was the very opposite of suffering for sin. It is of the utmost importance to distinguish between these two kinds of suffering. The confounding of them must lead to serious error. Suffering as a righteous One, standing amongst men, on God's behalf, is one thing; and suffering instead of men, under the hand of God, is quite another. The Lord Jesus suffered for righteousness, during His *life*. He suffered for sin, in His death. During His life, man and Satan did their utmost; and, even at the cross, they put forth all their powers; but when all that they could do was done — when they had travelled, in their deadly enmity, to the utmost limit of human and diabolical opposition, there lay, far beyond a region of impenetrable gloom and horror into which the Sin-bearer had to travel, in the accomplishment of His work.[1]

Baked in the oven speaks of being exposed to the heat of hidden sufferings. This may speak of how the Lord inwardly agonized over the fallen condition of humanity. How did the Lord Jesus suffer being under the authority of imperfect parents? What daily oppression afflicted His soul being reared in a poor home and with siblings often taking advantage of his kind, selfless nature? What did it mean to the Lord to be under the unrighteous and often brutal rule of the Roman Empire? During the Lord's first advent, His own countrymen were more concerned about religious form and rituals than true allegiance to Jehovah; how this superficial attitude must have disheartened the devoted One who was fully aware of their deepest thoughts. A sinless man who never had one ill notion His entire life certainly would feel the agonizing weight of those living in and suffering in sin around him. Commenting to this inward suffering by our Lord, L. M. Grant adds:

> He felt the condition of mankind far more deeply than appeared on the surface. We may feel sorrow because of the evil all around us and for the ways evil infiltrates the Church of God in its testimony on earth. He feels this more deeply than we, and when here on earth, His disciples did not enter into the sufferings of His heart, as in His weeping over Jerusalem (Luke 19:41-44) and in His prayer in Gethsemane (Luke 22:41-46).[2]

Accordingly, the various preparation methods of the meal offering picture different ways Christ suffered during His life. This oblation when baked in a pan (or griddle) indicates the open sufferings which the Lord endured from human enmity. He endured verbal insults, the condescending attitudes of sinners, and the jeers of a brutal crowd demanding His death. He endured the flesh-tearing whip, the pulling out of His beard, the blows of brutal men to His face, and a crown of thorns beat down upon His head. In the same way that baking the meal offering made it more acceptable to those who would taste it, Christ's outward sufferings draw out our deeper admiration for Him. The Lord shows us that there is something to be gained through patiently suffering in righteousness, for even the Creator of the universe *"learned obedience by the things which He suffered"* (Heb. 5:8).

Besides baking the meal offering in an oven or in a pan, it also could be cooked in a cauldron, presumably in boiling water, but also "with oil." L. M. Grant notes: "Since water is a symbol of the Word of God, then it appears that this offering implies the sufferings of the Lord Jesus because of His obedience to God's Word and because of His faithfully declaring it (Luke 4:25-29 and John 10:27-31)."[3] The Lord's example shows us that there is a cost associated with living according to and faithfully declaring God's Word. God's message of salvation is foolish and offensive to the world (1 Cor. 1:18), hence the believer should not be surprised by the disdain and the ridicule spewed at them by those dead in trespasses and sins.

In the final three verses of Leviticus 2, a meal offering consisting of corn still on the ear or grain beaten out of the ear is mentioned. This offering represented the firstfruits of the harvest, as the grain had not been processed (milled) by human hands. The memorial was to be burnt by the priest upon the altar with oil and frankincense. This would also be an acceptable sweet-smelling offering to God, for it declared the uniqueness of spiritual life within the Lord Jesus. He was the only man on the entire planet who had eternal life within His own person. Beyond the wonders of His holy character, He held within His own essence the origin of life: *"All things were made through Him, and without Him nothing was made that was made. In Him was life, and the life was the light of men"* (John 1:3-4). How lonely and distressing it must have been to be removed from the holy bliss of heaven to endure a harsh existence as a human being on a cursed planet surrounded by rebels.

Ingredients Mentioned

	Uncooked Dough	Baked in an Oven	Baked in a Pan	Cooked or Boiled	Roasted Grain
Fine Flour	X	X	X	X	
Oil	X	X	X	X	X
Frankincense	X				X
Leaven					
Honey					
Salt	X	X	X	X	X

The Procedure and Provision

The person who brought the meal offering was to prepare it at home and then present it to a priest at the tabernacle. The preparation of the various meal offerings differed; some were not exposed to heat (2:1-3), others were subjected to the heat of an oven or frying pan (2:4-10), and some directly to fire (2:14-16). The priest would then burn a portion as a memorial of the offering on the altar and receive the remainder for himself (2:10). If a priest offered a meal offering, it was to be completely burned on the altar (6:23).

Aaron and his sons were to share this offering, but it was to be eaten by all with the unleavened bread in the Holy Place (6:16, 7:9-10). In this way the meal offerings were a provision of sustenance for God's ministers. Practically speaking, there is no better spiritual diet than for believer-priests to feed on Christ daily, that is, to draw from Him all that is needed for spiritual life daily. Studying and meditating on His Word strengthens our inner man and increases our understanding of and appreciation for Him. In this sense Christ is the food of the believer: *"For the bread of God is He who comes down from heaven and gives life to the world"* (John 6:33); *"Jesus said to them, 'I am the bread of life. He who comes to Me shall never hunger, and he who believes in Me shall never thirst'"* (John 6:35).

One type of meal offering was the firstfruits offering. The firstfruits offering associated with the Feast of Firstfruits in early spring had a unique feature; it was not to be burned on the altar (2:12). The barley harvest normally commenced at this time and a wave sheaf of that harvest was to be presented before the Lord, but it was not to be burned on the altar; in fact, it would become part of the leavened wave loaves at the Feast of Pentecost (Lev. 23:9-14). As we will examine in a subsequent chapter, the leavened loaves represent the Church which is composed of redeemed sinners who, though they still have sinful natures, are positionally sanctified in Christ and enabled to glorify God in Christ through the power of the Holy Spirit, despite the corruption within themselves. In practice, the Church has many spots, but positionally speaking, she will never suffer the flames of the altar – God's wrath. Rather, Christ in His Church is waved before and presented to the Father unto the praise of His Glory! Thus, offering the oblation of the firstfruits as a sweet savor offering on the altar was prohibited.

There were, however, other unleavened first-fruit offerings, such as ears of green corn or corn removed from the ear. These represent Christ apart from our sin, and could be brought before the Lord as an acceptable meal offering (2:14). Oil would be poured over the grain, and salt would be added before it was burned on the altar. As the presentation of the first fruit was a representation of the entire harvest, the offerer was, in effect, placing the entire yield before the Lord in acknowledgement that he had been the recipient of God's blessing and that God was sharing with the offerer His own harvest (Num. 12:13).

The fine flour symbolizes our Lord's perfect moral character – His sinless perfection in all His doings. John wrote of Christ's demonstrated perfect character: *"And the Word became flesh and dwelt among us, and we beheld His glory, the glory as of the only begotten of the Father, full of grace and truth"* (John 1:14). The Lord's flesh concealed the outshining glory of God but allowed His divine moral excellence to be viewed by all. Of all the men who have ever walked on this earth, only the Lord Jesus Christ could say:

> *My judgment is righteous, because I do not seek My own will but the will of the Father who sent Me* (John 5:30).

> *I always do those things that please Him [His Father]* (John 8:29).

> *Whatever I speak, just as the Father has told Me, so I speak* (John 12:50).

> *If you had known Me, you would have known My Father also* (John 14:7).

> *I have manifested Your name to the men* (John 17:6).

In every respect of moral nature and divine character the Son was a perfect representation of the Father: *"The Son can do nothing of Himself, but what He sees the Father do; for whatever He does, the Son also does in like manner"* (John 5:19). This is why the Lord Jesus could adamantly declare to Philip on the eve of His death: *"He that has seen Me has seen the Father"* (John 14:9). He was perfect in all His doings, in every circumstance, in each word spoken, and in every thought mentally conceived – all to the glory of God and thus achieving in His life the full appreciation of His Father. In application, the Lord's example should be followed by all those who name Him as Savior – let us not be just balanced, but strive to be full of grace and truth, that we too can manifest His name among men.

The priests were to either "pour" (2:1) or "anoint" (2:4) the meal offering with oil. In some cases the oil was to be "mixed" into the meal offering (2:5). Olive oil was also to be used in the special holy anointing mixture used to consecrate priests and holy things within the tabernacle for the Lord's service (Ex. 30:22-32). Oil is fluid that is active and enabling as shown in the operation of a lamp where oil is drawn from a reservoir through a wick to produce light when burned. The Holy Spirit is generally depicted as an active fluid in Scripture, such as blowing wind (John 3), seven flames of fire (Rev. 4), or rushing water from a rock (John 7). The Holy Spirit enables and accomplishes the will of God through others in a powerful and invisible fashion. For example, in one of Zechariah's visions, he sees two olive trees supplying oil to a lampstand. God used the expression *"Not by might nor by power, but by My Spirit"* (Zech. 4:6) in reference to the influence of the oil. God was confirming that it would be His Spirit working in Joshua and Zerubbabel (the two trees) to accomplish His will and provide a testimony (as seen in the lampstand) of Himself in Jerusalem.

In summary, pure oil is repeatedly used in the Bible to represent the enabling power of the Holy Spirit. Scripture repeatedly acknowledges the enabling power of the Spirit during Christ's earthly sojourn. The conception of Christ was through the power of the Holy Spirit (Luke 1:35). The Lord Jesus was anointed by the Spirit of God directly after His baptism in preparation for His public ministry (Matt. 3:16). The Lord offered Himself up as a sinless sacrifice in the power of the Holy Spirit (Heb. 9:14). As J. N. Darby notes, the unleavened cake saturated with oil is a beautiful picture of the entire life of the Lord Jesus:

> The cake was made mingled with oil, just as the human nature of Christ had its being and character, its taste, from the Holy Ghost, of which oil is the known symbol. But purity is not power [alone, thus the oil expresses] another form of spiritual power, acting in the human nature of Jesus.[4]

Scripture confirms that the Lord Jesus was led by and enabled by the power of the Holy Spirit in all His doings (Luke 4:18-19; John 1:32-34, 3:31; Acts 10:38). This is pictured by the oil on and within the meal offering.

Frankincense is what distinguished the meal offering from an ordinary cake. The frankincense for the meal offering was kept separate until presented before the Lord (Lev. 2:1; 15); it was then placed on the offering. The gum from the frankincense tree is an unusual spice which does not release its aroma until it is burned. This speaks of those superb, indescribable qualities that the Father appreciates about His Son, especially those exhibited in the agony of Calvary. Edward Dennett further explains this point:

> This being the case, there is the additional thought that the graces of Christ were brought out through the action of the holy fire; that His exposure to the judgment of God's holiness (fire) upon the cross, as there made sin, did but bring out all that was most precious and fragrant to God. He was indeed never more precious in His eyes, His perfections were never more fully displayed, than when He proved His obedience to the uttermost in the very place of sin. Hence He could say, *"Therefore doth My Father love me, because I lay down My life, that I might take it again."* It was for God's glory that He passed through the fire of judgment, and in doing so all the "sweet spices" of His moral graces and the perfection of His entire devotedness were brought out, and ascended up as a sweet savor to God.[5]

The frankincense burning on the altar fully released its sweet aroma; likewise, the voluntary sufferings of Christ at Calvary produced a lovely fragrance which God the Father fully appreciated.

Salt was added to all the meal offerings, and when burned it created white smoke. Salt adds flavor to what is eaten, and also serves as a food preservative. Salt then stands in contrast with leaven, which corrupts. This is why Paul used salt as a metaphor to speak of uncompromised truth (Col 4:6), and why the Lord Jesus exhorted His disciples to have a "salty" testimony (Matt. 5:13). The Gospels confirm that the entire life of the Lord Jesus was marked by dedication to living and declaring truth – His testimony was thus pure (salty) and appreciated by God.

Leaven, in Scripture, speaks of sin, a corruptive influence, or evil doctrine (Matt. 13:33; 1 Cor. 5:8). Henry Morris explains: "Leaven, of course, being involved with the fermentation process, is a perfect symbol of decay and corruption, and it is important that spiritual fellowship not be contaminated with it."[6] During the Feast of Unleavened Bread, the Jews were not only prohibited from eating leavened bread, but also they were not permitted to have leaven in their homes. If a Jew wanted to have fellowship with God and His people (i.e., to remain a part of the general assembly), the leaven had to go (Ex. 12:19). Because the Lord lived an unleavened life, He always remained in perfect fellowship with His Father (John 1:18, 3:13).

The Lord Jesus warned His disciples against the influence of humanized traditions that oppose sound doctrine: *"Beware of the leaven of the Pharisees, which is hypocrisy"* (Luke 12:1). He also cautioned them concerning *"the leaven ... of the Sadducees"* (Matt. 16:6). Today the ideologies of the Sadducees live on in intellectualism, humanism, higher criticism, post-modernism, and naturalism. Lastly, the Lord Jesus commanded His disciples not to be influenced by *"the leaven of Herod"* (Mark 8:15). Herod, a Jew, was in cahoots with the Roman Empire, and was, therefore, a friend of the world (Jas. 4:4); his love for God and His Word had been supplanted by the love for materialism, fame, and political ambition. Not only was the Lord's life not leavened by sin (1 Cor. 5:6-7), but also He was not influenced in the least by these leavened influences of a God-hating world. Because it reflected these aspects of Christ's life, the unleavened meal offering was valuable and precious to God.

Honey symbolizes natural sweetness (Matt. 12:46-50; John 2:4). Because of the high sugar content in honey, it greatly enhances the reaction of leaven within a lump of bread dough. Drawing from this relationship and the premise that leaven represents sin or a corrupting influence, Bible commentators have speculated as to what "honey" typifies in Scripture:

"The affections of those we love after the flesh" (J. N. Darby).

"Nature and its relationships" (C. H. Mackintosh).

"The amiable side of human nature" (William Kelly).

We understand that Christ, as *holy humanity* (see Luke 1:35), could not sin, for there was nothing in His members that would respond to sin; there was no "honey" in Him per se. His very essence repulsed sin and loathed its working. Some have suggested that the external solicitations of Satan upon the Lord Jesus caused some internal moral struggle within His person. This is not the case. How could the Father, looking down from heaven, declare, *"This is My beloved Son, in whom I am well pleased"* (Matt. 3:17), if the Lord was struggling internally with thoughts of sin? As John declared, the Lord Jesus "was," not "might be," *"The Lamb of God who takes away the sin of the world!"* (John 1:29). The Father never questioned the impeccability of Christ – only Satan and men do that – He was blameless and perfect; there was nothing within Him that would disqualify Him as the only acceptable substitutional sacrifice for man's sin.

Summary

The meal offering portrays the perfect character and spotless life of our Lord Jesus Christ. It was consumed by the fire on the altar to speak of Christ's person being fully tested by the righteousness of God and not found wanting. During His earthly sojourn, our Lord exhibited a blameless and even character; this is represented in the fine flour. He was both anointed by and full of the Holy Spirit as represented by the olive oil poured over and mixed into the meal offering. His entire life was a sweet savor to God, but the fragrance of the burning frankincense with the meal offerings specially pictures God's appreciation of all His sufferings resulting from living on a cursed planet with a condemned people immersed in sin. The Lord was completely faithful, as symbolized by preserving salt, and sinless, as shown by the absence of leaven in the meal offering. Yet, beyond that, Christ was impeccable; that is, there was no capacity within Himself to sin, as shown by the absence of honey, which would stimulate the effectiveness of leaven, if present. We agree with the Shulamite bride when speaking of her beloved: *"He is altogether lovely. This is my beloved"* (SOS 5:16).

Application

The symbolism of the meal offering presents a significant application for the Church. Christ, as a man, sustained the harsh living conditions of a sin-plagued planet, the contradiction of sinners, the opposition of

Satan, and the hatred of the world. This is the type of suffering which pertains to the baking and cooking of the meal offering. To realize this concept should be a comfort to all believers, for our interceding High Priest in heaven can fully empathize with those who are suffering and enduring what He already has (but in no way to the extent that He did). He knows all about living for God in a wicked world. In this we find a solace and comfort for our distressed souls. Thus, the redeemed are invited to *"come boldly,"* and *"obtain mercy, and find grace to help in time of need"* (Heb. 4:16). May each believer take full advantage of the throne of grace in times of need.

Additionally, as we contemplate and further appreciate the sweet-smelling life of the Lord Jesus, may God stir our own hearts to pursue holy living. To share the gospel message with others without a solid testimony to corroborate the validity of the message is to mock Christ. To declare the gospel message accurately in word and deed without regard to personal suffering for doing so honors Him. This is Christ's example and we are shown through the meal offerings that such a dedicated life refreshes the heart of God.

Meditation

Take my life, and let it be consecrated, Lord, to Thee.
Take my moments and my days; let them flow in ceaseless praise.
Take my hands, and let them move at the impulse of Thy love.
Take my feet, and let them be swift and beautiful for Thee.

Take my will, and make it Thine; it shall be no longer mine.
Take my heart, it is Thine own; it shall be Thy royal throne.
Take my love, my Lord, I pour at Thy feet its treasure store.
Take myself, and I will be ever, only, all for Thee.

— Frances R. Havergal

The Peace Offering
Leviticus 3:1-17, 7:11-34

The peace offering is the third and final sweet savor offering mentioned in Leviticus. Whereas the burnt offering speaks of God's own appreciation for Christ's sacrifice, the peace offering expresses all the privileges and communion believers can enjoy with God through His sacrifice. In the burnt offering we see Christ treasured by God exclusively, but the peace offering speaks of the joyful fellowship that God and redeemed and cleansed worshippers share.

In the execution of the peace offering, the offerer was not a mere observer, as he was with the burnt offering, but a participant. This likely explains why it was permitted to bring a female sacrifice. The worshipper's capacity to enjoy communion with God through Christ is the primary view; that is, there is less focus on the victim directly representing specific aspects of Christ's character and sacrifice. The offering of a female as a burnt offering would not be permitted, as that sacrifice would poorly represent the devotion of the Son of God to His Father.

William Kelly further clarifies the distinct meanings of the various sweet aroma offerings as he compares and contrasts the other two with the peace offering:

> [The peace offering] is not here all going up to God (Christ surrendering Himself to God up to His death); nor only has God His portion, but the priestly family have theirs (Christ surrendering Himself in His life); but Christ is alike the means and object of communion. It rightly therefore follows both the offerings of a sweet savor – the holocaust [the burnt offering] and the oblation [the meal offering]; it approaches the former, in that it supposes the death of Christ; it resembles but it surpasses the latter, in that if part is for God, there is part for man. It was preeminently therefore what united all who partook

of it in joy, thanksgiving, and praise. Hence the fellowship of God, the priest, the offerer and his family is the impression engraved on it.[1]

The peace offering portrayed God's fellowship with His people made possible through the efficacy of Christ's sacrifice and His effectual work as the offering Priest. Thus, it was the only offering in which God, the offering priest, and the individual who brought the sacrifice received portions (i.e., were mutually blessed). This is likely why the fowls were not permitted as peace offerings; they would be an insufficient sacrifice for all parties to have a part. Everyone did benefit from and enjoy this offering; this portrays the fellowship that God and man are able to enjoy on the basis of Christ's past sacrifice for sin and as a result of His present intercessory work as High Priest. Because Christ and His Father are in perfect fellowship and union, believers in Christ can enjoy all the rich blessings appropriated to us through that lovely communion – this spiritual reality is pictured in the sweet savor of the peace offering.

The Types of Offerings and Portions

There were four types of animals which could be sacrificed: cattle or oxen from the herd (3:1-5), and a lamb (3:6-11) or a goat (3:12-17) from the flock. The peace offering was not gender-specific (3:1, 6). As just mentioned, it was also unique in that God, the offering priest, and the offerer all received a part of it. The Lord's portion is addressed first: The fat that covered the intestines and the liver, the kidneys (and the fat attached above them), and the sheep's fatty tail (3:9) were to be burned on the Bronze Altar as a sweet savor to God (3:3-5, 9-11, 14-17).

The fat and kidneys were burned on top of the ashes and smoldering remains of previous burnt offerings, such as those offered twice daily by the priests (3:5). The offering priest received the right thigh after it was presented to the Lord as a heave offering (7:14). The general populous of priests received the breast after it, too, was waved before the Lord (7:28-36). The remainder of the animal was returned to the offerer who then likely invited family and friends to a merry feast in thankful celebration of the Lord's goodness (7:15-16).

What is the spiritual significance of the breast, the thigh, the fat, and the kidneys? The breast represents endearment and love, while the thigh (the strongest muscle in the body) is an emblem of strength. This reminds us that to properly serve God, the believer-priest (1 Pet. 2:5-9) must draw his or her strength from the Lord and yearn for the embrace of His vast and changeless affection. This is the believer's food; this is what we are to live for!

Fat is where the energy of the body is stored for later use and, as indicated in the animal offerings, it readily piles up over the entrails (i.e., the belly area). We now recognize the fatty lobes attached to the top of the kidneys as the adrenal glands. These glands are primarily responsible for releasing hormones into our bodies to enhance our response during stressful situations. This is accomplished by the manipulation of carbohydrates, fats, and proteins, as well as the regulation of salt and water levels in our bodies. Adrenalin, which physiologically equips the body to respond to threatening or exhilarating circumstances, is secreted by these glands. The main idea here is that, not only was the fat to be offered on the altar, but the glands which enhanced the body's responsiveness were to be burned too.

The special emphasis on the fat of the animal suggests that it was considered the best part of the sacrifice (Gen. 4:4; 45:18). This symbolic association between "fat" and "one's best" is scripturally connected with the inward heart of man: *"Their heart is as fat as grease, but I delight in Your law"* (Ps. 119:70); *"They have closed up their fat hearts; with their mouths they speak proudly"* (Ps. 17:10). Thus, fat represents the energy of the inward will – the disposition of our heart. The Lord Jesus dedicated His best with full consecration to the Father. Hence, the fat of the peace offering was not to be eaten but rather to be burned on the altar to symbolize the Father's full esteem for and acceptance of the Son's devotion. All of Christ's energy was selflessly and purely expended for God.

God wants our best, too, which is only possible by following the Lord's example of wholehearted devotion. Our commitment to God is to be without reservation. This is why God delighted in David, a man whose heart beat strongly for the Lord (1 Sam. 13:14). David aspired: *"I will praise You, O Lord, with my whole heart"* (Ps. 9:1). The burning of the fat, representing human will, reminds us that God wants our whole heart in service to Him.

The kidney is the organ that actively filters toxic waste from the body. What might be the spiritual meaning represented in the burning the kidneys on the Bronze Altar? Scripture includes the testimony of many who personally valued the work of divine examination and cleansing.

David pleaded with the Lord to examine him and to show him his sin: *"Examine me, O Lord, and prove me; try my mind and my heart"* (Ps. 26:2). Jeremiah acknowledged that God tests the minds and the hearts of His people (Jer. 11:20). To serve the Lord properly, we need to see our sin clearly in order to confess it to God, and to this end we should desire the Lord to show us our sin. Only what is done for the Lord with clean hands and a pure heart counts for eternity (Ps. 24:5). For our energy (the fat) to be properly expended for the Lord, our hearts must have pure motives (the kidneys) – otherwise we will do more damage than good to the name of Christ. Christian service without a display of Christ's character is nothing more than humanism; it is a Christ-mocking gesture of the worst kind.

The Lord Jesus is the supreme object of the Father's delight. In grace, the Father has given His people that which He enjoys abundantly – Christ – that all may have fellowship together in Him. Though our estimation of the Lord is imperfect and will never rise to the standard of divine reckoning, we are permitted to enjoy and appreciate the very One whom God esteems so highly. This is the reality of the Christ-centered fellowship which is signified in the peace offering.

The General Procedure

The procedure for the sacrifice of the peace offering was the same regardless of the animal in question, and was as follows:

> The offerer brought his sacrifice before the Lord after gaining the assistance of a priest.
> The offerer laid his hand on the head of his sacrifice (on the north side of the altar).
> The offerer killed the sacrifice there before the door of the tabernacle.
> The priest sprinkled the blood around the outside of the altar.
> The priest offered the fat and the kidneys on the altar.
> The priest salted the sacrifice (Num. 18:19; Ezek. 43:24).
> The priest waved a memorial of the cakes and bread of the offering.
> The priests received their portion of meat and cakes.
> The offerer received what remained of the animal and the cakes.
> All enjoyed fellowship together.

The offerer was responsible for burning the remaining meat after the allotted time.

The peace offering was a sweet savor sacrifice, in contrast with the sin and trespass offerings, which related to the righteous handling of the offence and damage of sin, respectively. The peace offering does not relate to Christ's suffering for human sin, even though the blood of the sacrifice was sprinkled about the altar. It is quite important to understand that a sin-bearing Christ is not pictured in the peace offering; instead, we see Christ who, having already borne our sins, has secured our *peace with God*, this opens the way for us to enjoy the *peace of God* in happy fellowship with Him. And we are encouraged to do so, but God cannot come into the darkness to have fellowship with us; we must walk with Him in the light of divine truth (1 Jn. 1:7).

Thankfully, when we do sin there is a provision for cleansing through the effectual power of Christ's blood. As we confess sin to the Lord, His blood has the power to repeatedly wash and cleanse us from all the stain of sin:

> *If we say that we have fellowship with Him, and walk in darkness, we lie and do not practice the truth. But if we walk in the light as He is in the light, we have fellowship with one another, and* **the blood of Jesus Christ His Son cleanses us from all sin**. *If we say that we have no sin, we deceive ourselves, and the truth is not in us.* **If we confess our sins, He is faithful and just to forgive us our sins and to cleanse us from all unrighteousness** (1 Jn. 1:6-9).

This is likely why the blood of the peace offerings was sprinkled about the Bronze Altar – it represented the future cleansing power of Christ's blood for the sin that is within us. Notice that John does *not* say that God cleanses our unrighteousness when we pray to ask forgiveness of our sins. According to God's Word we know it is when we "confess" our sins to Him that we are purified and are returned to fellowship with God again. The act of confessing means that we stand with God against ourselves, that is, we agree with Him that our wrong behavior was sinful and that we are genuinely sorry for offending Him. Confession is the responsibility of the believer, and cleansing is God's; both processes must be performed on an ongoing basis as we have a constant need of *"the blood of Jesus Christ His Son* [which] *cleanses us from all sin"* (1 Jn. 1:7). This passage does not concern a person's eternal salvation or the believer's relationship with God – that is secured in Christ (John 5:24, 10:28-29); the focus here, as well as in the peace offering, is the believer's fellowship with God.

To summarize, although the peace offering involves the shedding and sprinkling of blood about the altar, it is not Christ's sin-bearing sacrifice that is symbolized (as in the sin offering), but, rather, it is our necessity for ongoing sin-cleansing by His blood. The effectual working of Christ's blood pictured in the sin offering is to purge the sin that is on us (Rom. 5:12) and to purge the sinner's guilty *"conscience from dead works to serve the living God"* (Heb. 9:12). That blood was shed two thousand years ago on our behalf, but it is as effectual today as then.

Motives for the Offering

There are three reasons given as to why an individual might be motivated to sacrifice a peace offering. The first, and apparently the most common, was to express thanksgiving to God (7:12-15). The birth of a child, the recovery from a severe illness, or some other special reason for gratitude could prompt the presentation of a peace offering. An individual might also offer a peace offering as a ritualistic expression of having entered into a vow with the Lord (27:9-10) or having fulfilled one, as in the de-consecration of a Nazirite (Num. 6:17-20). Lastly, an offerer wanting to contribute a voluntary gift to the Lord could offer a peace offering (22:18-23).

All peace offerings had a deadline for its consumption. If a sacrifice was presented for either of the latter two reasons, an extra day was permitted to eat the meat associated with the sacrifice. Yet, if the meat was eaten after the second day, the peace offering in its entirety would be unacceptable to the Lord and the offender would be unclean and cut off from his people (7:18-21). Either through human digestion or by fire the entire animal of the peace offering was totally consumed after the second day.

What application might we derive from this time limitation? While it is true that extending thanks to the Lord for His goodness is important, it is also true that more personal energy and time is required to affect real worship and devotion. True worshippers long to understand the heart of God. They are not satisfied with merely recognizing God's goodness to them, but they desire to know why He is so gracious. What within His holy character motivated His benevolent favor? This type of spiritual pursuit requires more sustained effort by the believer in God's Word with the assistance of the Holy Spirit and, consequently, has more lasting value.

Those who brought a peace offering would take an unblemished animal, either male or female (3:1, 6), from their herds or flocks to the tabernacle for sacrifice. Besides the animal sacrifice, the offerer also had to present unleavened cakes mixed with oil, unleavened wafers anointed with oil, fried cakes of fine flour and oil, and leavened bread to the priest (7:12-13). According to Jewish tradition, there were to be ten cakes of each kind of pastry in every peace offering for a total of forty. One of each type was presented to the Lord as a heave offering and then given to the officiating priest (7:14). The remaining ones were neither heaved nor burned, but after being dedicated to the Lord they were returned to the offerer and eaten in the communal meal that followed.[2] Through the peace offering God provided His priests with meat and bread to eat (7:16-17).

If leaven speaks of corruption, why was leaven included in the bread of the peace offering, when as we have seen it was prohibited in the meal offering? While it is true that the believer has "leaven" within, we also realize that positionally in Christ there is no sin or uncleanness in us. Until glorification, sin will remain within believers, but those in Christ should no longer be ruled and ruined by its presence. This is likely why both leavened bread and unleavened cakes were presented before the Lord: the redeemed, who still sin, are presented before the Lord because the Redeemer who cannot sin is with them. This aspect is not communicated through the meal offering, which pictures not the redeemed but the Redeemer's sinless humanity – thus, no leaven was to be used in the meal offering. The peace offering, on the other hand, demonstrates the amazing provision of grace that though we still sin (1 Jn. 1:10) we can be perfectly cleansed of that sin by the blood of Christ through confession (1 Jn. 1:9). This then allows us to come before the Lord and present acceptable unleavened sacrifices to Him, though we still have within us a nature that sins.

All of the meat associated with this sacrifice of thanksgiving had to be eaten the same day that it was offered (7:15); anything remaining until the next day had to be burned (v. 17). From a symbolic point of view, this stipulation connects the value of the believer's praise with the means by which it was made acceptable to God, that is through the priestly energy of Christ (as pictured in the burning fat on the altar). The Lord's people do not create spiritual fellowship with each other when they come together to consume food or have fun; rather, when believers are conscious of Christ's presence a certain reverential awe overshadows all that transpires in their doings. This is why the Jews were not permitted to hold private feasts; the Lord's people cannot enjoy spiritual fellowship together, in any form, apart from the One who binds them together in divine love. J. N. Darby comments on the fundamental link that real fellowship and worship must share:

> When the Holy Spirit leads us into real spiritual worship, He leads us into communion with God, into the presence of God; and then, necessarily, all the infinite acceptability to Him of the offering of Christ is present to our spirit. We are associated with it: it forms an integral and necessary part of the communion and worship. We cannot be in the presence of God in communion without finding it [worship] there.[3]

What man does apart from God's acceptance of His Son (and His sacrifice) has no value with Him – in fact is insulting to Him (Isa. 64:6). It is for this reason the Jews faced stern consequences if they ate the meat of the sacrifice after the day it was offered. The time limit for eating the meat reminds us we should not delay to give God thanks when we know that He has blessed us. Our tomorrows may never come, or, as is often the case, in our busyness we may forget to pause and praise Him. How often we act like spoiled children who are indifferent or even oblivious to expressions of their parents' love! Worse yet, we praise ourselves for our perceived achievements, or we extend to others the gratitude which the Lord deserves.

The story of Hosea and Gomer conveys a vivid picture to us of how God feels when we direct our praise and devotion, which He deserves, to others. The prophet Hosea was an honorable man, but his wife Gomer was lascivious and actually conceived children that were not Hosea's. In time, Gomer abandoned Hosea to pursue a fast-life with her various lovers. It wasn't long before Gomer found herself in a poor and desperate situation. Hosea demonstrated sacrificial love for Gomer and sent supplies to her. From a distance Hosea watched his wife Gomer praise her lovers for the very provisions he had sent to assist her (Hosea 2:5-8). God allowed Hosea to feel this hurt and to write of it that we might better understand how God feels when we rob Him of the praise that He deserves and value worldly pleasures more than our communion with Him. Gomer was abandoned by her lovers and sold into slavery. The redeeming love of God is exemplified when Hosea bought back his own adulterous wife during a public slave auction. After experiencing the magnitude of Hosea's love, she never departed from him again. May we learn this lesson before experiencing the harsh repercussions that Gomer experienced. Consistent gratitude is a guard against depression and regression.

Worship focuses on who God is inherently, His "worth-ship." Praise acknowledges God's blessings to us. The blind man of John 9 was thankful that Jesus healed his blindness, but it was only when he realized that he was in the presence of the Son of God that he fell down and worshiped Christ. This realization came after more exposure to the truth. He worshiped the Lord Jesus for who He was/is, not for what He had done. Praise has its place, but if worshippers focus only on the gifts God bestows and not upon why God has given them, our worship will become shallow and selfish. Worship focuses on the Giver, not the gift itself and thus requires more effort on the believer's part. L. M. Grant further clarifies this distinction as it pertains to the peace offerings for vows and spontaneous gifts:

> The Lord Jesus has plainly forbidden us to make vows today (Matt. 5:33-37), man in the flesh has been proven untrustworthy by the law of God, and we cannot promise what we may do in the future. Yet the vow would no doubt speak of the purpose of heart to devote oneself to the Lord in obedient faith. This is right, but not an actual vow. There is energy involved in this more than in a thanksgiving, so it was eaten two days.
>
> The voluntary offering, however, was not because of a single matter for thanksgiving, but a spontaneous appreciation of the Lord Himself. This too involved more energy than did one occasion of thanksgiving, so it could be eaten the second day; but if any remained later than the second day, it was to be burned (v. 17).[4]

Apart from Christ there can be no fellowship with God, and apart from the communion of the Spirit there can be no true worship. One must wonder if this is why the Church is weak in much of the world today. Could it be that many who name Christ today are crowding into spectacular, well-garnished buildings in which the Lord is nowhere to be found? Is it possible that we have permitted religious form and professional showmanship to drive the Lord from our church meetings? The peace offering declares that true worship of God and fellowship with God are not separated aspects of our spiritual life in Christ, but rather the former is a natural expression of the latter.

Prohibitions

The Israelites were not permitted to ingest the fat or the blood of the animals sacrificed for the peace offerings; these were Jehovah's portion (3:17). This is due to the symbolism involved: the blood was the life of the animal sacrificed and the fat was its excellence. The Jews were also forbidden to eat the meat of the sacrifice if it had come into contact with something unclean (7:19) or if they had become unclean themselves (7:20-21). To ignore this directive carried a stiff penalty – that individual was cut off from the nation. This may seem to us to be too severe, but the Lord wanted to stress the seriousness of pretending to be in fellowship with Him while secretly indulging in sin. This important message was also impressed upon the Christians at Corinth centuries later, some of which had died or were in danger of dying for not judging personal sin and yet continuing to gather with the Church to worship the Lord, as if there were nothing wrong (1 Cor. 5:4-8, 11:27-32).

The Necessity of Sweet Aroma Offerings

Besides the burnt offering, the meal offering, and the peace offerings described in the early chapters of Leviticus, the priests also were commanded to present daily sweet savor offerings for the nation of Israel (Ex. 29:38-42). These daily offerings were a perpetual sweet savor to God and were a continual sign to the nation of Israel that they were accepted into God's presence (i.e., that they were in proper fellowship with their God). Likewise, believers in the Church Age are accepted in the Beloved as a continual sweet savor offering unto God. The daily sacrifices included a meal offering and a drink offering which were to accompany the lamb slain as a burnt offering in the morning and afternoon. Logistically speaking, the fire on the Bronze Altar was occasionally extinguished and the sweet savor before God ceased for a time, but through Christ's redemptive work, all believers are made a continual sweet fragrance unto God forever!

The daily sacrifices, therefore, allowed God to tabernacle among His people and to communicate His will to them through Moses. Through the daily sweet savor sacrifices the tabernacle could continue to be "the tent of meeting." The billowing smoke of the burnt offerings was a continual testimony of the nation's acceptance with God. The absence of smoke from the Bronze Altar at any time except a God-directed relocation of the camp signaled to the nation that there was a problem that needed immediate attention. Where there is no smoke there is no sacrificial fire, and without substitutional sacrifices a holy God could not be in fellowship with His people. Jehovah was teaching His people the importance of properly and immediately dealing with sin in order to maintain communion with God. This is illustrated in the sweet savor of the peace offerings which were sacrificed by those who understood and desired the blessing of God's presence.

Application

As previously stated, the peace offering symbolizes God's fellowship with man through Christ; it was the only offering of which God, the offering priest, and the offerer all received a portion. As the believer's fellowship with God, provision from God, and ability to bless God are all figuratively demonstrated within the peace offering, there is much application for the Church to consider. It suffices here to suggest three points:

First, for centuries to come, the peace offering would be God's provision for the priests' food. Consequently, in the context of the peace offering, the altar of God was also called the Lord's Table for His serving priests. The Lord's Table is an expression that is used in both the Old and New Testaments to convey the concept of divine provision and fellowship (Ps. 23:5, 78:19; Mal. 1:7, 12; 1 Cor. 9:13, 10:18). Both the Levitical priests under the old covenant of the Law (Lev. 6:16, 26, 7:6, 31-32) and believer priests under the new covenant of grace (1 Cor. 10:20-21) have been invited to abide at the Lord's Table.

The story of King David's kindness to Mephibosheth, the crippled son of Jonathan (2 Sam. 9:13), is a fitting allegory of the Lord's Table.

Normally, a new king would exterminate all remaining heirs of the previous dynasty in order to prevent a potential takeover. However, King David, because of his love for Jonathan and the covenant he had made with him (1 Sam. 18:3), set a place at his table for Mephibosheth for the remainder of his life. Mephibosheth never had to worry about where his next meal would come from, and he could enjoy daily fellowship with the king. Similarly, though once the enemies of God, believers in Christ now have the opportunity to enjoy fellowship with Him and with other believers at His table and to receive daily wherewithal to serve Him.

Often the biblical term "the Lord's Table" (which speaks of a spiritual table where believers receive blessing and fellowship in Christ – see 1 Corinthians 10) is confused with the biblical term "the Lord's Supper" (which refers to the remembrance meeting of the local church – see 1 Corinthians 11). Consequently, most of Christendom refers to the Lord's Supper with the non-scriptural term "the communion service." There is *communion with Christ* at the Lord's Table, but more specifically, there is a *remembrance of Christ* at every Lord's Supper – the value of His death is proclaimed afresh. The Lord's Table is spiritual and is set by Him, whereas the table at the Lord's Supper is physical and is set by us; at the former we receive provisions from the Lord, but at the latter we worship and remember Him.

The Lord's Table speaks of the sum total of the spiritual blessings we have in Christ, while the Lord's Supper refers to the remembrance meeting of the Church. In the sense that the souls of believers are refreshed through Spirit-led worship, the Lord's Table probably includes the Lord's Supper, but the distinct terminology and significance of each should not be lost. It is a great privilege to remember and refresh the Savior during the Lord's Supper, and it is a blessing to the heart of every believer to commune with and receive from the Savior at His Table.

Paul thus exhorts the believers at Corinth not to remove themselves from the Lord's Table to partake of the world's resources; to do so is to fellowship with demons:

> *I do not want you to have fellowship with demons. You cannot drink the cup of the Lord and the cup of demons; you cannot partake of the Lord's table and of the table of demons. Or do we provoke the Lord to jealousy? Are we stronger than He?* (1 Cor. 10:20-22).

When ordering the priesthood and sacrifices, God wonderfully provided for the needs of His priests, mainly through the peace offerings just reviewed. While atoning blood was being applied to the altar to sanctify it, the priest also appropriated the offering by eating it. This repeats the same idea of Exodus 12 where the blood of a victim (the Passover lamb) was applied to sanctify the one who ate the victim's flesh. The themes of blood atonement, substitutional death, and sanctification to God are all inter-connected in Scripture and, ultimately, have their typological climax and fulfillment at Calvary.

The Bronze Altar would be God's Table to supply His priest's needs, but the priests had to eat what was provided by the Lord before Him in the tabernacle. May each believer realize the importance of eating at the Lord's Table and, accordingly, choose to abide with Him there. Failure to do so will provoke the Lord's jealousy and His chastening hand. Why would a believer ever want to sever his or her communion with the Lord? It is a great privilege and honor to sup at His Table!

Second, as shown symbolically in the burning of the fat (the animal's energy) and kidneys (the purifying organ), every believer should strive to have pure motives when dedicating his or her energy in service for the Lord. We do not want to waste time and resources to bolster an emotional experience, a religious cause, or just busy work. We should want what God wants and that means giving our best to what He says is best: *"Therefore do not be unwise, but understand what the will of the Lord is"* (Eph. 5:17). This will require the believer to expend much time meditating and studying God's Word.

In all three peace offerings the central focus is upon the blood which was sprinkled about the altar, and the fat and the kidneys which were burned on the altar: the blood is the basis of *redemption*, the fat the basis for *acceptance*, and the kidneys speak of the basis of holy *purification*. Through redemption, what a believer chooses to do through Christ in the will of God with pure motives is made acceptable to Him. This is only possible through the enabling power of the Holy Spirit as pictured in the oil of the cakes that accompanied the peace offering, thus the cakes and bread were a necessary part of the overall sacrifice.

Third, in the peace offering, our Lord is presented as the basis of our peace with God and with each other. How wonderful it is to be accepted by God in the Beloved! Through Christ alone can the believer enter God's presence in peace, with acceptable worship, and enjoy the benefits of divine communication and fellowship. The Lord Jesus Christ – *"He is our peace"* (Eph. 2:4).

When believers are in communion with the Lord, they will be in fellowship with each other. There is only one fellowship to be a part of, only one to actively pursue and maintain. Thus, Paul commanded fellow believers to *"keep the unity of the Spirit in the bond of peace"* (Eph. 4:3). If we are not in fellowship with God, it is impossible for us to be in fellowship with each other; His peace is what is missing.

The early Church *"continued steadfastly in the apostles' doctrine and fellowship, in the breaking of bread, and in prayers"* (Acts 2:42). In the Greek language, there is a definite article that precedes the word *koinonia* ("fellowship") in this verse. This means that all the believers in Jerusalem were enjoying "the fellowship." There is only one kind of spiritual fellowship that can be enjoyed by all believers and that is Christ's fellowship. The Lord instructed His disciples: *"Abide in Me, and I in you. As the branch cannot bear fruit of itself, unless it abides in the vine, neither can you, unless you abide in Me"* (John 15:4). As we choose to abide with Him, we learn that fellowship and fruitfulness cannot be separated. This is the message of the peace offering: because of God's past acceptance of Christ's redemptive work at Calvary and because of Christ's current intercessory ministry, both God and man are able to come together in sweet communion. The enjoyment of that fellowship is in the mutual appreciation of the beloved Son of God and our beloved Savior.

Meditation

> The King of Heaven His table spreads, and blessings crown the board;
> No paradise, with all its joys, could such delight afford.
>
> Pardon and peace to dying men, and endless life are given,
> Through the rich blood that Jesus shed to raise our souls to Heaven.
>
> Millions of souls, in glory now, were fed and feasted here;
> And millions more, still on the way, around the board appear.
>
> — Philip Doddridge

The Sin Offering
Leviticus 4:1-35, 5:1-13, 6:24-30

A transition between the sweet savor sacrifices and the non-sweet savor sacrifices occurs in Leviticus 4. The burnt offering, the meal offering, and the peace offering were voluntary offerings and, thus, a sweet fragrance to God. The two offerings yet to be described are the sin offering and the trespass offering which were mandatory and, therefore, did not smell sweet to God. The exception to this was the fat for the sin offering burnt on the Bronze Altar was a sweet savor to the Lord (4:31). The contrast between the sweet savor and the non-sweet savor offerings is significant and we would do well to understand and appreciate it.

A person who brought a sweet-smelling offering identified himself with the victim by laying his hands on the head of the sacrifice, and was recognized as an acceptable worshipper. Although the offerer of a non-sweet-smelling sacrifice also identified with the victim in this same way, his approach was much different. He was not a cleansed worshipper in communion with God, but rather a guilty sinner deserving judgment. With this said, William MacDonald reminds us that sin and trespass offerings were to be offered by the redeemed alone:

> The sin offering was appointed for a redeemed people. It does not speak of a sinner coming to the Lord for salvation, but of an Israelite, in covenant relationship with the Lord, seeking forgiveness. It has to do with sins committed unconsciously or unintentionally.[1]

The Law, the covenant that Jehovah and the Jewish people entered into at Sinai, was chiefly conditional: God would bless them for obedience and punish them for disobedience. Their relationship with Jehovah in that covenant was maintained by the annual observance of the Day of Atonement. On that day, the high priest sprinkled the blood of a bull and of a goat on the mercy seat to atone for all the failures of the people (including himself) in upholding their part of the covenant. It is important to understand that the purpose of these five offerings is to maintain Jehovah's presence among His people, not to establish it initially. As a nation, they had already been redeemed by the blood of the Passover lamb in Egypt.

In the sweet aroma offerings the offerer was accepted because of his union with the victim, which God fully accepted and appreciated. This, as mentioned previously, pictures our acceptance in Christ before God. However, in the non-sweet-smelling offerings the opposite was true – the victim took on the guilty and unacceptable status of the offerer and was judged in his place. This does not mean that Christ in Himself was unacceptable, but that with our sin upon Him, He received God's judgment. In the sweet-smelling offerings the offerer is brought up in status, but in the non-sweet-smelling offerings the victim is brought down in position.

With that clarification on the differences between the sweet and non-sweet savor offerings, let us now examine the distinctions between the two different non-sweet savor offerings. The sin offering was demanded for the *offense of sin*, but the trespass offering was required for the *damages of sin*. The sin offering deals with the guilt of sin; Christ's blood purges the believer's conscience from that. The trespass offering deals with the damage that sin causes; through Christ's offering, full restoration of the sinner to God is made possible. Thus, Christ as pictured in the sin offering resolves *who we are* by nature, but in the trespass offering He absolves *what we have done*. Both the sin offering and the trespass offering were commanded by God for those who committed sins of ignorance against Him (inadvertent actions done in weakness or negligence; 4:13, 22, 27, 5:15) – these were not for premeditated acts of defiance against God, and for offenses against one's neighbor (6:2-5).

Leviticus 5:1-4 provides four examples of such offenses: someone who negligently withheld information in a public charge against another person, accidental defilement from touching something dead, some human uncleanness (e.g., a leper), and a rash oath (e.g., a soon-forgotten vow). If Jephthah would have recalled the provision of the sin offering, he could have atoned for his tragic vow and have been forgiven, thus sparing his daughter from his own foolishness (Judg. 11).

Although there were a variety of reasons a person might present a sin offering unto the Lord, Leviticus 4:1 through 5:13 groups these occasions into two classes:

1. When the conscience of the offerer was violated – no specific sins are listed (Lev. 4)
2. When the offerer became ceremonially unclean per the stipulations of the Law (Lev. 5:1-13)

Leviticus 4 provides instructions for the wounded conscience. It is often after the fact that we realize we have sinned: perhaps it was a hasty word ill-spoken, a passing comment about someone else that we later realize was gossip, or some mental comparison that we held onto just long enough to prompt our pride. Because we have a nature within us that is prone to sin, these types of sins readily occur. While it is true we are not responsible for the sin nature we inherited, we are completely responsible for how it expresses itself – the sin offering reminded the Jews that they were each personally accountable to God for sin.

There were no Levitical sacrifices that an individual could sacrifice to the Lord to atone for willful sin: *"But the person who does anything presumptuously, whether he is native-born or a stranger, that one brings reproach on the Lord, and he shall be cut off from among his people"* (Num. 15:30). God is holy, and for Him to dwell among His people, they had to be holy too; as this was an impossibility, sin and trespass offerings were needed. At the national level, all sin was atoned for on the annual Day of Atonement, a matter discussed further in Leviticus 16. The sin offering dealt with what every man was by nature – a sinner, whereas the trespass offering highlighted what every man does – sinful acts.

The History of the Sin Offering

The sin offering was first introduced to us in Exodus 29 when Aaron and his sons were consecrated as priests. Before they could serve before the Lord in the tabernacle, the matter of their sin had to be addressed. For this, an unblemished bullock was to be sacrificed for a sin offering (Ex. 29:14). Aaron and his sons were to place their hands upon the head of the bullock to symbolically show their identification with the innocent substitute, which was to take their place in the judgment of their sin.

The bullock was killed, its blood collected, and its carcass prepared for sacrifice. The fat above its liver and its two kidneys was burned on the Bronze Altar, but the remainder of the animal was burnt in a clean place outside the camp. Because the sacrifice symbolized the transfer of sin and judgment, it had to be done outside the camp, lest there be defilement within the camp. Moses took some of the blood from the bullock and applied it to the horns of the Bronze Altar with his finger; the rest was poured out at the base of the altar. The sin offering was a non-sweet savor offering (except for the burned fat, according to Lev. 4:31) because God demanded it in order to make atonement for the sins of the newly-installed priests.

The formalized procedure for presenting a sin offering in Leviticus 4 follows the pattern of its introduction in Exodus 29 during the consecration of the priests (which is revisited in Lev. 8), except in two points. First, the sin offering was limited to atoning for sins of ignorance only. Second, it was now available for anyone who realized that they had unwontedly sinned against the Lord (4:2). As shown in Exodus 29, no burnt offering would be accepted by God until a sin/trespass offering had first been presented (Lev. 5:7-10). This was true for all rituals requiring a burnt offering (e.g., the purification ritual of the cleansed leper in Lev. 14).

The General Procedure

Instructions for this sacrifice were provided for six different people groups: the high priest (4:3-12), the whole congregation (4:13-21), a ruler of the people (4:22-26), a common person (4:27-35), the poor (5:7), and the very poor (5:11-13). A young bull was the required sin offering for the first two groups (4:3, 14), a male kid (goat) was the obligation of a ruler (4:23), a common person could offer either a female lamb or kid (goat) (4:28, 32), while the poor were permitted to offer two birds and the very poor, fine flour (5:7-13).

The high priest had to officiate the offerings for himself and for the congregation, and these required him to purge the sanctuary with the blood of the young bull. Because the blood was taken into the sanctuary, eating any part of the bull sacrifice was prohibited (6:30). Although a sinning ruler needed to bring a male kid from the goats (4:23), and common people needed a female kid or lamb for their sins (4:28), the procedure for both was identical. Portions of the kids and lambs could be eaten by the officiating priest in the courtyard of the tabernacle because the blood of these animals was not carried into the sanctuary (6:25-29). As expected, all animals presented had to be without blemish (4:3, 23, 28).

When any individual or the Jewish elders (who represented the entire congregation) became aware that a sin of ignorance had been committed, a sin offering was to be presented to atone for the sin and to receive Jehovah's forgiveness. The procedure for the first four groups was similar, except for the type of animal to be presented and the application of blood within the sanctuary:

> The offerer brought the animal to the door of the tabernacle of the congregation (4:4, 14).
> The offerer and priest brought the animal to the north side of the altar (1:11, 4:24, 29, 35).
> The offerer put his hand on the head of the sin offering and killed the sacrifice before the Lord (4:4, 15, 24, 29, 35).
> The priest collected and smeared the blood of the sheep and goats on the horns of the Bronze Altar and poured out the remaining blood at the base of the altar (4:25, 30, 34).
> The high priest collected the blood of the bull and brought it into the Holy Place and with his finger he sprinkled the blood before the veil seven times and then smeared blood on the horns of the golden altar of incense; the remaining blood was poured out at the base of the Bronze Altar (4:6-7, 17-18).
> The high priest/priest burned the fat and the kidneys on the Bronze Altar as in the peace offering to make atonement (4:8-10, 19-20); the fat (presumably with the kidneys) of the kids and lambs were also burned on the altar (4:26, 31, 35).
> The priest salted the sacrifice (Num. 18:19; Ezek. 43:24).
> The high priest took the remainder of the bull (as offered for the high priest or for the congregation) where the ashes of the burnt offering were poured out and there burned it on a wood fire (4:11-12, 20-21).
> The priest received the remaining portion of the sin offerings presented by the rulers and common people (i.e., the kids and lambs). This portion was to be eaten in the Holy Place (6:25-27, 10:17).

The procedure for the poverty-stricken was unique and less involved. The poor could offer two turtledoves or two young pigeons – one for a sin offering, which first had to be presented by the priest, and the other for a burnt offering. After the offerer provided the priests with the two birds, the priest was to wring off the head of one of the birds, sprinkle its blood on the sides of the altar, and drain out the remaining blood at the altar's base – this was the sin offering (5:7-9). The priest then offered the second bird as a burnt offering in the manner described in Leviticus 1 (5:10).

If the offerer was so severely impoverished that he could not supply two birds, he could bring one tenth of an ephah of fine flour for the sin offering. The priest was then to burn a memorial of it on the altar, without oil or frankincense because it was a sin offering, to atone for sin (5:11-13). This practice begs the question: "How can a meal offering, which does not have blood, atone for sin?" After all, we read in Hebrews: *"According to the law almost all things are purified with blood, and without shedding of blood there is no remission"* (Heb. 9:22). Although the meal offering itself did not have blood, it was carefully burned on the remains of other animals which did have blood. As the meal was burned with the blood sacrifices, it assumed the value of a blood sacrifice for those who could not afford to offer one. This ensured that anyone who wanted atonement for their sin had a provision to come near God and be forgiven.

The remaining portions of the sacrificed bull not placed on the Bronze Altar were burnt on top of the ashes of the burnt offering located in a ceremonially clean place outside of camp (6:11). Whether the sin offering was burnt on the altar or the ash pile, the procedure showed that the basis of its approval directly related to God's acceptance of the burnt offerings, which pictured God's immense appreciation of His Son's sacrificial devotion. The portions of the lambs and kids that were not burnt on the altar were given to the officiating priest, who had to eat the sacrifice in the courtyard of the tabernacle. This was because the flesh of the offering was considered holy; a reality which even required special considerations for cleaning or destroying the pots the holy meat was cooked in (6:25-29).

Looking back, we recall the priests were permitted, indeed invited, to eat portions of the meal offering, the peace offering, and the sin offering. When the priests fed on the cakes of the meal offering, this symbolized

God's people, in holy priestly character, feeding on (i.e., seeking and appreciating) the perfections of Christ. Their consumption of the peace offerings symbolized the fellowship with and blessings we have in Christ due to what He accomplished for us at Calvary and also due to His ongoing intercession for us. But why would God permit the priests to eat of the non-sweet-smelling sacrifices? J. N. Darby remarks that when they partook from the sin offerings, it symbolized:

> Christ and even those who are His, as priests, in devoted love and in sympathy with others, identifying themselves with their sin and with the work of Christ for that sin. To Him alone it was, of course, to bear the sin; but founded on His work, our hearts can take it up in a priestly way before God. They are connected in grace with it according to the efficacy of the sacrifice of Christ; they enjoy the grace of Christ therein.[2]

The believer's union in Christ from a positional standpoint is complete in every aspect, including the fact that we died with Him two thousand years ago (Rom. 6:6). Though Christ bore the judicial penalty of sin for us, we nonetheless experienced the fellowship of His death in an ongoing way (Phil. 3:10) – this truth is conveyed in the eating the meat of the sin offering in the holy place. It is noted that while the meat and cakes/bread of the peace offerings could be enjoyed by everyone outside of the tabernacle, the priest's portion of the meal, sin, and trespass offerings was considered "most holy," and had to be eaten in the Holy Place. However, their eating within the Holy Place conveyed a different tenor: Consumption of the meal offering celebrated their communion of God's grace as redeemed men, but in the sin and trespass offerings they ate as sinners in His propitiation, that is, subjects of God's mercy.

God only required blood to be sprinkled before the veil to purge the sanctuary when a bull was sacrificed for the high priest or the congregation. L. M. Grant suggests a possible reason why this purification was required for a sinning high priest or for an offense committed by the entire congregation, but not for the sins of common people:

> The reason for this seems to be that the priest was the spiritual representative of the people and he had access into the sanctuary:

therefore the sanctuary was "purged by blood" on his account. The case of the sin of the whole congregation is evidently connected in such a way with the priest as their representative that a similar ritual was necessary.[3]

J. N. Darby further explains how the procedural difference highlighted the level of communion that sin had interrupted, thus determining the sacrificial process for restoration:

> In the case of the high priest and the body of the people sinning, it is evident that all communion was interrupted. It was not merely the restoration of the individual to communion which was needed, but the restoration of the communion between God and the whole people; not the forming a relationship (the Day of Atonement effected that), but the reestablishment of interrupted communion. Hence the blood was sprinkled before the veil seven times for the perfect restoration of the communion, and the blood also put on the horns of the altar of incense.[4]

Under God's Levitical order, a common person who sinned could not come to God directly to resolve the problem; he had to approach the priest to effect the sin offering on his behalf. As a whole, the access of the nation to Jehovah rested on His anointed high priest. However, if the whole congregation sinned, or if the priest who represented the people sinned, the result was the same – they all were cut off from the Lord. This is why the blood was carried in and sprinkled before the veil in these cases. The sanctuary was not purged in this way for the sin of a single person, as that would suggest that the sin of one individual severed all communion of the nation with God.

The blood from the sweet savor offering was not sprinkled before the veil, because the burnt offering and peace offering did not purge sin; also, the blood from these sacrifices was sprinkled on the outside of the Bronze Altar and not applied to the horns of the altar. However, the sin offering does speak of purging from sin. In this particular sacrifice we see Christ suffering apart from God under the judgment for our sin, and doing so in the place of total rejection – "outside the camp" (Heb. 13:11). Our Lord by His own blood entered the Holy Place once for all (Jew and Gentile) after He had suffered outside the city of Jerusalem (Heb. 9:12). In the Church Age, any Jew who wants to be saved must leave the deadness of Judaism, with its system of encumbering works, to identify with Christ by grace alone. The Gentile also must meet Him there. The sin offering tells us that the guilt of sin can only be taken away by Christ's blood. All sin severs communion with God; the good news is that Christ has already been judged for all sin, thus permitting the sinner to simply identify with Him in His sacrifice in order to be made right with God.

The Great Exchange

Before the sin offering was killed the offerer placed his hands upon the head of the animal, presumably confessing his sins and symbolically transferring the offense to the animal. If the whole congregation committed an offense, then the leaders of the people put their hands on the head of the bull and confessed the sin. The sacrifice was then killed and completely burned. This indicated the sin had been fully atoned for and forgiven. The picture of the sin offering is clear; Christ identified with us by becoming a man, took our sin upon Himself at Calvary, and was judged by God in our place:

> *But God demonstrates His own love toward us, in that while we were still sinners, Christ died for us. Much more then, having now been justified by His blood, we shall be saved from wrath through Him* (Rom. 5:8-9).

> *For Christ also suffered once for sins, the just for the unjust, that He might bring us to God, being put to death in the flesh but made alive by the Spirit* (1 Pet. 3:18-19).

The sin offering was completely consumed by fire and the Lord Jesus was completely consumed in the judgment for our sin. David prophesied that the billows and waves of God's wrath would break upon the Sin-bearer, the Messiah (Ps. 42:7). During those three hours of darkness, while hanging between heaven and earth nailed to a cross, the Lord Jesus was forsaken by God the Father (Matt. 27:45-46). He was stripped of His clothing and His dignity – as a public spectacle He endured the persistent insults, the demeaning jeers, and the blatant blasphemy. Having completed His task as the sin offering, the Lord declared with a loud voice, *"It is finished;"* He then offered up His spirit to the Father (Matt. 27:50; John 19:30). This fulfilled His own prophetic words:

Therefore My Father loves Me, because I lay down My life that I may take it again. No one takes it from Me, but I lay it down of Myself. I have power to lay it down, and I have power to take it again. This command I have received from My Father (John 10:17-18).

The Lord presented Himself as an offering for sin; He was *"the Lamb of God who takes away the sin of the world!"* (John 1:29). The Lord Jesus was both the Mediator of a New Covenant (Heb. 8:7-9) and the ransom that established it: *"For there is one God and one Mediator between God and men, the Man Christ Jesus, who gave Himself a ransom for all, to be testified in due time"* (1 Tim. 2:5-6). The priest who presided over the sin offering was innocent of the offerer's sin, but yet became connected with it in order to apply the blood of the sacrifice to make atonement for the sinner – this pictures Christ as the Mediator between God and men. Furthermore, Christ was the ransom God paid for human sin. While Old Testament sacrifices merely atoned for sin (i.e., provided a temporary covering), Christ's sacrifice was the propitiation which satisfied God's wrath concerning all of man's sin for all of time:

Being justified freely by His grace through the redemption that is in Christ Jesus, whom God set forth as a propitiation by His blood, through faith, to demonstrate His righteousness, because in His forbearance God had passed over the sins that were previously committed, to demonstrate at the present time His righteousness, that He might be just and the justifier of the one who has faith in Jesus (Rom. 3:24-26).

But we see Jesus, who was made a little lower than the angels, for the suffering of death crowned with glory and honor, that He, by the grace of God, might taste death for everyone (Heb. 2:9).

And He Himself is the propitiation for our sins, and not for ours only but also for the whole world (1 Jn. 2:2).

Through Adam's sin, the special creature formed in His own image and likeness was lost to God (Gen. 1:26), but by the blood of Christ, God is able to restore all that was lost in Eden. The shed blood of the Lord Jesus is the only basis in which God the Father can redeem sinful man;

Christ's blood is more valuable than all the precious metals and gems in all the earth combined:

> *You were not redeemed with corruptible things, like silver or gold, from your aimless conduct received by tradition from your fathers, but with the precious blood of Christ, as of a lamb without blemish and without spot. He indeed was foreordained before the foundation of the world, but was manifest in these last times for you who through Him believe in God, who raised Him from the dead and gave Him glory, so that your faith and hope are in God* (1 Pet. 1:18-21).

His sacrifice was *foreordained*; none of the events associated with Calvary was an accident, including the disdain, brutality, and betrayal of God's own Son. The devil did not outsmart God or catch Him by surprise. Rather, that horrific day had been intricately prearranged before the foundation of the world; however, God's redemptive purposes were kept secret until accomplished in Christ (1 Cor. 2:8-9). The innocent took the place of the condemned (Col. 2:12), so that the guilty could have the opportunity to be redeemed and receive the righteous standing of the innocent. This is the great exchange pictured in the sin offering – Christ took our place in eternal death that we might receive everlasting life in Him.

Summary

In the sin offering, our Lord is presented in His substitutionary death on the cross. We see the awfulness of sin and also the adequacy of the work of the Lord Jesus to satisfy every demand of God against us. God judges sin in accordance with the revelation the sinner has received from Him. Since God dwelt in the very midst of the Israelites, they incurred great accountability. Wherever God extends privilege, it is adjoined with responsibility. However, as shown in the sin offering, God also extends tremendous mercy to those sinners who approach Him, having agreed with Him on the matter of sin and its terrible consequences, and seeking only a divine resolution for it. Thankfully, at such times God's mercy is extended without reservation; He chooses to judge man not according to what he has become in sin, but rather what becomes Himself in grace.

This is God's grand prerogative and the purpose of the Law, that is, to make man conscious of his sin (Rom. 3:20) and his need of a Savior, and then to point him to the only One who could save – Christ (Gal. 3:24). David understood that though the Law of God was pure, it brought condemnation to man, for no one could keep it. Furthermore, he had committed murder and adultery, and under the Law should have been put to death: there was no sacrifice to atone for such blatant subversion of God's Law. Yet, David understood the gracious heart of God and that the Law could not be the end in itself. Without knowing how God would righteously deal with his gross sin, he knew that God would do so and David could thus plead:

> *Have mercy upon me, O God, according to Your lovingkindness; according to the multitude of Your tender mercies, blot out my transgressions. Wash me thoroughly from my iniquity, and cleanse me from my sin. For I acknowledge my transgressions, and my sin is always before me* (Ps. 51:1-3).

We, in the Church Age, understand God dealt with David's sin the same way He dealt with ours: in the death of Christ: *For He made Him who knew no sin to be sin for us, that we might become the righteousness of God in Him* (2 Cor. 5:21). This is the message of the sin offering. God hates sin but loves the sinner, and because He judged His Son for our offenses, God can righteously restore repentant sinners to Himself.

Application

Did you notice what the first unintentional offense requiring a sin offering was in Leviticus 5? It was for the omission of accurate information or refusing to testify altogether when required to by a governing authority. This explains why the Lord Jesus responded when the high priest invoked the name of Jehovah and implored Him to explain Himself. The Lord, who otherwise did not open His mouth, was obliged to answer the charge; not to do so would be a sin (Matt. 26:63-64).

Two notes of application are suggested. Firstly, the Lord is honored when our speech is fully truthful. He instructed His disciples: *"But let your 'Yes' be 'Yes,' and your 'No,' 'No.' For whatever is more than these is from the evil one"* (Matt. 5:36-37). Furthermore, we should not be guilty of omitting important testimony to the end that governmental authorities derive a skewed conclusion; this perverts justice and does not reflect God's holy character. There are unusual circumstances which may require us to be silent rather than declare the truth in order to protect the innocent from perverted justice. At such times we should bear the consequences of that decision willingly, while still taking care not to distort the truth in any way.

Secondly, not long after the Lord Jesus chose His disciples He told them of His light-bearing ministry to the world and that they would be responsible to continue it: *"I am the light of the world. He who follows Me shall not walk in darkness, but have the light of life"* (John 8:12). *"You are the light of the world ... Let your light so shine before men, that they may see your good works and glorify your Father in heaven"* (Matt. 5:14-16). The light of Christ (i.e., His truth) was to shine out of them wherever they went. After His resurrection, the Lord formally commissioned His disciples to do just that: *"You will receive power when the Holy Spirit comes on you; and **you will be My witnesses** in Jerusalem, and in all Judea and Samaria, and to the ends of the earth"* (Acts 1:8). They were to preach the gospel message and to teach those responding to it all they knew to be true concerning Christ. That work has continued to the present day and will continue until the end of the Church Age (Matt. 28:19-20).

Each and every Christian is to be a witness for Christ – an instrument of God to illuminate the way of salvation for the lost. Those who respond to the gospel message are then to receive the teachings of Christ, so that they too can share the good news message with others. Paul engaged in this important work while at Ephesus and those who received the truth from him passed it on to others also (Eph. 4:20-21). True followers of Christ are willing to be witnesses for Christ wherever He has them, and whenever the opportunity arises to share the gospel message with the lost.

Meditation

"In the Beloved" accepted am I,
Risen, ascended, and seated on high;
Saved from all sin through His infinite grace,
With the redeemed ones accorded a place.

"In the Beloved," God's marvelous grace,
Calls me to dwell in this wonderful place;
God sees my Savior, and then He sees me,
"In the Beloved," accepted and free.

"In the Beloved" – how safe my retreat,
In the Beloved accounted complete;
"Who can condemn me?" In Him I am free,
Savior and Keeper forever is He.

— Civilla D. Martin

The Trespass Offering
Leviticus 5:14-19, 6:1-7, 7:1-10

As previously mentioned, under the Levitical system the sin offering was commanded for the *offense of sin*, but the trespass offering was required for the *damages of sin*. The sin offering deals with the guilt of sin; Christ's blood purges the believer's conscience of that. The trespass offering deals with the damage that sin causes and seeks to offer restitution. The sin offering targets who we are by nature, while the trespass offering highlights what we have done (sinful acts). Through Christ's sin and trespass offering, full restoration of the sinner to God is permitted. Neither the sin offering nor the trespass offering were designated as "sweet savor" offerings; each was demanded by God. They could only be used for sins of ignorance towards God (there were no personal offerings which atoned for willful sin) and for trespasses against one's neighbor. On a national level, all sin, including willful sin, was atoned for on the annual Day of Atonement. Through these two offerings, God was practically teaching His people that they were sinners by nature and that to properly deal with their offenses they needed to offer atonement to God, confess their sins, and make restitution to those wronged.

The contextual challenge is to discern whether Leviticus 5:1-13 belongs with the discussion of the sin offering or whether it is an introduction to the trespass offering. It is the author's opinion that this section best belongs with the instructions for the sin offering (i.e., it is a supplementary section to Leviticus 4). The fact that the word "trespass" is used (5:6) in the discussion of the sin offering confirms the close tie between these two sacrifices. It is noted that at times Scripture does refers to both of these distinct offerings with a singular identification (7:7; Ps. 40:6).

The following reasons are submitted to justify the conclusion that Leviticus 5:1-13 is a continuation of discussion of Leviticus 4. First, the phrase *"And the Lord spoke unto Moses, saying..."* occurs in both Leviticus 4:1 and 5:14 and appears to introduce a new topic. Second, the animals mentioned in Leviticus 5:6-7 agree with those involved in the sin offering (Lev. 4:23, 28, 32); that is, there is no mention of a ram, as required in the trespass offering (5:15, 18). Third, the offerings for the poor (Lev. 5:7-13) complete the remaining people groups not addressed in chapter 4. Rich or poor, ruler or common citizen, priest or not, anyone with a wounded conscience had the opportunity to receive God's forgiveness and be restored to Him through the sin offering. Fourth, there is no mention of "restitution" in Leviticus 5:1-13, which is a key principle of the trespass offering. Fifth, the instructions for the sin offering (and those of this passage) are arranged by various people groups, but the trespass offering is organized according to various types of sins. Thus, the clear distinction between who we are in the sin offering (sinners by nature) and what we do (sin) in the trespass offering is shown in the organization of the text.

William Kelly further warns us not to mistakenly assume that because the Hebrew word in Leviticus 5:6, *asham*, is rendered "trespass" that it is the trespass offering that is in view. He explains:

> Guard against the mistake of referring Leviticus 5:6 to the trespass offering, since it relates to *the sin offering* alone. The passage says that if one be guilty in any of the things mentioned in Leviticus 5:1-4, he shall confess that he has sinned, and bring his *ashamo* his debt, his due compensation, or simply *his offering*. The word has the same sense in Leviticus 5:15 and Numbers 5:7. *Asham* has three meanings: *guilt,* as in Genesis 26; *debt,* or *what is due* for contracting for guilt; and sacrifice for certain sins, *i.e., sin offering.* Thus the term *asham* is not appropriated to trespass offerings wherever it occurs, but is of wider significance.[1]

The context and content of verse 6 clearly relates to the sin offering and since *asham* may be translated as "sin" (Jer. 51:5) or as "a sin offering" (Isa. 53:10), there is no reason to assume that Leviticus 5:1-13 is speaking of the trespass offering or to conclude that the sin and trespass offering are one and the same.

Atonable Offenses

The term "offenses" refers to sins committed in ignorance. The trespass offering could be invoked for two specific classes of offenses. The first case is when a person sinned against God (Lev. 5:14-19); the second, when a person sinned against his neighbor (Lev. 6:1-7).

In the first category, there are two further types of trespasses which are mentioned: the first is an offense concerning God's *holy things* (5:15-16) and the second is unknowingly doing something God had forbidden (5:17). Besides the sacrifice of the ram (offered for the expiation for the sin), restitution was required; a shekel of silver was to be paid into the Lord's treasury. The actual procedure for sacrificing the ram is not specified until Leviticus 7:1-10. Through the trespass offering and the payment of a silver shekel, the damage of the offense was atoned for (5:16, 18).

A trespass against one's neighbor also required restitution and a ram sacrifice (Lev. 6:1-7). Matthew Henry explains the type of trespasses specified in verses 1-3, which admittedly seem to be more than matters of ignorance, but perhaps were not obvious public crimes:

1. Denying a trust: If a man lie to his neighbor in that which was delivered him to keep, or, which is worse, which was lent him for his use. If we claim that as our own which is only borrowed, left in our custody, or committed to our care, this is a trespass against the Lord, who, for the benefit of human society, will have property and truth maintained.

2. Defrauding a partner: If a man lie in fellowship, claiming a sole interest in that wherein he has but a joint interest.

3. Disowning a manifest wrong: If a man has the front to lie in a thing taken away by violence, which ordinarily cannot be hid.

4. Deceiving in commerce, or, as some think, by false accusation; if a man has deceitfully oppressed his neighbor, as some read it, either withholding what is due or extorting what is not.

5. Detaining what is found, and denying it (v. 3); if a man have found that which was lost, he must not call it his own presently, but endeavor to find out the owner, to whom it must be returned; this is

doing as we would be done by: but he that lies concerning it, that falsely says he knows nothing of it.[2]

When it came to restitution for these wrongs, the offender was to restore what had been wrongfully appropriated plus twenty percent of its intrinsic value (6:4-5). Moses had already revealed to the Jewish nation what restitution was required for *willful* offenses against others in the matter of property rights (Ex. 22:1-15). Thus, the Jews were already familiar with the concept of restitution: that true remorse over sin is shown by the offender's desire to right a wrong. In fact, true repentance is shown by a desire to over-compensate for the damage that was done by sin, if possible.

As an example, Moses had commanded, *"If a man steals an ox or a sheep, and slaughters it or sells it, he shall restore five oxen for an ox and four sheep for a sheep"* (Ex. 22:1-2). David referred to this verse centuries later as the rightful restitution for someone whose lamb had been *willfully* stolen (2 Sam. 12:6). Nathan told a story of a rich man stealing a poor man's only ewe to make David feel the weight of his own sin against God and his fellowman. David was a thief and a murderer; he had stolen Uriah's wife, Bathsheba, and had Uriah murdered in an attempt to cover up his sin. His restitution to God for his sin would be four "lambs" – in God's timing, He took four of David's sons in judgment. All this to say that restitution for offenses is an important matter to God.

The Procedure

The procedures for the presentation of a trespass offering are contained in Leviticus 7:1-10. Because the trespass offerings typify the ministry of the Lord Jesus Christ in correcting the damage caused by our sin, the flesh of the sacrifice and the place where it was offered were deemed "most holy" (7:1, 6).

The trespass offering follows the pattern of the burnt offering in that the ram was killed on the north side of the altar and before the Lord. The blood was collected and sprinkled around the altar and the fat and kidneys were put on the altar in the same fashion as described for the peace offering. The instructions pertaining to the consumption and disposal of the sacrificial flesh correspond with those of the sin offering. Two noteworthy differences between the sin offering and the trespass offering are that the ram's blood was not sprinkled before the veil as was the blood of the bull in the sin offering, and the ram's blood was sprinkled round about the altar (7:2) instead of being poured out at its base as with the sin offering.

Though many aspects of the sacrificial procedure parallel those of other offerings, the trespass offering served a unique purpose in calling man's attention to the necessity of offering restitution for offenses. Hence, the Lord Jesus is superbly pictured in the trespass offering as the One who compensates for all the destruction caused by man's sin.

The Psalm of the Trespass Offering

David prophetically confirms this correlation in Psalm 69. It is generally agreed there are sixteen psalms that are messianic in nature, that is, these are prophetic poetry pertaining to the future Jewish Messiah. These psalms carefully trace the Son of God's path from eternity past, through His spotless life on earth, and His exaltation after returning to heaven. Psalm 69 is of particular interest for us in our study of the trespass offering, for it portrays Christ as the future trespass offering for human sin. Because of its significance, it is quoted on seven occasions in the New Testament in direct application to the Lord Jesus Christ.

Psalm 69 describes what Christ was to accomplish and suffer as God's Trespass Offering. There may be no other text in our Bibles that so personally reveals the personal anguish of our Lord, suffering as our Trespass Offering:

Those who hate me without a cause are more than the hairs of my head; they are mighty who would destroy me, being my enemies wrongfully; though I have stolen nothing, I still must restore it (Ps. 69:4).

Because for Your sake I have borne reproach; shame has covered my face (Ps. 69:7).

Because zeal for Your house has eaten me up, and the reproaches of those who reproach You have fallen on me (Ps. 69:9).

Deliver me out of the mire, and let me not sink; let me be delivered from those who hate me, and out of the deep waters. Let not the

> *floodwater overflow me, nor let the deep swallow me up; and let not the pit shut its mouth on me* (Ps. 69:14-15).

> *Reproach has broken my heart, and I am full of heaviness; I looked for someone to take pity, but there was none; and for comforters, but I found none. They also gave me gall for my food, and for my thirst they gave me vinegar to drink* (Ps. 69:20-21).

Christ restored all that was lost by Adam in Eden and more. To accomplish this, in His rejection Christ both tasted the gall and drank the vinegar. Matthew records the exact fulfillment of this prophecy (Matt. 27:22-50). Before being nailed to the cross, the Lord was offered gall to drink; He tasted it but He would not drink the pain-numbing narcotic in order to ensure full cognitive awareness throughout His suffering. He did, however, drink the vinegar furnished just before His death to completely fulfill the prophecy.

The fulfillment of every messianic detail in *The Psalm of the Trespass Offering* further confirms the Lord Jesus is the antitype of this Levitical offering. Having Christ as our trespass offering liberates our minds from the guilt we too experience when we *"sin through ignorance against the holy things of the Lord"* (Lev. 5:15). C. H. Mackintosh expounds on the importance of this realization for the believer:

> It would be impossible to enjoy true peace and liberty of heart, if one did not know that the claims connected with "the holy things of the Lord" had been perfectly met by our divine Trespass Offering. There would ever be, springing up in the heart, the painful sense that those claims had been slighted, through our manifold infirmities and shortcomings. Our very best services, our holiest seasons, our most hallowed exercises, may present something of trespass "in the holy things of the Lord" – "something that ought not to be done." How often are our seasons of public worship and private devotion infringed upon and marred by barrenness and distraction! Hence it is that we need the assurance that our trespasses have all been divinely met by the precious blood of Christ. Thus, in the ever-blessed Lord Jesus, we find One who has come down to the full measure of our necessities as sinners by nature, and trespassers in act. We find in Him the perfect answer to all the cravings of a guilty conscience, and to all the claims of infinite holiness, in reference to all our sins and all our trespasses; so that the believer can stand, with an uncondemning conscience and emancipated

heart, in the full light of that holiness which is too pure to behold iniquity or look upon sin.[3]

Well put, Mr. Mackintosh, and praise the Lord! The believer has total liberation in Christ to be all that God calls him or her to be!

Summary of the Sweet and Non-sweet Aroma Offerings

In Leviticus chapters 1 through 7, five offerings are specifically described as crucial for maintaining Jehovah's presence among His covenant people. Three offerings (the burnt offering, the meal offering, and the peace offering) were designated as sweet aroma offerings because they were associated with one's choice to freely praise and thank God for His goodness. These present Christ's devotion and excellences, and indicate our approach to God is through Him on the basis that the price of sin has already been paid. When God looked down on the Levitical sacrifices, He could see His Son's finished work on man's behalf because He is not bound by time.

The final two offerings, the sin and trespass offerings, were demanded by God because of the offerer's sin, and thus were deemed non-sweet aroma offerings. In these offerings the perfections of Christ, though apparent and needful, are not the emphasis; rather, He is extolled as the suffering Sin-bearer who satisfies God's righteous demand for justice and restitution (Isa. 53:10). To summarize:

- In the **burnt offering**, we see what God the Father thinks about the freewill death of the Son.
- In the **meal offering**, we see the perfect humanity of the Lord Jesus.
- In the **peace offering**, we see Christ as the grounds of our fellowship with God.
- In the **sin offering**, we see the work of the Lord Jesus as our substitute.
- In the **trespass offering**, we see how the Lord Jesus restored what our sin took away.

This entire sacrificial system was replaced some two thousand years ago by what it symbolized, that is, Christ's achievements in redemption (2 Cor. 3:11-14). This being the case, a believer in the Church Age has much more scriptural revelation with which to behold the Savior in the sacrifices than the Jews did. We are utterly amazed God would stoop so low as to represent such spectacular wonders of His Son in the slaughtered animals, the splattering of blood, the wringing off of heads, the smoke of burning fat, and the stench of smoldering flesh. However distasteful all this may seem to our dignified humanity, this is exactly the point we are to appreciate. How much more repugnant would it be for the Creator of all things to personally experience all that is pictured in the Levitical sacrifices! The writer of Hebrews confirms the purpose of these Old Testament pictures and lessons is to further our appreciation of the Lord Jesus Christ and His finished propitiatory work (Heb. 10:1-4).

Throughout their history, the Jews offered tens of millions of animals and various fowls in sacrifice to Jehovah. Millions of gallons of innocent blood was shed, collected, spattered, smeared, and poured. Yet in all this exhaustive labor, not one human sin could be judicially resolved: the entire sacrificial system was to call our attention specifically to one sacrifice, one innocent Victim, and one particular blood to be shed – that of the Lord Jesus Christ!

This draws to a close our contemplation of Christ as seen in the five offerings of Leviticus 1-7. At this junction, the words of C. H. Mackintosh well express the author's own feelings concerning the holy ground we have transversed together:

> We shall here close our meditations upon one of the richest sections in the whole canon of inspiration. It is but little we have been enabled to glean from it. We have hardly penetrated below the surface of an exhaustless mine. If, however, the reader has, for the first time, been led to view the offerings as so many varied exhibitions of the great Sacrifice, and if he is led to cast himself at the feet of the great Teacher, to learn more of the living depths of these things, I cannot but feel that an end has been gained for which we may well feel deeply thankful.[4]

Application

As we seek to apply this passage to our own lives, let us return to the story of David's sin and restitution. The anger David felt after hearing Nathan's story of the stolen lamb was just, but hypocritical; he himself was guilty of theft and murder, and under the Law deserved the death penalty. David was enraged at the injustice done to a poor man, yet he had committed a much worse offense and had remained unrepentant for more than a year. This demonstrates how easy it is for anger to cloud rational thinking and logical conclusions. When we are not in communion with God, our anger has the greatest opportunity to be provoked and to cause ungodly behavior. It is also good to remember that though others may not know your secret sins, both God and you know all about them and *"Be sure your sin will find you out"* (Num. 32:23). David's sins had made his life miserable, but after repenting of his offenses, his fellowship with God was fully restored.

In Psalm 51, David acknowledges that he had received unmerited mercy from God, as under the Law, adultery and murder were punishable by death. The Law also demanded four lambs be given in restitution for a stolen lamb that had been killed. David had stolen Bathsheba and then had her husband Uriah killed; God would exact a heavy price for these sins. Though forgiven, in restitution for his crimes, David experienced the loss of four sons: his newborn son conceived in adultery with Bathsheba, Amnon, Absalom, and Adonijah. God spared David's life, but God's justice cost David dearly and his household never knew peace afterwards.

No doubt as David looked back over his life, he greatly regretted that moment of uncontrolled lust. The message of the Law is *"the wages of sin is death"* (Rom. 6:23) and God will judge all that offends His holy character. Though believers in the Church Age are not under the Law, the underlying principles related to human sin still apply: all sin has consequences, all sin brings separation in fellowship, all sin will be judged, and there should be restitution for all sins committed. Although the judicial aspects of all this were accomplished in Christ, believers must realize personal sin involves consequences for both us and the Body of Christ. We may choose our sin, but God always chooses the consequences of our sin to effect His glory. Additionally, if we have sinned against another, we should not only apologize to the offended party and ask for forgiveness, but also seek to make restitution for the offense. For some offenses this will not be possible, but the humble attitude exhibited in trying to do so will in itself be the salve that initiates the healing process.

Meditation

Thou, O Son of God, wert bearing
Cruel mockings, hatred, scorn;
Thou, the King of Glory, wearing,
For our sake, the crown of thorn;
Dying, Thou didst us deliver
From the chains of sin forever:
Thousand, thousand praises be,
Precious Saviour, unto Thee.

All the shame men heaped upon Thee,
Thou didst patiently endure;
Not the pains of death too bitter
Our redemption to procure.
Wondrous Thy humiliation
To accomplish our salvation:
Thousand, thousand praises be,
Precious Saviour, unto Thee.

— Ernst Homburg

Consecration and Service
Leviticus 8 - 9

With the Levitical sacrifices having been thoroughly explained in chapters 1-7, a new subject matter, the consecration and service of the priests, is introduced in the three subsequent chapters. The chapter themes are: the consecration of the priests (Lev. 8), the commencement of their service (Lev. 9), and the proper execution of their office (Lev. 10). These three chapters form the second major section of Leviticus.

In the previous section we read that animal blood was sprinkled before the veil in the tabernacle and around the base of the Bronze Altar, but in this chapter blood will be sprinkled directly on the priests themselves. In all of the Old Testament, there are only three instances in which individuals were sprinkled with blood for ceremonial cleansing. The Israelites as a congregation were sprinkled with blood by Moses at the giving of the Law at Mount Sinai (Ex. 24:8). In this chapter, which parallels Exodus 29, Moses sprinkles blood on Aaron and his four sons to consecrate them as priests. Lastly, a priest was to sprinkle a healed leper with a mixture of water and blood on the day of his cleansing (Lev. 14:7). Although this ritual may have been performed for someone who recovered from an innoxious form of this disease, leprosy was generally considered incurable and there is no Old Testament record of a leper undergoing the rites of Leviticus 14.

All the furnishings of the tabernacle and the tent itself had been manufactured and set in place. The holy garments to be worn by the priests and the high priest had been fashioned. But the priests required more than just special garments to serve in the tabernacle; they had to be ceremonially cleansed and consecrated for "holy" service. Moses was to gather the entire assembly to the tabernacle to observe this momentous occasion (8:3-4). Moses would supervise the ceremony, which required the slaughter of one bullock and two rams and the preparation of unleavened bread with the anointing oil (8:1-2). The bread and oil were to be brought in a basket to the door of the tabernacle when the priest arrived. There, Moses oversaw the bathing of the priests, likely at the Bronze Laver (8:6).

Moses then dressed Aaron in high priestly attire: the tunic, the sash, the blue robe, the ephod, the band of the ephod, the breastplate (which held the Urim and the Thummim), and the miter (or turban) which displayed the gold frontal plate (Ex. 28). Moses consecrated the tabernacle, and all that was inside it, and the Bronze Laver and the Bronze Altar in the courtyard with special anointing oil (8:10-11). He then poured the anointing oil over Aaron's head (8:12). Once Aaron was consecrated as high priest, Moses then put tunics, sashes, and head pieces on Aaron's sons who would serve as priests.

Only one thing remained before Aaron and his sons could serve the Lord as priests – the matter of sin atonement. For this, an unblemished bullock was sacrificed as a sin offering (8:14-17). Aaron and his sons placed their hands upon the head of the bullock to symbolically show their identification with the innocent substitute for the judgment of their sins (8:14).

As the priests were not yet sanctified, Moses performed all the priestly tasks in the ceremony. He killed the bullock, collected its blood, and prepared its carcass for sacrifice as previously discussed in Leviticus 4 and 5. The fat above its liver and its two kidneys was burned on the Bronze Altar, but the remainder of the animal was burnt in a clean place outside the camp. Because the sacrifice symbolized the transfer of sin and judgment, it had to be done outside the camp, lest there be defilement within the camp. Moses took some of the blood from the bullock and applied it to the horns of the Bronze Altar with his finger; the rest was poured out at the base of the altar.

Upon the completion of the sin offering, Aaron and his sons laid their hands on the head of one of two rams before Moses slaughtered it. Its blood was then sprinkled about the altar, and its carcass (after being washed and cut into pieces) was completely consumed by fire upon the altar as a burnt offering (8:18-21). Aaron and his sons then laid their hands on the head of a second ram (8:22), which served as a trespass offering. Moses took some of the blood of the second ram and applied it to the tip of the right ear, the right thumb, and the right big toe of each of the priests (8:23-24). Throughout Scripture the right side is designated as a place of honor; for example, we read that the Son sits at the right hand of God in heaven (Heb. 1:3), and that only those on Christ's right hand at the Judgment of Nations enter into His kingdom (Matt. 25:34-41). As believer-priests in the Church Age, our hearing (pictured in the ear), our service (typified by the thumb), and our walk (portrayed by the big toe) are to be consecrated for the honor and glory of God.

Moses mixed some of the remaining blood with the anointing oil and then sprinkled it on Aaron and his sons, who were dressed in their priestly attire (8:30). This fully consecrated the priests and their garments; from that day on they were to be considered holy – set apart solely for God's use. This initial act of cleansing and anointing designated Aaron and his descendants as perpetual priests for as long as the dispensation of the Law would be administered (Ex. 29:9).

Unleavened bread, an anointed cake, and a wafer were taken from the aforementioned breadbasket by Moses and were placed in the hands of Aaron and his sons, along with the fat and right thigh of the second ram (8:25-27). They waved all of these before the Lord and then Moses placed these on the altar (8:28). Apparently, a portion of this ram was considered as a peace offering, a sweet savor sacrifice (Ex. 29:28); God received the fat, the kidneys and the right thigh (the priests' portion normally) on the altar and the acting priest (Moses in this case) received the breast after waving it before the Lord (8:29). The remainder of the animal was returned to the offerer (Aaron and his sons, in this situation); this was to be boiled at the door of the tabernacle (8:31). The meat from the sacrifice and the bread from the basket located at the entrance of the courtyard were to be eaten by Aaron and his sons, and any leftovers were to be burned (8:32). The newly-commissioned priests were not permitted to leave the tabernacle courtyard for seven days and nights to conclude the ritual of their consecration (8:33-35). We see Aaron and his sons did exactly what they were commanded to do (8:36).

The Eighth Day

On the eighth day, Moses called Aaron and his sons and the elders of Israel together for the commencement of the Aaronic priesthood. As mentioned previously, the number *eight* is used in the Bible to speak of new beginnings. L. M. Grant affirms that the Levitical priesthood and sacrifices indicated a new beginning for the nation in their relationship with God; thus, it was appropriate for the new system to begin on the eighth day of the consecration ceremony:

Having completed all the instructions concerning the offerings and their laws, and now also having completed the consecration of the priests, Moses indicates the beginning of the priestly service in connection with the people. This was on "the eighth day," for it was a new beginning for the people as regards their relationship to God.[1]

The word "eighth" thus appears in the book of Leviticus more than any other book in the Bible to highlight the Jewish nation's new era of opportunity through the provision of blood atonement.

On this day Aaron was to offer a young calf as a sin offering and a ram as a burnt offering (9:2). The elders of Israel, on behalf of the people (9:15), were to offer a kid of the goats as a sin offering, a young calf and a lamb as burnt offerings, and a young bull and a young ram as a peace offering, which was to include a meal offering mixed with oil (9:3-4). Moses promised all those who came to the tabernacle that the glory of the Lord would appear to them that day (9:4-6). Indeed, this was the grand purpose of the preceding activities. Jehovah wanted His people to understand that though they were sinful by nature, they could still have access to Him through blood atonement, as offered by His priests on their behalf.

The priests and the elders both offered sacrifices to God as representatives of the nation. Hence, this inaugural event strongly resembled the Day of Atonement described in Leviticus 16. The main difference between these two ceremonies is that at this time the people, or representative elders, offered peace offerings instead of a second goat for the scapegoat as required on the Day of Atonement. This substitution in procedure made the commencement day of the Aaronic priesthood a day of feasting and celebration, instead of a solemn fast.

The priests executed all the offerings as previously instructed (9:7-21). After Aaron had placed the appropriate portions of the sin offering, burnt offering, and peace offering on the Bronze Altar, he lifted up his hands and blessed the people, then returned down the southern ramp from the altar (9:22). Aaron's benediction for the people at the conclusion of the sacrifices was not improvised, but rather he was obeying the Lord's command as received through Moses:

And the Lord spoke to Moses, saying: "Speak to Aaron and his sons, saying, 'This is the way you shall bless the children of Israel. Say to them: The Lord bless you and keep you; the Lord make His face shine upon you, and be gracious to you; the Lord lift up His countenance upon you, and give you peace.' So they shall put My name on the children of Israel, and I will bless them" (Num. 6:22-27).

Moses and Aaron went into the tabernacle and after a period of time departed together; it was at that moment that the dazzling glory of the Lord appeared to all the people (9:23). Fire blazed out from the Lord and consumed what remained on the altar all at once. When the people witnessed this spectacular event, they cried out in fear and fell to the ground in awe (9:24). The supernatural feat demonstrated God's approval of the entire consecration process and His approval of Aaron as Jehovah's high priest. Aaron would make atonement on behalf of the people and be their representative before the Lord in worship and in intercession.

Application

The symbolism associated with the priest's consecration in Leviticus 8 presents significant applications for the Church. Christ has already borne the judgment for the sins of humanity and the provision for redemption is available to all who want to be purchased by His blood (1 Pet. 1:19). In addition to the specific types of Christ portrayed in the offerings of these two chapters, the work of the Holy Spirit in the converting and saving of sinners is also symbolized.

First, note that Aaron and his sons willingly came to the door of the tabernacle to be cleansed by Moses. No one dragged them there; God appointed them to come and they chose to come. God forces no sinner into heaven or into service, but through the invitation of His Word (Rom. 10:17) and the illumination of the Holy Spirit (1 Cor. 2:14), vile sinners are made aware of their lost condition and are brought into agreement with God on the matter of sin and its only solution – Christ. The foreknowledge of God and His predetermined actions in concert with human choice is, thus, a fascinating and mysterious ramification of salvation and also of service (Eph. 2:10). We do choose whether or not to serve the Lord; however, it should be observed that the spiritual response of a redeemed sinner is to gladly serve the Lord in whatever capacity He determines.

Second, the fact that the priests had to bathe before they donned their new attire parallels the reality that each believer priest has been regenerated and cleansed when he or she trusted Christ for salvation (Tit. 3:5). Like the Aaronic priest's initial washing at the door of the tabernacle, this act of the Holy Spirit need never be repeated. Later, the Laver would be used by the priests for their daily purification. They had to pause at the Laver to wash their hands and feet before serving before the Lord, but this was not the same as their initial full-body washing. The work of the Holy Spirit enables the lost to understand the ungodliness of our sinful attitudes and desires. He makes us feel their uncleanness, and leads us to repent of them, and so we cry out to God regarding our need to be saved. At conversion, the Holy Spirit works to cleanse the new believer from evil bents and polluted things. Although the lusting nature of the flesh remains in the new believer, he or she has a new attitude towards uncleanness and the Spirit's continuing help to repudiate that which displeased God. The act of regeneration, also occurring at conversion, implants new life and a new order of living within him or her. Those who were dead are made spiritually alive (Eph. 2:1-3)!

Third, just as the priests were anointed with oil at their consecration, the Holy Spirit likewise anoints the believer at his or her conversion (1 Jn. 2:20). Priests, prophets, and kings were often anointed when they were consecrated (set apart) for the Lord's use. Indeed, the Lord Jesus Himself was anointed by the Holy Spirit (Acts 10:38) at the commencement of His ministry. Likewise, each believer is anointed and called to serve the body of Christ. Not only does this separate out the believer for God's purpose, but this anointing actually provides divine discernment of the truth, which enables the believer to follow after God's will in his or her ministry. It is through this provision of the Holy Spirit a new believer becomes part of a holy priesthood which is *"to offer up spiritual sacrifices, acceptable to God by Jesus Christ"* (1 Pet. 2:5) forever.

Fourth, the priests were completely equipped by the Lord with all the necessary implements and clothing to fulfill the office of priest. Similarly, the Holy Spirit distributes spiritual gifts to believers *"as He wills"* (1 Cor. 12:11). The number of gifts per believer will vary (1 Cor. 12:4), but each will receive at least one spiritual gift (1 Cor. 12:7). Also, the manner in which these gifts will be used will differ (1 Cor. 12:5), and the beneficiaries (those who receive the spiritual ministry) will vary (1 Cor. 12:6). Thankfully, the Lord equips us for the service to which He calls us.

Fifth, the priests were sealed by God; that is, they would be protected by Him from outside harm while fulfilling their office. Numbers 16 records a revolt against Moses, God's chosen leader of the nation, and Aaron, God's chosen high priest for the nation. Korah, Dathan, Abiram, and others sought to intrude into the priesthood – it cost them their lives. In the believer's case, God does not promise immunity from physical harm, but the Christian's eternal security is indeed assured. The Holy Spirit Himself is the seal of God (Eph. 1:13). This eternal seal is likened to the wax seal placed on a letter or scroll in ancient times. Such a seal protected and secured the letter from being opened, and it also indicated who was the originator and owner of the letter. In some cases, seals were used to indicate approval of a contract or an agreement. Through the sealing ministry of the Holy Spirit the believer is both approved of and secured in Christ forever!

The pattern of the Levitical priesthood typifies with astonishing foreknowledge the eternal spiritual realities now accomplished in Christ through the power of the Holy Spirit on the believer's behalf. As each believer priest is infused by the power of the Holy Spirit and serves the Lord with pure motives, the Lord Jesus is honored and God Himself is refreshed. The sweet aroma of His Son permeates all such sacrifices that ascend to His throne, and when God breathes it in, that which was freely offered on earth reminds Him of His Son now in heaven.

Meditation

> Jesus, the Christ! Eternal Word! Of all creation Sovereign Lord!
> On Thee alone by faith we rest, and lean our weakness on Thy breast.
>
> Thy blood hath washed us from our sin; Thy Spirit sanctifies within;
> And Thou for us in all our need, at God's right hand dost ever plead.
>
> O keep us in the narrow way, that never from Thee our footsteps stray;
> Sustain our weakness, calm our fear, and to Thy presence keep us near.
>
> — Morshead

Strange Fire
Leviticus 10

This is indeed one of the most sorrowful portions of Scripture. Jehovah had selected Aaron and his four sons Nadab, Abihu, Eleazar, and Ithamar to officially minister in the tabernacle on behalf of the nation. But shortly after their consecration, before the Israelites moved northward from Mount Sinai, Nadab and Abihu, Aaron's oldest two sons, were fatally judged for intruding into God's presence with "strange fire" (vv. 1-5).

What a contrast to the scene which had just concluded! At the initiation of the Aaronic priesthood all was done *"as the Lord commanded,"* and the result was the glory of God appeared to the entire nation. In Leviticus 10, something is done *"which He had not commanded,"* and the result was prompt, irrevocable judgment. Hardly had the last echoes of exaltation faded away before the entire camp was shocked by grief at the cost of presumptuous worship. The newly installed priests had failed to properly execute their high office and holy vindication was swift and final. Such is the story of man, says C. H. Mackintosh:

> Thus, man spoils everything. Place him in a position of highest dignity, and he will degrade himself. Endow him with the most ample privileges, and he will abuse them. Scatter blessings around him, in richest profusion, and he will prove ungrateful. Place him in the midst of the most impressive institutions, and he will corrupt them. Such is man! Such is nature, in its fairest forms, and under the most favorable circumstances![1]

Having kindled their own censors of incense, the two sons brought them into the tabernacle to offer worship to the Lord (v. 1). The Lord had yet to give instructions as to how the holy incense should be kindled and presented before Him; those directives were forthcoming (Lev. 16:12-13). The reference to "strange fire" may speak of fire that did not come from the Bronze Altar, which is where atonement for sin was accomplished and thus pictures God's ultimate judgment of human sin at Calvary. To approach God on any other basis than through Christ's propitiation would be intensely insulting to God. One way this is done today is when people tell God they can earn their way to heaven through good church attendance, water baptism, giving to the poor, etc. instead of trusting in Christ's finished work alone. Like many today, Nadab and Abihu had good intentions, but they were intruding on the things of God without having the mind of God. Their actions angered the Lord and fire came out, perhaps from above the Ark of the Covenant, and the two lads died (v. 2).

Moses reminded Aaron what Jehovah had previously declared: *"By those who come near Me, I must be regarded as holy; and before all the people I must be glorified"* (v. 3). Aaron held his peace! Moses called on Uzziel's sons Mishael and Elzaphan (Aaron's cousins) to carry the bodies of Nadab and Abihu from the sanctuary to a location outside of camp (vv. 4-5). Because Nadab and Abihu had been rightly judged for their offense, Moses did not permit Aaron to grieve for his sons in the customary way. Aaron had to remain in the tabernacle and was not to uncover his head or tear his clothes, which were normal Jewish gestures of mourning. Aaron had anointing oil upon him, and thus no dust was to be put on his head, nor was there to be any degradation to what God had declared holy, including the priestly garments. Moses warned him that if he did not obey, God's wrath would also come upon him and the people. Although Aaron was not permitted to outwardly grieve for his sons, the nation did (vv. 6-7).

We know Aaron's younger sons, Eleazar and Ithamar, were not yet twenty years of age when the Jewish adults were judged the following year at Kadesh-barnea (Num. 14). This indicates Eleazar and Ithamar were teenagers at this time, which meant Nadab and Abihu were likely in their twenties when they died. Later, when the Israelites were in the Promised Land, Eleazar replaced his father as high priest.

This entire scene demonstrates God's hatred of humanized religion. Fallen humanity has a natural propensity towards religious pride (i.e., making religious choices that neither show faith in God nor turn us from a path of sin). Nadab and Abihu offered strange fire to God in worship just after God had given them specific instructions as to the proper way for priests to offer sacrifices to Him. God struck them both dead for their arrogance. Mere religious deeds do not impress God, nor do they have any eternal value. Endeavoring to worship God through any means or method other than what His Word authorizes does not please the Lord: rather, the activity mimics the sin of Nadab and Abihu in Leviticus 10.

How utterly putrid to God, then, are all the ceremonies, the holidays, and the rituals which the Church has created to obtain some religious experience or to try impress Him. In the Church Age, believers are commanded by the Lord to pray, to learn the teachings of Christ, to be water baptized and to regularly observe the Lord's Supper in remembrance of Christ. Furthermore, believers are to be living sacrifices by mortifying their fleshly desires and yielding to God's will, they are to fulfill their work of ministry within the body of Christ, and they are not to forsake the gatherings of the local church. Whatever is beyond God's pattern of body-life for the Church is humanized religion, an offense to God, and distracts the lost from learning the truth.

Recalling God's Holiness

No matter the dispensation God's people find themselves in, one inescapable truth remains the same: when God's holiness is disregarded or forgotten, humanized religion and sin will abound among His people. One need only recall the incredible scene which occurred just a few weeks prior to the tragic events of this chapter to discern the validity of this statement. After Moses sprinkled the Israelites with blood at Mount Sinai, Moses, Aaron, Nadab, Abihu, and the seventy elders of Israel ascended part of the way up the mountain to meet with God, although only Moses was permitted upon the summit. The description of what the leaders of Israel saw and did is astounding:

> *Then Moses went up, also Aaron, Nadab, and Abihu, and seventy of the elders of Israel, and they saw the God of Israel. And there was under His feet as it were a paved work of sapphire stone, and it was like the very heavens in its clarity. But on the nobles of the children of Israel He did not lay His hand. So they saw God, and they ate and drank* (Ex. 24:9-11).

Originally, the people fled from God's holy presence when they witnessed His grandeur in this smoking and quaking mountain, but then the leaders, with Nadab and Abihu, were permitted to come a little ways up the mount to view the base of Jehovah's throne. They joyfully feasted while gazing on this display of God's magnificence. This is not the only time in Scripture that man was permitted, in some degree, to witness the awesome scene of God upon His majestic throne.

Centuries later, the spectacular sight of God's throne totally overwhelmed the prophet Isaiah. Above a rumbling, smoked-filled temple Isaiah saw seraphim flying overhead, crying out to each other, *"Holy, holy, holy is the Lord of Hosts; the whole earth is full of His glory!"* (Isa. 6:3). Centuries later, John was caught up in the Spirit to witness a similar heavenly scene. John saw four living creatures flying above God's throne, and these declared a similar message as those Isaiah observed: *"Holy, holy, holy, Lord God Almighty, Who was and is and is to come!"* (Rev. 4:8). These spiritual beings continue to declare God's holiness as a warning of His unapproachable nature. He is the almighty, holy God; His character, attributes, and ways are unique. This is what "holy" means, "to be set apart." His very essence and attributes of holiness set God apart from all that He has created. Redeemed souls and elect angels are declared positionally holy and are thus *set apart* for His glory. God is pure and alone in majesty; there is absolutely no sin or evil in God (1 Jn. 1:6). Because God is holy, He cannot approve of anything within us which is less than His own perfect nature.

> One great hindrance to holiness in the ministry of the word is that we are prone to preach and write without pressing into the things we say and making them real to our own souls. Over the years words begin to come easy, and we find we can speak of mysteries without standing in awe; we can speak of purity without feeling pure; we can speak of zeal without spiritual passion; we can speak of God's holiness without trembling; we can speak of sin without sorrow; we can speak of heaven without eagerness. And the result is a terrible hardening of the spiritual life.
>
> — John Own

It is when man loses sight of God's holiness that we enter into sin. Nadab and Abihu saw the glory of God on at least two occasions (the second time being after their consecration in Lev. 9), yet lackadaisically entered into God's presence to offer "strange fire." God had just provided instructions as to how the priests could approach Him and affect worship on behalf of the nation; Aaron's sons, however, had other thoughts as to how a holy God could be worshipped. Their mistake, as previously noted, was deadly, and the offense was so great that Aaron was not allowed to mourn the death of his two sons. The holiness of God is a serious matter.

Recalling God's words concerning His holiness to Moses on Mount Sinai, Peter reminds believers in the Church Age that God remains holy and desires His people to reflect His moral nature: *"As obedient children, not conforming yourselves to the former lusts, as in your ignorance; but as He who called you is holy, you also be holy in all your conduct, because it is written, 'Be holy, for I am holy'"* (1 Peter 1:14-16). Paul reminds the believers at Corinth that their bodies had become the temple of the Lord and that they should not desecrate God's dwelling place (1 Cor. 6:19). To be mindful of God's holiness is a strong defense against engaging in sin. God will not tolerate filthiness or wickedness in His presence. God is holy and He will not settle for anything less than holiness in us. There are no degrees of righteousness and holiness with God, so His people should not be satisfied with conduct which God does not approve.

> There is a danger of forgetting that the Bible reveals, not first the love of God, but the intense, blazing holiness of God, with his love as the center of that holiness.
>
> — Oswald Chambers

Prohibitions and Instructions

The remainder of Leviticus 10 contains three prohibitions (vv. 8-11) and further instructions concerning the sacrifices offered by the priests (vv. 12-20). For the first time, and the only time mentioned in Leviticus, God spoke directly to Aaron, without the mediation of Moses. This is no doubt because the new regulations God gave pertained only to the priests, a result of the failure that had just occurred. The first restriction Aaron received was that the priests were not to drink wine and other fermented beverages while in the tabernacle. This would ensure their minds were clear when they were executing their priestly duties If their cognitive abilities were muddled by alcohol, they might mistakenly alter the prescribed sacrificial procedures. This, as already seen, could have fatal ramifications. This constraint seems painfully obvious, but perhaps Nadab and Abihu were intoxicated when they angered the Lord, and thus the specific warning is stated to preclude a repeat offense. F. B. Hole suggests a valuable application for believers today:

> All who have come to the Lord, while He is still disallowed of men, are constituted priests, as we learn in 1 Peter 2:3-4, and all of us should be in right priestly condition. But the **position** is one thing; and the **condition** which answers to it is another. Hence that important word, "Be not drunk with wine, wherein is excess; but be filled with the Spirit" (Eph. 5:18). When thus filled we can offer the sacrifice of praise, as the next verse indicates. The contrast is between what is fleshly and what is spiritual. We are to decline what excites the flesh that we may know the power of the Spirit. The same thing, of course, is true not only of our praise but also as to our powers of spiritual discernment, and as to our ability to teach others that which we may have learned from God of His things.[2]

The second regulation was that the priests maintain a clear distinction between the *holy* and the *profane* (v. 10); the third, that a similar difference between *clean* and *unclean* should be observed. These latter two injunctions (i.e., laws concerning uncleanness) are further explained in Leviticus 11-15. Aaron was now responsible to both discern the difference between holy and unholy, clean and unclean, and to instruct the people in the same. The observance of these three prohibitions was necessary for the priests to be effective teachers of the people. One cannot teach what is right if one does not do what is right (v. 11).

In verses 12-15, Moses again reiterates what portions of which sacrifices were to be eaten by the priests. Moses soon discovered, and was angered by, a breech in this protocol committed by Eleazer and Ithamar (vv. 16-18). They had completely burned up the people's sin offering (the goat carcass) instead of eating their portion of it in the Holy Place. If the blood of the sin offering was not used to cleanse the sanctuary, the remaining portion of the animal was to be eaten by the priests in the courtyard – for it was "holy." Aaron apparently endorsed this isolated incident and explained to Moses that the irregularity was tied to the judgment of Nadab and Abihu. F. Duane Lindsey summarizes Aaron's defense:

Aaron asked his brother, "Would the Lord have been pleased if I had eaten the sin offering today?" Apparently he either had a genuine fear of eating what was "most holy" (v. 17) in the wake of his sons' deaths, or he was confused by grief and inadvertently mishandled the sacrificial procedure. If so, this would seem to be a case in which he should have brought his own sin offering for a ritual violation, though this is not indicated.[3]

In either case, Moses was satisfied with Aaron's explanation and the matter was forgotten.

Application

We learn much of God's will for our lives by studying what He has declared in His word, and this leads to one of two major outcomes. We are put under deeper responsibility if we ignore God's revealed will, or we become more useful to God if we obey it. On this point, there is an important application for the believer to learn from the lives and deaths of Nadab and Abihu. In view of their privileged inclusion in the group that was allowed onto Mount Sinai in Exodus 24, and their subsequent untimely deaths due to their own presumption, F. B. Hole remarks:

> It is noticeable that of the sons of Aaron only Nadab and Abihu are mentioned [in Exodus 24]. The two who died under judgment, almost as soon as they were consecrated as priests, had no excuse for their sin. They fell in spite of this great privilege; whereas Eleazar and Ithamar, who carried on as priests, did not apparently have this unique experience. It is often the way that failure is most pronounced in those who are most highly privileged.[4]

This is a valuable point for the Church to consider. God judged Nadab and Abihu with death for offering strange incense-fire to Him after having witnessed His glory and having received specific instructions as to the proper way to offer sacrifices to Him. What accountability does the Church, which has far more revelation than Nadab and Abihu did, have with God concerning the matter of executing proper worship? Much! Christians then should make a special effort to worship God in the way God has deemed appropriate.

The Lord Jesus instituted the "Lord's Supper" as a time for the local church to remember Him corporately (1 Cor. 11:17, 20). He said to do it often, understanding our tendency to forget Him and His work. Yet the command set down no rules for how frequently Christians should gather to remember the Lord; our love for Him will determine this matter. The early church transitioned from "breaking bread" daily in Acts 2 to the established practice of remembering the Lord once a week on Sunday (Acts 20:7). Every believer should confess their sins before partaking of the Lord's Supper (1 Cor. 11:23-32), just as the Levitical priests washed their hands and feet at the Bronze Laver before entering into the tabernacle with their offerings to worship God (Ex. 30:17-21). If a Levitical priest did not prepare properly to offer worship, he was in danger of dying, and Paul acknowledges that the Christian (a believer priest, 1 Pet. 2:5, 9) faces the same peril if he or she approaches God in worship with unconfessed sin. God has appointed a way for the Church to offer corporate worship to Him. Let us not seek our own method for extending honor to God.

When believers assemble for worship, they should do so in the beauty of holiness (having humbly confessed their sins) and with a spiritual offering ready to present to the Lord (1 Chron. 16:29). The audible ministry should be done by Spirit-led men, as the man represents God when speaking (1 Cor. 11:7), and this is in accordance with the instructions given for church order (1 Cor. 14). The women are to attend to the visual ministry in the assembly of revealing God's glory by covering all competing glories: the woman, the glory of man, and her hair, the glory of woman (1 Cor. 11:7, 15). In this way, only God's glory, as represented by uncovered men, is seen by God and the angels overlooking the gathering. This pictures the scene in heaven as seraphim and cherubim cover their own intrinsic glories with their wings in the presence of God, so that God's glory is preeminent (Isa. 6:2; Ezek. 1:11). Satan was a covering cherub (Ezek. 28:14-16) who rebelled against God's creation. He didn't want to conceal his own glories anymore, but wanted to have the position of God. Satan continues to oppose God's arrangements, whether it be civil, church, or family order.

May the Church do what Satan failed to do – show submission to God's order by obeying scriptural practices. Leviticus 10 illustrates just how much God hates humanized religion and also the extraordinary means He will invoke to remove its repulsive devices from His people. Let us not be indignant when He purges from us what is putrid to Him and harmful to us, but rather, let us thank Him for caring enough to take action.

Meditation

Not all the blood of beasts, on Jewish altars slain,
Could give the guilty conscience peace, or wash away its stain.
But Christ, the heavenly Lamb, took all our sins away,
A sacrifice of nobler name and richer blood than they.

— Isaac Watts

Clean and Unclean Food
Leviticus 11

Chapters 11-15 comprise the third major section of Leviticus: The Laws of Cleanliness (or Purity). When the word "clean" is used in this context, we are not speaking of good hygiene or even the absence of filth, but rather a ritual state of purity that the general population of Israel was to maintain. While some laws within these chapters do promote good personal hygiene and a healthy diet, this is not their primary focus. Rather, the Lord wanted His people to be consistently thinking about His holiness and the necessity of maintaining "cleanliness" in order to have communion with Him. A holy people must strive for holiness in all areas of their life.

In the things pertaining to God, there were only three ceremonial classifications: holy, clean, and unclean. For example, the priests, their garments, the sacrifices, and the things of the tabernacle were specifically cleansed by blood and anointed with special oil in order to be declared "holy" before the Lord. The Israelites could not participate in any of the feasts or sweet-smelling sacrifices unless they were "clean." If "unclean," they were required to take specific actions to remedy the situation and become ceremonially "clean" again. For major issues, offerings were required, but for lesser and more common matters of uncleanness, one simply washed and remained isolated until evening.

"Holy" status could only be gained by divine imputation, usually through the means of blood purification and anointing oil. What God deemed holy was holy. Likewise a "clean" status was only obtained through the means which God set forth; this typically involved washing and waiting, or, depending of the type of uncleanness, blood purification. God labors to keep His people holy and clean, but man pollutes what God has accomplished (i.e., making that which is holy, unholy, and that which is clean, unclean). The prophet Haggai emphasizes this point to his fellow countrymen at a time when they had settled into spiritual complacency and materialism. Jehovah instructed Haggai to ask the following questions of the priests:

> *"If one carries holy meat in the fold of his garment, and with the edge he touches bread or stew, wine or oil, or any food, will it become holy?" Then the priests answered and said, "No." And Haggai said, "If one who is unclean because of a dead body touches any of these, will it be unclean?" So the priests answered and said, "It shall be unclean." Then Haggai answered and said, "So is this people, and so is this nation before Me," says the Lord, "and so is every work of their hands; and what they offer there is unclean"* (Hag. 2:12-14).

What is holy does not change what is not, but that which is unholy does influence what is holy. Haggai was to inform the people that having an altar and performing sacrifices did not make the Jews a holy people. In reality, they had made themselves unclean before Jehovah, and nothing they offered Him with defiled hands would be accepted. They were supposed to be building Jehovah a temple, but instead they used the supplied resources for that task to build themselves nice homes. Though they were performing religious gestures, the Jews had lost the joy, the privilege, and the status of a holy people. Haggai challenged them to cleanse their hands (i.e., to repent); they did and a temple was quickly raised up against overwhelming opposition as a testimony of God's greatness. Only those with "clean hands" can be known as God's holy people among the nations.

With this said, it is important to understand that the distinction between "clean" and "unclean" cannot be directly equated with "non-sinful" or "sinful" conduct, for much of the ceremonial defilement the Jews faced was due to certain bodily functions or unintentional actions, neither of which were morally wrong (e.g., accidently touching a dead carcass). To ensure that there would be no confusion about what God regarded as clean and unclean, Leviticus chapters 11 through 15 supplied specific laws governing Israelite conduct for: diet (chp. 11), motherhood (chp. 12), leprosy (chps. 13-14), and other forms of bodily uncleanness (chp. 15). Instructions regarding the Day of Atonement directly follow this section (Lev. 16). The Day of Atonement permitted God to maintain His relationship and presence among His people in a corporate sense until the next atonement for sins was offered. In the meantime His people were to be mindful of God's holiness and their responsibility, to the extent possible, to maintain the prescribed purity before Him.

Dietary Laws (Leviticus 11)

The dietary laws listed in this chapter are nearly identical to those that Moses highlights some forty years later in Deuteronomy 14. Previously, the Jews had been prohibited from eating the fat or consuming the blood associated with sacrifices. In this chapter the Jews were to be mindful of not eating any creature that God deemed as unclean. While there may be health-related reasons for abstaining from certain foods, verses 44-45 indicate the primary reason for these stipulations:

> *For I am the Lord your God. You shall therefore consecrate yourselves, and you shall be holy; for I am holy. Neither shall you defile yourselves with any creeping thing that creeps on the earth. For I am the Lord who brings you up out of the land of Egypt, to be your God. You shall therefore be holy, for I am holy.*

The Lord was using stringent dietary laws to teach the Israelites a disciplined thought life, as they had to be mindful of maintaining "clean" conduct throughout their daily routine. Meal times would be a regular opportunity for the Israelites to not only thank God for His goodness, but also to remember His holiness and His expectation for personal holiness in their own lives. In His unbounded grace, Jehovah had chosen them to be a holy ("set apart") people for Himself and for His purposes. The dietary laws were one distinctive which would ensure His covenant people would be a peculiar nation among all others.

Accordingly, the Jews were not permitted to eat just anything that struck their fancy. Some of God's directives (i.e., those regarding moral matters) are commanded because they are right, while others are right simply because they are divinely commanded; the dietary laws fit best into the latter category. For these and similar ordinances, the practical value, if any, is not always expounded. God does not need to explain Himself to be obeyed; in fact, the lack of exposition imposes a grander test of our faithfulness. Generally speaking, however, if God does not explain His rationale for what may seem like a mundane matter to us, He is not only testing our obedience but also revealing something which is important to Him. So while there may have been health benefits in abstaining from eating certain creatures, as already stated, the primary emphasis of these dietary edicts was to affirm Israel's election in the broader sense as God's peculiar and special covenant people.

Instructions in this part of Leviticus seem to come in threes. Just as there were three ceremonial classifications for Jewish individuals, there were three designations for creatures also: sacrificially acceptable (e.g., "holy"), clean (could be eaten and touched), and unclean (could not be eaten or touched). F. Duane Lindsey further suggests that Leviticus 11 can be outlined according to three main prohibitions against uncleanness:

> (1) Unclean animals were not to be eaten, though no punishment is stated for violation of this command. (2) All dead animals, whether unclean or clean (unless ritually slaughtered at the tabernacle), rendered those who touched their carcasses ceremonially unclean, but this was only temporary if they washed in water and waited till evening. (3) Household articles touched by certain carcasses were also unclean (vv. 32-38).[1]

The first instruction is a dietary law against eating unclean animals, of which there are three sub-classes: land-bound creatures (vv. 1-8), creatures living in water (vv. 9-12), and flying creatures (vv. 13-23). There was one simple rule for the land-bound creatures: animals with a cloven hoof and that chewed their cud were considered clean (edible); all others were not. To prevent confusion a list of clean animals are given: ox, sheep, goat, deer, gazelle, roe deer, wild goat, ibex, antelope, and mountain sheep. The camel, the badger, the rabbit, and the swine were unclean animals because they either did not have a cloven hoof (e.g., the camel), or did not chew the cud (e.g., the swine).

The second class of creatures addressed lived in the water. In short, only fish that had scales and fins could be eaten (vv. 9-12). All other seafood was considered unclean and therefore inedible. The final group to be discussed was flying creatures (vv. 13-19): nineteen types of birds and the bat (a flying mammal) were deemed unclean; most were birds of prey (e.g., the eagle, the buzzard, and the raven). In feeding directly on their prey, these birds were eating the blood of the flesh and were thus deemed unclean. Clean birds, (such as sparrows, pigeons, doves, and quail) could be eaten, although these are not specifically listed in Leviticus 11 or in Deuteronomy 14. Along similar lines, the only flying insects allowed in the Jewish diet were four varieties of locust (vv. 20-24). The reader might recall that John, the forerunner of Christ, made locust his staple food when he dwelt in the wilderness; this was permitted per Leviticus 11. For many the thought of eating insects is disgusting, but presently about one tenth of humanity's protein worldwide is derived from the consumption of insects. The Israelites were also prohibited from eating worms, snakes, rodents, and other insects not already approved. Anyone eating these would be, ritualistically speaking, "unclean."

While the other peoples of the world could eat what they most enjoyed, the Jews would be a nation marked by the high privilege of only eating what Jehovah pleased – thus, their separation as Jehovah's peculiar people would be plain for all to see. They could exercise free choice in their diet, but only within the limits laid out by their God. This was not their only distinctive; the Jews were obviously different in their attire (Lev. 19:19; Deut. 22:5), their physical appearance (Lev. 19:28), and even in what they were physically permitted to touch (Lev. 11-15). A Jew who wanted to honor Jehovah would have to be mindful of what was "clean" and "unclean" every moment of every day.

This chapter details what creatures are clean and unclean so the people would know what ones they were not to eat; in fact, they were not even to touch these unclean things! This shows the extent to which Jehovah was jealously guarding His people; He did not want them even near to what was unclean, lest they be tempted to defile themselves. Thus, contact of any kind with what God deemed as unclean was forbidden (vv. 8, 24, 26-27, 31-40). How much sin in the Church today would be avoided if God's people enacted this same principle; that is, to not only *"abhor what is evil and cling to what is good"* (Rom. 12:9-10), but also to *"abstain from all appearance of evil"* (1 Thess. 5:22)?

The second major prohibition against uncleanness in Leviticus 11 dealt with touching what was dead. Limiting direct contact with the various bacteria present in rotting tissue would certainly impede the spread of disease. Whether the animal itself was designated unclean (vv. 24-28) or clean (vv. 39-40) did not matter; if someone touched an animal's carcass, that person was instantly made unclean. The remedy was to thoroughly wash oneself and to avoid contact with others until evening. No one who was ceremonially "unclean" could participate in worship or feasts, or any social event for that matter, until the evening after he or she had washed.

Swarming creatures are addressed in verses 29-38. Although this group is not specifically identified, the Hebrew word *sherets*, which means "swarm" or "creeping things" is translated as "insects" in verse 20. This word, as shown by its usage in Genesis 7:21, refers to any group of creatures which move together. As we know, insects often do. A vessel which was found to have a dead "swarming thing" in it was deemed unclean. It therefore had to be purified or destroyed. From a public health standpoint, the practical advantages of this practice are obvious. An exception was permitted for a running spring of water in verse 36. These precious water sources cleansed themselves of contamination and were, therefore, not considered unclean if a dead insect (for example) was found floating on the water. Though contamination was still a remote possibility in such cases, it would be an impractical imposition if the Israelites had to purify or destroy each stream. This was especially true during their wilderness sojourn, as "swarming things" would be drawn to scarce water supplies and no doubt some insects would die there.

Application

Two points of application are suggested, one pertaining to our attitude towards others we might think are "unclean," and the second in connection with our convictions about proper diet. There is a narrative in the book of Acts that addresses both. Peter was abiding in the house of Simon, a tanner living in Joppa. At noon Peter ascended to the housetop to pray. While in the spirit of prayer, Peter received a vision. He saw a great sheet bound by its four corners coming down from heaven; it contained an assortment of unclean creatures. The Lord commanded, *"Rise, Peter; kill and eat"* (Acts 10:13). Peter refused because the edicts of Leviticus 11 forbade it. The Lord responded: *"What God has cleansed you must not call common"* (Acts 10:15). Peter learned through this thrice-repeated vision that what God calls clean is clean, and that all men, not just Jews, could now be cleansed by the blood of Christ.

Peter later explained what he had learned from the vision to Cornelius, a Gentile who feared and honored the Lord: *"You know how unlawful it is for a Jewish man to keep company with or go to one of another nation. But God has shown me that I should not call any man common or unclean"* (Acts 10:28). The Law prohibited the Jews from having any contact with Gentiles lest the Jews be defiled, but in the Church Age, the gospel message is for everyone, Jew and Gentile (Rom. 1:16).

The Law was glorious in that it pointed the nation to what would replace it, which was still more glorious – salvation in Christ by grace (2 Cor. 3:6-13; Gal. 3:24). Thus, Peter already understood that much of the Law was no longer in effect. This is evident in that Peter had been staying with a new believer named Simon, a Jew, who made his living by skinning dead animals and tanning their hides. By Levitical standards he would be unclean, yet Peter gladly passed many days in his home (Acts 9:43).

In the vision, the Lord not only affirmed that the Levitical dietary laws were no longer in effect for the Jews, but also that the wall of partition between Jew and Gentile had been broken down; the two could become one in Christ (Rom. 15:16; Gal. 3:28; Eph. 2:11-18). The Jews were no longer to think of anyone as "clean" or "unclean;" the important distinction is whether a person is "saved" or "lost." Those justified in Christ are saved; those who are not are lost. This is the mindset that believers should have today. While we tend to think of others in terms of social and economic classes, spiritually speaking, there are only two groups of people in the world today: "saints" and "ain'ts." James reminds us other estimations are based on the world's standards and devalue the worth of another's soul; in fact, we actually blaspheme the name of the Lord when we show such partiality (Jas. 2:1-7).

Concerning the second point of application, we understand today that whatever food is given thanks for is thereby sanctified for our bodies' use. This was also the situation in the days of Noah (Gen. 9:2-3). Paul confirms this truth with Timothy, a Jew and his spiritual son in the faith: *"For every creature of God is good, and nothing to be refused, if it be received with thanksgiving: For it is sanctified by the word of God and prayer"* (1 Tim. 4:4). However, it is also understood that our bodies are the temple of God (1 Cor. 6:19) and we should not, therefore, willfully harm our bodies by ingesting contaminated, poisonous, or digestively-disagreeable foods. This would include any mind-altering or body-stimulating substances of a non-medical nature.

Furthermore, there may be cultural or practical reasons for abstaining from certain foods if eating such things would offend others. In Paul's day, the consciences of some Christians were offended when other believers ate meat that had been offered to idols. Idols do not eat much, so there was always plenty of high-quality, second-hand meat available at a reasonable price in the marketplace. Paul writes: *"I know and am convinced by the Lord Jesus that there is nothing unclean of itself; but to him who considers anything to be unclean, to him it is unclean"* (Rom. 14:14). This indicates it would not be a sin to eat meat that had been offered to idols if one had a clear conscience in the matter (Rom. 14:23). However, whatever the believer's persuasion might be on the matter of proper healthy diet, or economical purchases, it should be understood to be an area of liberty. Such liberties are to be forfeited, if need be, to avoid offending others unnecessarily. Paul explains:

> *But food does not commend us to God; for neither if we eat are we the better, nor if we do not eat are we the worse. But beware lest somehow this liberty of yours become a stumbling block to those who are weak. For if anyone sees you who have knowledge eating in an idol's temple, will not the conscience of him who is weak be emboldened to eat those things offered to idols? And because of your knowledge shall the weak brother perish, for whom Christ died? But when you thus sin against the brethren, and wound their weak conscience, you sin against Christ. Therefore, if food makes my brother stumble, I will never again eat meat, lest I make my brother stumble* (1 Cor. 8:8-13).

This means we do not cause division by promoting our alimentary convictions among those who see things differently (Rom. 14:1-3), and that we gladly yield our rights if there is the potential for stumbling another believer by our eating and drinking, especially those younger in the faith.

Our meal times should be characterized by thanksgiving and joyful fellowship, not unprofitable arguments and meddling pride. The dietary laws issued to the Jews were specific to them; these were to accentuate their need for holiness in all areas of life, for holy Jehovah resided with them. Thus, at that juncture of time, non-compliance with these specific "dos and don'ts" would be a sin. However, in the Church Age, the matter of what a believer eats is not a moral issue, but rather one of wisdom. The believer would be wise to eat what is good for the body and likewise foolish to ingest or drink what is harmful to the body. A believer would also be wise not to eat or drink what might offend others who are of a different conviction.

The restrictive diet given to Israel was never confirmed for the Church; rather, believers today are to be mindful of what they "eat" spiritually. The believer grows by having an appetite for the sincere milk of the Word and by learning the meatier doctrines of the faith (Heb. 5:12-14; 1 Pet. 2:2). If the believer is going to expose his mind to violence, pornography, filthy language, course jesting, and extravagant indulgences, the heart will readily be conformed into a stagnant cesspool of carnal ambitions: *"For as he thinks in his heart, so is he"* (Prov. 23:7). Physically you are what you eat, but spiritually you become what you think upon and the believer is to think on Christ and learn how to better please Him.

Meditation

> Blest are the pure, whose hearts are clean,
> Who never tread the ways of sin;
> With endless pleasures they shall see
> A God of spotless purity.
>
> — Isaac Watts

The Law of Motherhood
Leviticus 12

This chapter specifies the durations in which a new mother was considered unclean followed by a period of time she was merely regarded ceremonially unclean. She was considered contagiously unclean (i.e., was not to have direct contact with others) for seven days after the birth of a boy and fourteen days after the birth of a girl; this related to postnatal discharge. The limitations of this period of uncleanness were the same as experienced during her monthly menstruation cycle (v. 2).

If a mother gave birth to a boy, the flesh of his foreskin was to be circumcised on the eighth day. Prothrombin is necessary for the clotting process; we now know the amount of this protein present in a baby boy's blood climbs to more than one hundred percent of normal levels on the eighth day after birth. Under normal conditions, this is the only day in the male's life in which such levels are reached. If circumcision is to be performed, the eighth day of life is the best time to do it as vitamin K and prothrombin levels are at their peak to enhance blood clotting.[1]

As noted earlier, the number eight signifies a new beginning in Scripture. A Jewish boy began his journey among God's covenant people after being circumcised. Without circumcision he was considered an outsider and could not benefit from the blessings and privileges extended to the Jewish nation through Abrahamic covenant.

Besides marking a Jewish male as one under God's covenant blessing, the physical act of circumcision also has a practical lesson for us. Through circumcision a portion of flesh is cut off and dies. In the spiritual sense, circumcision occurs when believers do not put confidence in their flesh or make a provision for it to fulfill its lusting (Rom. 13:14; Gal. 6:12-13). The Lord reminded His disciples: *"It is the spirit that gives life; the flesh profits nothing"* (John 6:63). To profitably serve the Lord, believers must understand that there is nothing in "the flesh" that can please the Lord (Rom. 7:18). Even when seemingly good deeds are accomplished in the power of our flesh, our impure motives and inner intentions ruin the gesture. From a human perspective, the good we do may appear godly, but yet, from God's perspective, if it was accomplished in the flesh, it is tainted with sin. Only what is fully done through the Spirit of God in us can perfectly represent Christ-like selflessness. Such acts have God's full stamp of approval; all else has diminished value and can even be offensive to God.

After the days of the new mother's separation were fulfilled, an additional period of thirty-three days for the birth of a boy and sixty-six days for that of a girl were to be added before she could be ceremonially purified (vv. 4-5). During this time she could not touch anything that had been consecrated in the service of God, nor could she enter the sanctuary. The total time of purification for a boy was then forty days, and for a girl, eighty days. Some see this regulation as God's tender care for mothers. By limiting a new mother's visitors, her exposure to germs in her weakened state after childbirth would be minimized.

At the end of this time she was to venture to the tabernacle and offer a yearling lamb as a burnt offering and a pigeon or dove as a sin offering. If poor, as in the case of Mary the mother of the Lord Jesus, she could offer two birds: one as a sin offering and the other as a burnt offering (vv. 6-8; Luke 2:22-24). The atonement was necessary for ritual purification only. The mother had not sinned in giving birth, but she had brought a child into the world having a fallen nature, a nature that adamantly opposes God and His interests.

We are not given a rationale for why the different timeframes for purification after childbirth are based on the gender of the baby. Although our modern culture has difficulty with pondering gender related restrictions, these matters are contained in Scripture for a purpose. Perhaps there were medical or social ramifications which we are not aware of, or maybe there was a spiritual lesson to consider. For the latter possibility, the distinction may have served as a reminder to the mother that in the beginning it was a woman who was deceived and sinned first: *"And Adam was not deceived, but the woman being deceived, fell into transgression"* (1 Tim. 2:14). The different purification durations also would remind every mother of God's creation order: the man was created first and the woman was created from the man and for the man. What is certain is that there is nothing sinful about carrying and delivering a baby, although every baby born adds to the sin of the world! Nor does God favor the birth of a boy over that of a girl, as the purification offering was the same for both male and female offspring. Both genders are necessary to honor God's command to our first parents to *"be fruitful and multiply and fill the earth"* (Gen. 1:28). Leviticus 12 then reminds us of how humanity fell and also the condition of defilement in which sin has plunged all men and women since that dreadful day in Eden.

Application

While in general it is God's plan for children to be born from the marriage union of a husband and wife, Malachi reminds us that God is not seeking offspring merely, but rather a "godly seed" that will live for Him (Mal. 2:15). In principle, God is more interested in quality than quantity of children. In other words, parents should not be having babies for the sake of obtaining a large family, but rather for the added capacity of serving the Lord and bringing honor to His name. To have more children than what parents can spiritually, emotionally, educationally, and economically care for is not wise. As the prophet Ezekiel informed the parents of his day, children are born unto the Lord – they are for Him (Ezek. 16:20). The psalmist declares that *"children are a heritage from the Lord"* (Ps. 127:3), and then explains:

> *As arrows are in the hand of a mighty man, so are children of one's youth. Happy is the man who hath his quiver full of them; they shall not be ashamed, but they shall speak with the enemies in the gate* (Ps. 127:4-5).

The psalmist reminds us that we parents are mere stewards, and not owners, of the children God graciously entrusts to our care. If reared in the ways of the Lord, these skillfully sharpened and straight arrows become a rich blessing to all.

Children must be trained up for the Lord. Untrained children, not surprisingly, remain foolish (Prov. 22:15) and predictably absorb what outside influences fill their void of understanding. Children are natural sponges – they are compelled to learn and to develop an understanding of the world in which they live. Billy Graham highlights the danger of neglecting the spiritual aspects of a child's development: "Parents have little time for children and a great vacuum has developed, and into that vacuum is going to move some kind of ideology."[2] Peter Marshall acknowledges the unfortunate outcome: "Let us not fool ourselves—without Christianity, without Christian education, without the principles of Christ inculcated into young life, we are simply rearing pagans."[3] God forbid that as His stewards we should rear up pagans to revile His name!

A Christian family is not a large household or even a household of Christians, but a Christian household. It is more than Christ dwelling within the hearts of family members; it is a family that is pursuing the heart of God. If the Bible is not at the center of family life and all home affairs, that home cannot be called a true Christian home. The vital focus and end objective of every Christian household is the glory of God!

Meditation

> O blessed home where man and wife
> Together lead a godly life
> By deeds their faith confessing!
> There many a happy day is spent,
> There Jesus gladly will consent
> To tarry with His blessing.
>
> — Magnus B. Landstad

Inspection and Diagnosis of Leprosy
Leviticus 13, 14:33-53

In the previous chapter, the atonement associated with childbirth called our attention to the inherited sinful *nature* within all newborns. Leviticus 13 speaks of the visible outbreak of that nature in sinful *activity*, as represented in the disease of leprosy. Leprosy, as a type, focuses on the corrupting and defiling power of the sin within, rather than its guilt or the fallen nature itself. Leprosy speaks, not of what we are in Adam, but rather of who we prove we are by our lives. Although we are not responsible for being born with a sinful nature, we are fully responsible for what it does and how it affects others.

While certainly family and friends suffer for our wrong actions, this chapter illustrates sin's menace to the congregation as a whole, and the group's need to take action against someone who is threatening its wellbeing. Today this would relate to our interactions within the local church and dealing with those in unrepentant sin. Chronic leprosy must be dealt with, and someone suspected of leprosy was to be "brought" to a priest for examination, as he or she may not want to come voluntarily. Similarly, those living in continuing sin rarely want it to be noticed and repudiated by others.

The Hebrew word *tsara`ath*, translated "leprosy," describes a broad range of spreading surface discolorations and flaking in both people and objects. It has a variety of meanings depending on what was suspected of infestation. For example, mold and mildew on clothing, household articles, and the walls of a home were also referred to as "leprosy." This is why elaborate instructions were provided to the priests so that they could identify leprosy of the flesh (13:1-28) or of the head (13:29-44), and also recognize it in the form of mold and mildew within garments and other personal articles (13:47-59) and in houses (14:33-53).

As used in reference to people, this generic Hebrew term not only described Hansen's disease (the chronic infection typically associated with the Old Testament description of leprosy), but many other skin diseases as well. While Hansen's disease is stubbornly persistent, other skin inflammations and distortions also labeled "leprosy" often cleared up in time. In biblical times, leprosy spoke of a variety of skin diseases; some were highly contagious and were without any curable medical treatment. Those who were diagnosed with such were forced into isolation and left to fend for themselves. The provision for ceremonial cleansing in Leviticus 14 seems to indicate that natural healing did occur for some types of skin diseases, but not for dreaded Hansen's disease.

Hansen's disease is primarily a granulomatous disease of the peripheral nerves, skin, and mucosa of the upper respiratory tract; skin lesions are the primary external sign.[1] Left untreated, leprosy is usually a progressive disease causing permanent damage to the skin, nerves, and eyes. Hansen's disease does not directly cause body parts to fall off or lead to death, as often construed, but the numbness resulting from nerve damage allows dangerous secondary injuries and infections to develop. Often, leprous persons do not know they have been injured or have developed open lesions because they cannot feel pain in the affected area. Even apart from secondary infections, left untreated the disease readily advances and causes fingers and toes to become shortened and deformed, and in some cases leads to blindness and even death.

While today there is effective treatment for Hansen's disease, there was none in Old Testament days, meaning that if someone contracted the disease, he or she was isolated from the Jewish society to suffer a slowly deteriorating and miserable existence. To prevent the spread of the disease, lepers normally communed together in remote colonies and were dependent on loved ones to supply their necessities. For this reason, leprosy was intensely feared and no doubt led to an understandable paranoia among the Israelites.

Hence, Leviticus 13 supplied the priests with detailed procedures for properly inspecting various infections and correctly diagnosing the disease. As there was no cure for leprosy, the priests were not acting as physicians, but rather as public health officials protecting their brethren from an epidemic crisis. To this end, the twenty-one specific cases mentioned followed a similar procedure for detection:

- Preliminary symptoms noticed (vv. 2, 7, 9).
- A priestly inspection or reinspection (vv. 3, 10, 13).

- A statement by the priest of symptoms found (vv. 3, 1, 13).
- A diagnosis:
  — clean (vv. 6, 13, 17).
  — unclean (vv. 3, 8, 11), then isolation (vv. 44-46).
  — inconclusive, requiring a week's quarantine and reinspection (vv. 4, 21, 31).
  — still inconclusive, requiring another week's quarantine and reinspection (vv. 6, 22).

Proper inspection was a crucial task, as a wrong diagnosis could either allow a highly contagious person to freely roam through the camp and unknowingly spread the disease, or place a healthy person in close proximity to truly infectious lepers. In order to preclude either of these disastrous outcomes, the proper diagnostic procedure often required individuals to be quarantined and to undergo repeated inspections. The thought behind this was that if a person was truly a leper, they would only get worse, not better.

The process for detecting leprosy in the skin (13:2-17), in scars (13:18-23), in burns (13:24-28), in the scalp or the beard (13:29-37), or in a bald spot (13:40-44) were similar. If individuals noticed a raised place, a discolored spot, or a boil in their skin, they were to be brought to a priest for examination. If it was an obvious case (i.e., raw flesh, white hair in a boil, a spreading condition), the individual would be declared "unclean." If, however, the spot was white but did not appear to be deeper than the skin and the hair in the spot was not white, the priest was required to delay his diagnosis. For these cases, the individual would be quarantined for seven days and then inspected again. Oddly enough, if all the infected area turned white, it meant that the disease was inactive and the priest was to declare that individual "clean" (13:12-13, 16-17). F. B. Hole explains the spiritual meaning of this seemingly unusual circumstance:

> If the disease should come completely to the surface, so that the flesh is white and covered, and so further spreading became impossible, the man was to be pronounced **clean.** This may have seemed a remarkable ruling in Aaron's day, but its typical meaning for us is simple and striking. Sin defiles as long as it is working beneath the surface, but when it is brought completely to the surface by honest and thorough

confession on the part of the sinner, it ceases to defile. In confession the sinner has judged himself, and the spreading and defiling power of his sin is broken.[2]

This special situation highlights an important truth concerning the disease and also how unconfessed sin continues to harm us; that is, our "unclean" condition keeps us from communion with God. The priestly procedures were meticulous; the priests were even given guidelines for differentiating ordinary baldness from that which was caused by leprosy (13:40-44).

If an individual was declared "unclean," he or she was put out of the camp of Israel. Not only did this protect uninfected Jews from the contagious person, but it also kept those who were "clean" from becoming ceremonially "unclean," as to not ruin their active fellowship with Jehovah and His people. What was unclean could not abide with holy Jehovah in the camp. Likewise, those believers that continue in gross sin cannot be permitted to abide within the local fellowship: *"Do you not judge those who are inside?... Therefore 'put away from yourselves the evil person'"* (1 Cor. 5:12-13). For many "uncleannesses" the Jews simply washed and remained isolated until evening; this pictures confessing and repenting of sins on an ongoing basis. In Scripture, leprosy generally pictures an individual in a chronic debilitating sin who must be isolated to protect others until the problem is alleviated.

Paul used another well-known illustration to warn the Church at Corinth of sin's influence: just as the influence of leaven spreads quickly in a lump of dough, the willful sin of one person can readily corrupt others in the local assembly. Such an individual must be removed from the local fellowship until there is repentance (1 Cor. 5:6-7). However, as C. H. Mackintosh acknowledges, protecting the Lord's people from infection and defilement was only one aspect of priestly care; the priests were also to guard against unneeded isolation which would harm individuals:

> There were two things which claimed the priest's vigilant care, namely, the purity of the assembly, and the grace which could not admit of the exclusion of any member, save on the most clearly-established grounds. Holiness could not permit anyone to remain in who ought to be out; and, on the other hand, grace would not have anyone out who ought to

be in. Hence, therefore, there was the most urgent need, on the part of the priest, of watchfulness, calmness, wisdom, patience, tenderness, and enlarged experience. Things might seem trifling which, in reality, were serious; and things might look like leprosy which were not it at all. The greatest care and coolness were needed. Judgment rashly formed, a conclusion hastily arrived at, might involve the most serious consequences, either as regards the assembly or some individual of it.[3]

Not only did the leper suffer persistent discomfort, but he or she experienced devastating emotional and social effects as well. An infected husband might never embrace his wife again. A mother would not be permitted to hold and caress her children. Leprous grandparents would not be allowed to interact with their grandchildren. As Hansen's disease was agonizing on several counts, the priests had to use great care in properly diagnosing it.

Those declared "unclean" had to wear torn clothes and keep their heads bare as to be easily identified from a distance. If approached by a passerby, the disheveled leper had to cover his or her upper lip and cry out, "Unclean! Unclean!" (13:45-46). Lepers suffered a humiliating and miserable existence. From a practical standpoint, it is thought Hansen's disease is spread chiefly via respiratory droplets, so covering one's nose and mouth would help limit the reach of the infection.

Besides examining people, the priests were also charged with inspecting clothing and personal articles which evidenced discoloration, flaking, or peeling (13:47-59). Articles that contained mold or mildew were a health hazard. These were to be isolated for seven days and then inspected again by a priest. If the contamination had spread, the article was to be burned. If not, it was to be washed, isolated for another seven days and inspected again. If the mildew had faded, only the contaminated area was to be torn out and burned; the remainder was deemed clean. If the contamination had spread, the item was to be burned.

Another duty that fell to the priests was the inspection of houses, made of stone or clay, after the Israelites had settled in Canaan (14:33-53). The procedure for inspecting houses and the appropriate quarantine periods were similar to those for personal items. If mold or mildew was found, the infected portions of the house were to be removed and replaced and the house cleansed. If unclean conditions reoccurred, the house was to be destroyed. If the procedure for ridding the house of mold and mildew was successful, the house was purified by a two-bird ceremony similar to the one used to ritualistically declare a cured leper clean.

There is no biblical record of leprosy being found in a Jewish house, but these scriptural stipulations sound a warning for Christians in the present age: we must be alert for corrupting influences within the "House of God," which today is the Church. Peter warns, *"for the time has come for judgment to begin at the house of God"* (1 Pet. 4:17). Though not pertaining to the Church Age, Leviticus 13 suggests both a provision and a principle that the Church should learn from. William Kelly explains:

> A man is not made the judge of his own sin. It was laid down in the law that the Israelite should submit his condition to the inspection of another, and this other the type of a spiritual man, for a priest means that. It is really one who is called to have title of access to God, and who therefore should have his senses exercised to discern both good and evil according to the standard of the sanctuary. As such he is bound not to be carried away by conventional opinions, or traditional thoughts, or what men call public opinion – one of the most mischievous sources of depraving the holy moral judgment in the children of God.[4]

Only those who are walking close to the Lord will be able to discern issues of sin clearly and be able to have the mind of the Lord to humbly handle such loathsome situations. In his writings, Paul provided "bookend" instructions to compass both our attitudes and activities in relating to others in sin:

> *Brethren, if a man is overtaken in any trespass, you who are spiritual restore such a one in a spirit of gentleness, considering yourself lest you also be tempted* (Gal. 6:1).

> *But as for you, brethren, do not grow weary in doing good. And if anyone does not obey our word in this epistle, note that person and do not keep company with him, that he may be ashamed. Yet do not count him as an enemy, but admonish him as a brother* (2 Thess. 3:13-15).

So with a humble disposition we are to labor to restore those in sin, but without condoning what is wrong or being adversely influenced by those in the wrong. Peter reminds us God has not changed since the days of the Old Testament, nor has His expectation for His people altered: *"But as He who called you is holy, you also be holy in all your conduct, because it is written, 'Be holy, for I am holy'"* (1 Pet. 1:15-16). As believers, we need each other to be walking with the Lord, so that someone has the spiritual sense to tell us when we have gone our own way, especially when we ourselves might be ignorant of this.

Application

Leprosy pictures the troubling and deadly disease of sin. Like sin, leprosy exists within an individual long before it works its way outward and becomes evident to observers. In fact, Hansen's disease has an incubation period of about 3-5 years. Consequently, a leper did not become a leper because of his or her external sores; what was hidden within eventually became visible. In reality, all lepers were lepers long before they became aware of their symptoms. Likewise, a man does not become a sinner because he got falling-down drunk or stole his neighbor's belongings. We are all born into sin, and sooner or later the worst of us comes to light (Rom. 5:12).

Leviticus 13 identifies two main types of leprosy that infected people: leprosy of the flesh and leprosy of the head. Spiritually speaking, these relate to two classes of deadly sins. Leprosy of the flesh refers to fleshly lusts and includes gluttony, drunkenness, fornication, lasciviousness, etc. Leprosy of the head speaks of lusting in the mind which results in pride, unbelief, arrogance, envy, humanism, etc. There are two biblical examples of proud individuals whom God smote with leprosy. The first was Miriam, the sister of Moses, who with Aaron spoke against their brother, God's chosen leader for the people (Num. 12:1-4). Because Aaron was the high priest, he was spared judgment as that would have cut off the nation from Jehovah, but Miriam was punished:

> *So the anger of the Lord was aroused against them, and He departed. And when the cloud departed from above the tabernacle, suddenly Miriam became leprous, as white as snow. Then Aaron turned toward Miriam, and there she was, a leper. So Aaron said to Moses, "Oh, my*

> *lord! Please do not lay this sin on us, in which we have done foolishly and in which we have sinned"* (Num. 12:9-11).

The entire nation paused in their journey while Miriam suffered seven days with leprosy; then, the Lord healed her. Although the text does not state where the leprosy was located, it was likely her face and head that were infected. Jewish women were well-covered in public; thus, only her face would have been observable for Aaron's quick assessment. Forty years later, Moses recalled this event to warn the people of the dangers of both leprosy and of pride:

> *Take heed in an outbreak of leprosy, that you carefully observe and do according to all that the priests, the Levites, shall teach you; just as I commanded them, so you shall be careful to do. Remember what the Lord your God did to Miriam on the way when you came out of Egypt!* (Deut. 24:8-9).

Besides Miriam, King Uzziah was also struck with leprosy because of his pride. King Uzziah was better than many kings who ruled over the Southern Kingdom: *"King Uzziah did what was right in the sight of the Lord, according to all that his father, Amaziah, did"* (2 Chron. 26:4). Uzziah was divinely blessed for his determination to follow the Lord: *"as long as he sought the Lord, God made him prosper"* (2 Chron. 26:5). His leadership brought Judea economic prosperity, technological improvements, and vast military strength (2 Chron. 26:6-15). However, these accomplishments caused him to think more highly of himself than he did of his God. In arrogant pride he brought a censer into the temple to offer worship to Jehovah. This was an intrusion upon the priesthood which God had strictly forbidden (i.e., only priests could perform such tasks and then only per the Law). What happened next is astounding:

> *But when he was strong his heart was lifted up, to his destruction, for he transgressed against the Lord his God by entering the temple of the Lord to burn incense on the altar of incense. So Azariah the priest went in after him, and with him were eighty priests of the Lord– valiant men. And they withstood King Uzziah, and said to him, "It is not for you, Uzziah, to burn incense to the Lord, but for the priests, the sons of Aaron, who are consecrated to burn incense. Get out of the sanctuary, for you have trespassed! You shall have no honor from the Lord God."*

Then Uzziah became furious; and he had a censer in his hand to burn incense. And while he was angry with the priests, leprosy broke out on his forehead, before the priests in the house of the Lord, beside the incense altar. And Azariah the chief priest and all the priests looked at him, and there, on his forehead, he was leprous; so they thrust him out of that place. Indeed he also hurried to get out, because the Lord had struck him. King Uzziah was a leper until the day of his death. He dwelt in an isolated house, because he was a leper; for he was cut off from the house of the Lord (2 Chron. 26:16-21).

When King Uzziah served the Lord obediently, he was blessed. Yet, when he went his own way, God humbled him. The Lord will not tolerate pride, especially in those ruling His people. King Solomon posed several warnings concerning pride: *"The fear of the Lord is to hate evil; pride and arrogance and the evil way"* (Prov. 8:13), *"By pride comes nothing but strife"* (Prov. 13:10), *"Pride goes before destruction, and a haughty spirit before a fall"* (Prov. 16:18), *"A man's pride will bring him low, but the humble in spirit will retain honor"* (Prov. 29:23). God hates pride (Prov. 6:16-17). God judged King Uzziah's pride and he suffered with leprosy of the head for the remainder of his life. We do well to remember this valuable lesson and bestow the Lord the honor He deserves instead of trying to retain it for ourselves.

There was no cure for leprosy (i.e., Hansen's disease); it brought social isolation and a slow, agonizing death. Its damage to the nervous system often prevented individuals from being properly treated for injuries, as often no pain was felt when the injury occurred. Likewise, individuals who continue in sin will eventually become numb to the pangs of their conscience and further injure their souls (1 Tim. 4:2). Pain is generally a good thing because it alerts us to what needs attention. Likewise, our conscience prompts us to take moral action when it has been offended: God forbid that we become numb to it. Today there is a cure for leprosy and, thankfully, there is a cure for the sin it represents – the Lord Jesus Christ.

Be Holy and Come Near

Meditation

>Behold a fountain deep and wide,
>Behold its onward flow;
>It was opened in the Savior's side,
>And cleanses white as snow!
>
>Come to this fountain!
>It is flowing today;
>And all who will may freely come,
>And wash their sins away.
>
>— Ira Sankey

The Cleansing of a Leper
Leviticus 14

The priests must have read Leviticus 13 many times in order to familiarize themselves with proper inspection and diagnosis protocol. A wrong decision on their part could needlessly split a family apart or expose their community to a dangerous health risk. However, Leviticus 14, which supplies the regulations for ceremonially cleansing a healed leper, likely received much less attention, as there is no Old Testament record of a Jew being cleansed of leprosy (as it refers to Hansen's disease), and undergoing the ritual. Miriam's disciplinary punishment, in which she was a leper for seven days, seems to have been a special situation; we understand she did not undergo the eight-day ceremony as the entire camp moved on directly after her healing (Num. 10:14-15).

The Lord Jesus confirmed that the healing of leprosy was a rare event in the Old Testament: *"And many lepers were in Israel in the time of Elisha the prophet, and none of them was cleansed except Naaman the Syrian"* (Luke 4:27). Direct miracles in the Old Testament mostly occurred in the ministries of Moses, Joshua, and the prophets Elijah and Elisha; these served as signs to validate God's message and messenger. Even during these spectacular periods, only Naaman, the Syrian, was healed of leprosy by Elisha.

Leprosy was still considered a deadly disease in New Testament times. At one point, being discouraged in prison, John the baptizer questioned whether or not Jesus Christ was truly the Messiah. The Lord answered his doubts by confirming that He had healed numerous people of their infirmities, including many lepers (Luke 7:22). The Lord Jesus specifically noted this because His healing of so many Jewish lepers showed that His ministry was endorsed by God and that He was offering the people something the Law could not – newness of life.

As previously noted, leprosy is a picture of the deadly disease of sin. In Leviticus 14, no cure is named, as this belonged to God alone. No ceremonial rite could heal a leper; as shown through the ministry of the Lord Jesus Christ, only divine power could cure a leper. Leprosy was an incurable disease that destroyed one's flesh from the inside out, meaning that an individual was a leper long before there were visible signs of the disease. Likewise, we are all born in sin (Ps. 51:5; Rom. 5:12), and in time our rotten nature becomes apparent in works of the flesh (Gal. 5:19-21). The only remedy for our leprosy is also divine cleansing through Christ.

Three Cleansings

According to Leviticus 14, there were three cleansings which were to occur for a Jewish leper to be declared cured of the disease. In the spiritual sense, these same three cleansings parallel significant events in a believer's life as God miraculously deals with our sin.

The first cleaning was the miracle itself – the leper was healed: *"For the day of his cleansing, he shall be brought to the priest"* (v. 2). This pictures spiritual regeneration through trusting Christ; this is *"Not by works of righteousness which we have done, but according to His mercy He saved us, through the washing of regeneration and renewing of the Holy Spirit"* (Tit. 3:5). On the day that a sinner agrees with God about the matter of sin and receives God's solution – salvation in Christ alone – spiritual rebirth occurs through the power of the Holy Spirit. The Lord Jesus told Nicodemus that no one would get into heaven without being *"born again"* (John 3:3). John reminds us that we can only be born again by trusting the Lord Jesus as Savior (John 1:12-13). The spiritual leper, then, sees no solution to his or her dire problem of sin except to stand with God against himself or herself and be cleansed through Christ.

Although the supposedly cured leper was to seek out a priest for inspection, he or she could not enter the camp and approach the tabernacle to find a priest. It will never end well if the unclean approaches the clean; what is clean must approach that which is unclean for it to obtain purification, hence the command, *"the priest shall go out of the camp"* (v. 3). The leper had been previously declared "unclean" by a priest and therefore remained unclean until inspected again by a priest, pronounced "clean," and then ritually purified to receive the status of "clean." Only then could the cleansed leper be again included within the Jewish society. This Christ did for us – He suffered outside the camp (literally, Jerusalem; figuratively, Judaism and the workings of the Law) for us that we might come to Him there and experience salvation in Him:

> *Therefore Jesus also, that He might sanctify the people with His own blood, suffered outside the gate. Therefore let us go forth to Him, outside the camp, bearing His reproach* (Heb. 13:12-14).

The Lord Jesus became unclean outside of the camp and it is there that we, who were dead in trespasses and sins, must go to experience regeneration and be made alive in Christ.

After the priest had confirmed the physical cleansing of the leper, the next task was to declare him or her ceremonially clean; this procedure involved two birds (vv. 4-7). One bird was placed in an earthen vessel and was killed with water running over the vessel. The priest was then to dip the second bird, cedar wood, scarlet (yarn), and hyssop into the blood-water mixture in that vessel. The second bird was then released in an open field and it flew away. The priest then took the cedar wood, scarlet, and hyssop and sprinkled the healed leper seven times with the blood-water mixture and declared him "clean." Scarlet was used as it is associated with the judgment of sin through the shedding of blood (Isa. 1:18). The cedar is a lofty tree while hyssop a lowly plant; this pictures that all men, no matter their social status, are under God's condemnation and need to be cleansed by Christ's blood to be healed of sin.

Why was the bird killed in an earthen vessel? The Bible speaks of individuals as vessels of wrath and of mercy (Rom. 9:20-24), vessels of honor and of dishonor (2 Tim. 2:20), weaker vessels (i.e., a man's wife; 1 Pet. 3:7), and earthen vessels carrying precious treasure (2 Cor. 4:7). The latter example refers to the gospel message being joyfully transported within the Christian's body to be heard throughout the world (2 Cor. 4:7). As vessels are used to carry or hold things, Scripture often uses vessels as a symbol of service or to represent the means of accomplishing something. In the latter respect, the wicked are also used to accomplish God's purposes, such as Pharaoh in the days of Moses (Rom. 9:21-22). In Leviticus 14:5, the bloody earthen vessel speaks of the work of redemption accomplished in the body of the Lord Jesus through the power of the Holy Spirit, who is symbolized in the running water. The cleansing work of the Holy Spirit is further discussed in Hebrews 9:14: *"How much more shall the blood of Christ, who through the eternal Spirit offered Himself without spot to God, cleanse your conscience from dead works to serve the living God?"* Through His body, the Lord served us unto death that we may have the opportunity to serve Him through our bodies in life.

As the living bird flew off into the heavens, it did so with the visible marks of the death of the other bird upon it. Likewise, Jesus Christ will bear the marks (wounds) of His crucifixion forever (Zech. 10:12; John 20:24-29). Even though highly exalted and glorified in heaven, the Lord Jesus is described as *"a Lamb as though it had been slain"* (Rev. 5:6). Scars fade over time, but not the marks of Calvary in our Lord's body – these will testify of His love for His Father and for us throughout all of eternity.

The final portion of the leper-cleansing ceremony pictures *justification*; that is, God declares a believer positionally righteous in Christ after he or she trusts in the Lord Jesus as Savior. The birds represent both the death of Christ (the bird that died in the earthen vessel) and the resurrection of Christ (the released bird that ascended up into the heavens). The blood of the first bird links these two aspects together, and both have their place in reflecting today's gospel message:

> *Moreover, brethren, I declare to you the gospel which I preached to you, which also you received and in which you stand, by which also you are saved ... that Christ died for our sins according to the Scriptures, and that He was buried, and that He rose again the third day according to the Scriptures* (1 Cor. 15:1-5).

The resurrection of Christ is as important to the believer as Christ's sufferings and death at Calvary! Imagine for a moment that I am visiting you in your home and there is a knock at the front door. You open the door and are greeted by a close friend whom you know is terminally ill. As we converse, suddenly your friend convulses, falls to the floor, and dies. Your heart is broken with grief. Suppose I turned to you and said, "I have the power to heal your friend's disease. Would you desire me to do that?" You ponder the situation for a moment and rightly answer, "No, thank you; a cure would not help my friend; he is dead." But then suppose I proclaim, "I have the power to raise your friend back to life again. Would you like me to do that?" Your response is sensible, "No, thank you; my friend has a deadly disease and would just suffer and die again." What your friend needs is to be healed of his deadly disease *and* to be raised back to life; this is what Christ alone can do for the repentant sinner. At Calvary, God judicially dealt with the deadly disease of sin. Furthermore, all those who were once dead in trespasses and sins are made alive in Christ through His resurrection – all believers share in His life, which is eternal and abundant (John 10:10, 28). The above illustration shows how important both the death and resurrection of Christ are to the believer. After years of trying to keep the Law in order to cure his sin problem, Paul finally realized he was in a hopeless situation before God, unless he trusted Christ alone for salvation:

For I through the law died to the law that I might live to God. I have been crucified with Christ; it is no longer I who live, but Christ lives in me; and the life which I now live in the flesh I live by faith in the Son of God, who loved me and gave Himself for me (Gal. 2:19-20).

Like Paul, when we trust the gospel message, we are healed of the deadly disease of sin (speaking of its judicial penalty) and are made alive in Christ; this truth is illustrated by the two birds used in the cleansing ceremony of the leper.

Although the use of the cedar wood, scarlet yarn, and hyssop is not explained, these are associated with purification elsewhere in Scripture (Num. 19:6; Ps. 51:7). For example, at the first Passover in Egypt, a handful of hyssop was used as a primitive paintbrush to smear the blood of the Passover lamb on both sides and the top of the doorframe. Hyssop was a common bushy plant that grew on rocky surfaces. Interestingly, it was commonly used in Levitical purification ceremonies, but never used directly in any offering which foreshadowed the Lord Jesus Christ Himself. In Jewish rites, the hyssop was always held in a human hand, and it was not a part of the sacrifice; it was rather used to perform ceremonial purification on behalf of those who desired restoration. Metaphorically, then, hyssop speaks of a sinner's humility before God in true repentance. By picking up the hyssop at the first Passover, the Jews declared both the value of the lamb's blood for redemption and the fact that they wanted to be redeemed. In Leviticus 14, the priest grasped the hyssop with the same determination, but on behalf of the one who was still unclean.

The third cleansing detailed in Leviticus 14 required the healed leper to shave off all the hair on his body (including the eyebrows) and bathe himself; he was to repeat the same procedure seven days later (vv. 8-9). In the interim, the healed leper remained in semi-quarantine. This washing pictures the cleansing of sin after salvation through confession: *"If we confess our sins, He is faithful and just to forgive us our sins, and to cleanse us from all unrighteousness"* (1 Jn. 1:9). Confession prompts the cleansing of Christ which allows believers to remain in fellowship with God after they have disappointed Him through disobedience. The diligence of the healed and cleansed leper in this matter of bathing should encourage all who have experienced rebirth and justification in Christ to keep short accounts with Him and be attentive to confessing sin.

Hair is something our body produces in an ongoing manner for various reasons, but chiefly as a covering; in fact, long hair is a woman's glory (1 Cor. 11:15). Technically speaking, hair is a filamentous biomaterial that grows from follicles in our skin. Only that portion of the hair within the follicle is alive, meaning what we actually see is "dead." Hair, then, represents a history of past dead works accomplished by the body. The symbolism is astoundingly specific; the blood of Christ purges our consciences from past dead works to serve God in a new and living way (Heb. 9:14) and, as just noted, continues its effectiveness after our justification in Christ to cleanse us from unrighteousnesses as we confess them. No one else could bathe or shave the leper; he had to do it himself. Likewise, no one else can cleanse our conscience from guilt and dead works; we must personally ask the Lord Jesus to do it. And He will be glad to do so!

The Eighth Day

On the eighth day, after bathing and shaving a second time, the leper was to offer four sacrifices (vv. 10-20): a trespass offering (a male lamb), a sin offering (a female lamb), a burnt offering (a male lamb), and a meal offering (fine flour mixed with oil) and one log of oil. The sacrifices were presented before the Lord in accordance with the instructions previously set forth in the first seven chapters of Leviticus. Perhaps the trespass offering was required to compensate the Lord for the leper's lack of worship and sacrifice during this uncleanness. The application of blood and oil to portions of the cleansed leper's body closely aligned with the consecration procedure for the priests (Lev. 8). The anointing oil was also sprinkled before the Lord seven times. If the healed leper was poor, a young ram was still required for the trespass offering but two doves or young pigeons could be substituted for the sin and burnt offerings; the amount of fine flour required was also reduced (vv. 21-22).

Why was the leper and his or her offerings to be presented before the Lord on the eighth day? The number *eight*, as we have noticed previously, is used in the Bible to speak of "new beginnings," such as new life or a new order. William Kelly notes the significance of this numeral as related to the ceremonial cleansing of a cured leper:

> But on the eighth day we have the types of Christ in the fullness of His grace, and all the efficacy of His work before God applied to the man, so that the soul might realize the place of blessing into which it is brought.[1]

After being healed by God, declared clean by a priest, and twice bathed clean by his own doing, he was ready to offer sacrifices to God and experience *a new beginning*. On the eighth day the leper who had undergone all the cleansing protocol could return to live with his family and associate with old friends. Likewise, the believer also experiences new life in Christ through rebirth, justification, and through the ongoing cleansing of confessed sin. We cannot praise or serve the Lord acceptably, or even have confidence that He hears our prayers, unless we have clean hearts before Him. The heart affects the entire person. A good example of this can be found in the religious Pharisees at the time of Christ's earthly sojourn; they had impure hearts, and the Lord denounced them as unclean (Luke 11:39-40).

To signify the leper's renewed consecration to God, the priest took some of the blood of the trespass offering and smeared it on the right big toe, the right thumb, and the right ear lobe of the healed leper (14:14) This signified that the new life of the cleansed leper should be marked by dedicated serving hands, by a sound walk (i.e., a God-honoring testimony), and by allegiance to hear and do God's Word. In the Church Age, believers are also to be characterized by clean hands that serve (1 Tim. 2:8), clean feet that walk with the Lord (John 13:10), and clean attentive ears that listen to God's Word (John 15:3). In so doing we experience the new and eternal life of Christ.

Reaching the Priests With the Gospel

During Christ's earthly ministry, He healed many lepers so that the priests would have a testimony of Himself (Luke 5:14). Each time a Jewish leper went to locate a priest to undergo the Leviticus 14 ritual, the priests were forced to acknowledge something which had never happened before was now occurring regularly. One can only image the shock of the priests when the first lepers healed by Christ came knocking on their door. On one particular day nine came all at once to be inspected by the priests – they had all been healed by Christ:

> *Now it happened as He went to Jerusalem that He passed through the midst of Samaria and Galilee. Then as He entered a certain village, there met Him ten men who were lepers, who stood afar off. And they lifted up their voices and said, "Jesus, Master, have mercy on us! "So when He saw them, He said to them, "Go, show yourselves to the priests." And so it was that as they went, they were cleansed. And one of them, when he saw that he was healed, returned, and with a loud voice glorified God, and fell down on his face at His feet, giving Him thanks. And he was a Samaritan. So Jesus answered and said, "Were there not ten cleansed? But where are the nine? Were there not any found who returned to give glory to God except this foreigner?" And He said to him, "Arise, go your way. Your faith has made you well"* (Luke 17:11-19).

Although the Lord physically cleansed ten lepers that day, only one thankful Samaritan received spiritual healing. The other nine were satisfied with their physically clean status, and saw no need for further cleansing by the One who had healed them of leprosy.

On another occasion the Lord actually touched and healed a leper who had pleaded with Him to make him clean (Luke 5:12-14). According to the Law, anyone touching a leper would be tainted. The spiritual depiction is clear; the Lord became unclean in order to cleanse the impure: *"For He* [the Father] *made Him* [Christ] *who knew no sin to be sin for us, that we might become the righteousness of God in Him"* (2 Cor. 5:21). The leper the Lord Jesus touched was instantly cleansed, but then Christ gave him these instructions: *"But go and show yourself to the priest, and make an offering for your cleansing, as a testimony to them, just as Moses commanded"* (Luke 5:14). One can only imagine the shock on the priests' faces when this exuberant pilgrim began to tell them his story: "A man named Jesus touched me, cured my leprosy, and told me to come to you to proclaim what had happened and to offer the appropriate sacrifices!" In reaching out to touch one leper, the Lord Jesus was showing His love, not just for this individual, but also for the religious elite of Israel. The priests laboring at the temple needed to hear the kingdom gospel message too.

A steady stream of ex-lepers with amazing stories of healing over a three-year period was the Lord's means of reaching the priests. Consequently, Luke records the fact that a large number of priests turned from trying to earn their salvation through religious doings to trusting Jesus Christ alone for salvation (Acts 6:7). The priests thoroughly knew the Law; they had copied it and taught it to their brethren. The miraculous healing of so many lepers by one man awakened them to the fact that the Healer was the One the Law was calling their attention to – their Messiah had indeed come and was fulfilling Scripture before their eyes (Gal. 3:24). The Lord himself acknowledged this one Sabbath as He read from the scroll of Isaiah:

> *"The Spirit of the Lord is upon Me, because He has anointed Me to preach the gospel to the poor; He has sent Me to heal the brokenhearted, to proclaim liberty to the captives and recovery of sight to the blind, to set at liberty those who are oppressed; to proclaim the acceptable year of the Lord." Then He closed the book, and gave it back to the attendant and sat down. And the eyes of all who were in the synagogue were fixed on Him. And He began to say to them, "Today this Scripture is fulfilled in your hearing"* (Luke 4:18-22).

One sure way that the Jews would know that Messiah had come was by the extraordinary number of healings that He would perform. Seeing Jews healed of leprosy for the first time in their recorded history was sufficient proof to many that Messiah had come to deliver those who, like the leper of Luke 5, would say, *"Lord, if You are willing, You can make me clean"* (v. 12). It seems many priests realized they too needed to come to Christ and be spiritually cleansed by faith in Him.

Application

In the closing days of the Lord's earthly ministry, we read of Him enjoying a meal in the house of an ex-leper named Simon. Lazarus, who had been raised from the dead, was also present:

> *Being in Bethany at the house of Simon the leper, as He sat at the table, a woman came having an alabaster flask of very costly oil of spikenard. Then she broke the flask and poured it on His head (Mark 14:3-4).*

> *Then, six days before the Passover, Jesus came to Bethany, where Lazarus was who had been dead, whom He had raised from the dead. There they made Him a supper; and Martha served, but Lazarus was one of those who sat at the table with Him. Then Mary took a pound of very costly oil of spikenard, anointed the feet of Jesus, and wiped His feet with her hair. And the house was filled with the fragrance of the oil (John 12:1-3).*

Because of the Lord's healing power, two individuals who had been previously declared "unclean" could now sit down with the Lord and enjoy a meal with Him: Simon, a healed leper, and Lazarus, a resurrected dead man. Because of Mary's adoration and personal sacrifice, the house of a cleansed leper was transformed into a house of worship. Those who had been made clean by the Lord Jesus not only enjoyed His presence, but were also refreshed by the selfless worship of one who loved the Lord. Likewise, as cleansed lepers, we are afforded the same opportunity to enjoy fellowship with the Lord and freely worship Him. The One who reached forth with His love and became unclean that we might have our sins cleansed away deserves our affection and devotion too. How wonderful it is to be a cleansed leper in the house of God!

Meditation

Savior give, oh, give me rest
For this torn and troubled breast;
Sin has bound me with its chain,
Come Thou Lamb for sinners slain.

Come, oh, come, with me abide,
Let me feel Thy blood applied;
Humbly at Thy feet I bow,
In my weakness heal me now.

— Jesse P. Tompkins

A Needy People
Leviticus 15

Leprosy was a debilitating disease with consequences that could not be concealed for long. When the disease was observed, an immediate and deliberate response was required by the Law. Likewise, the disease of sin within each of us eventually manifests itself by ungodly deeds of the flesh. Naturally speaking, a depraved nature can respond no other way, no matter how hard one tries to suppress it – eventually our "leprosy" becomes visible too. This, however, is not the viewpoint of the following chapter; rather, Leviticus 15 speaks of frail humanity suffering the consequences of original sin. F. B. Hole provides this summary:

> Leviticus 15 is occupied with a variety of lesser defilements, which entailed a temporary separation and diligent washings before re-admission to the camp and its privileges was possible. These defilements sprang from the weakness of human nature and conditions as they exist today, as the result of the fall. Many of them were of an unavoidable nature but nevertheless they were to be recognized as being of a defiling nature and treated as such. Thus Israel was to be impressed with the holiness of their God and how everything of a defiling nature must be removed, if His presence was to be enjoyed. We do well to remember that the fall has produced in us many a weakness affecting our spirits as well as our bodies.[1]

The majority of the bodily discharges described in Leviticus 15 were natural and unavoidable, and therefore not sinful. The purifying procedures were to remind both men and women that they suffered weaknesses and infirmities because of Adam's sin. The protocols of this chapter are, consequently, not as involved as those associated with leprosy, and were self-initiated. Whereas leprosy was outwardly noticeable, most of the cases discussed in this chapter would only be known to an individual or, in some cases, his or her spouse. There would be no way of knowing whether or not individuals were actually obeying these stipulations, but regardless, a reminder of human frailty would be evident.

There are four types of bodily discharges and purifications addressed in Leviticus 15: a chronic male discharge (vv. 2-12), a periodic male discharge (vv. 16-18), a periodic female discharge (vv. 19-24), and a chronic female discharge (vv. 25-27). F. Duane Lindsey summarizes the first category of male exudation:

> The chronic or long-term male discharge described in this section was probably gonorrhea. The major concern was the man's ceremonial uncleanness and its consequences because other persons and objects he contacted became not only ceremonially unclean but also secondary sources of further uncleanness, for example, his bed (pallet, vv. 4-5), his chair (v. 6), his person (v. 7), his spittle (v. 8), his saddle (v. 9), and anything under him (subject to contact from his discharge, v. 10). In this sense, his uncleannesss was more infectious than that from skin disease (chps. 13-14) or from unclean animals (chp. 11) which were limited to direct contact. However, since a man with chronic discharge was not isolated outside the camp (13:45-46), his uncleanness was apparently less serious (though more ritually infectious) than that associated with skin disease. A probable conclusion to be drawn from this is that the purpose of the uncleanness codes was not primarily hygienic but religious and theological.[2]

In summary, the contagious safeguards for a male with a discharge pertained to ceremonial uncleanness, rather than limiting the infection. Once the pus from the infection ceased, the man was to initiate the purification rite (vv. 13-15). This included a seven-day waiting period, after which the man was to bathe and wash his clothes. On the following day, the eighth day, he was to bring two doves or two young pigeons to the priests to make atonement. One of the two birds was sacrificed as a sin offering and the other as a burnt offering.

The second category of male discharges discussed were those associated with an ejection of semen, whether a nocturnal emission (i.e., wet-dream) or one occurring during sexual intercourse. As this matter dealt with ritual purification solely, there was no guilt and therefore no sin offering was required. Sexual activity between a husband and wife is normal, expected, and was designed by God to enhance the couple's intimacy and to produce children. There is nothing sinful about this tender interchange between a husband and wife: *"Marriage is honorable among all, and the bed undefiled; but fornicators and adulterers God will judge"* (Heb. 13:4). The ejection of semen rendered those in contact with it ceremonially unclean. The solution was just to wash and wait; at evening time the unclean status was removed from the couple.

Before sinning in Eden, Adam and his wife enjoyed wondrous communion, full disclosure, and pleasurable intimacy with each other. After the fall, independence, guilt, selfishness, etc. marred this blissful union. Unfortunately, a certain aspect of estrangement now characterized their relationship; this new individuality soon led to the woman receiving her own name, Eve (Gen. 3:20). Previously, the man and woman were completely one, so when God called "Adam," both of them responded (Gen. 5:2). The Jewish stipulation of cleansing after sexual relations would constantly remind a husband and wife of their human frailty and all that had been lost due to their first parents' disobedience. From a medical point of view, this hygienic practice would certainly reduce urinary tract infections.

The third category of discharge related to a woman's regular (monthly) menstruation cycle (vv. 19-24). A woman with an issue of blood was ceremonially unclean and would be set apart from the community for seven days (whether her period lasted one day or all seven), after which she was to bathe and her "unclean" status would be removed (vv. 19, 24). During this time she was excused from normal household duties. If she engaged in sexual relations with her husband and afterwards it was discovered that she had commenced menstruation, then both would be ceremonially defiled and subject to the same separation criterion – both would be, in the practical sense, treated like lepers for seven days (Num. 5:2). It is noted that sexual relations were strictly forbidden during a woman's monthly period and thus the stipulation of verse 24, which gives the seven-day isolation period for the husband, relates to a surprise situation at the onset of menstruation (18:19, 20:18). After studying the regulations, one can see why there are several references to married women having their own tents in Scripture (Gen. 24:67, 31:33; Judg. 4:17).

It is hard for our modern culture to relate to such things; certainly from our viewpoint, women especially bore the hardness of these regulations. Pregnancy and nursing provided natural relief from the ordinance, this no doubt adding to a Jewish woman's desire to marry early and have many children. From a practical sense this mindset would more quickly build up the Jewish nation. There is, however, some evidence that would suggest that Jewish women nursed their children longer than our western culture deems necessary; this practice would allow naturally spacing their children. According to Section 1:31 of the Shemmot Rabbah, which is a rabbinic commentary of Exodus, Moses was nursed by his mother for approximately two years. 2 Maccabees 7:27 refers to a Jewish mother that nursed her son for three years.

These were days of poor sanitation, so perhaps there was some health benefit in feminine separation which we do not understand, but the entire matter seems best understood from a ceremonial perspective – a reminder of man's imperfect and unclean condition before God.

The last category of discharge related to a woman's chronic issue of blood for one of several possible gynecological or urinary problems (vv. 25-30). A Jewish woman remained unclean for seven days after the discharge ceased. She was then to offer two birds for a sin and burnt offering in the same manner as a man who had been healed of his chronic discharge. Besides the physical discomforts associated with chronic bleeding, there were the emotional ramifications of being perpetually unclean. Her condition isolated her from family and friends in much the same way that leprosy did. Such was the case with the woman who had suffered a discharge for twelve years, until the Lord Jesus healed her:

> *Now a certain woman had a flow of blood for twelve years, and had suffered many things from many physicians. She had spent all that she had and was no better, but rather grew worse. When she heard about Jesus, she came behind Him in the crowd and touched His garment. For she said, "If only I may touch His clothes, I shall be made well." Immediately the fountain of her blood was dried up, and she felt in her body that she was healed of the affliction. And Jesus, immediately knowing in Himself that power had gone out of Him, turned around in the crowd and said, "Who touched My clothes?" But His disciples said to Him, "You see the multitude thronging You, and You say, 'Who touched Me?'" And He looked around to see her who had done this thing. But the woman, fearing and trembling, knowing what had happened to her, came and fell down before Him and told Him the*

whole truth. And He said to her, "Daughter, your faith has made you well. Go in peace, and be healed of your affliction" (Mark 5:25-34).

After reviewing Leviticus 15, we understand why the woman was attempting to secretly approach the Lord; she was an unclean person in the midst of a crowd. Anyone touching her would also become ceremonially defiled, and, given the description of the situation, many did. But her faith in the Lord overcame the limitations that the Law pronounced on her and she was healed. The Lord knew all about what had happened, but He posed an open question to the crowd to allow the woman to declare the reality of the miracle so that all could glorify God. No earthly physician could heal her infirmity, but the Great Physician did without any explanation or medical examination.

Returning to Leviticus 15, although verses 32-33 relate to the specific instructions of this chapter, verse 31 provides a concise capstone for the laws of uncleanness in chapters 11-14: *"Thus you shall separate the children of Israel from their uncleanness, lest they die in their uncleanness when they defile My tabernacle that is among them."* The purpose of these purity regulations was to ensure that the Jews were consistently mindful of their tremendous privilege and responsibility of being in communion with holy Jehovah, the Self-Existing One and Creator of all things. In Adam, they were inherently unclean, but through blood atonement and the washing of water, God was permitting them to come near. No other people group on the planet was extended that opportunity, nor was any other nation chosen to represent Jehovah among the nations. The Law served as a constant reminder that Jehovah was holy and His people must be holy, too.

Application

As reviewed in the previous chapter, the Lord willingly touched an unclean leper to heal him and, in so doing, became unclean Himself. We have also seen that the unclean woman with the issue of blood was healed when *she* touched the Lord, who was clean but subsequently became unclean under the Law. Both stories illustrate the idea of substitution, but they do so from the different vantage points of Leviticus 14 and 15. The disease of sin which reaps chaos in the world must be radically dealt with through the death and resurrection of Christ (this is pictured in Lev. 14). However, human frailty resulting from sin's influence on us requires ongoing grace from above to overcome the suffering below (shown in Lev. 15). Whereas Christ had no experiential familiarity with inherited sin or sinful deeds, as symbolized by leprosy, He did suffer in His humanity upon a sin-cursed planet – He understands what it is like to be poor, hungry, thirsty, fatigued, ridiculed, and disdained for righteousness. In this sense, the Lord Jesus as our High Priest can fully empathize with our infirmities (Heb. 5:1-2), and longs to provide us with His compassionate grace that we might rise above them.

The Lord Jesus is the believer's High Priest (Heb. 3:1). As our High Priest, Christ perfectly represents us to God. Furthermore, Christ, being *holy humanity*, demonstrated compassion for others and felt the infirmities of mankind, yet not as we do in our sin. After His resurrection, Christ experienced glorification. Presently, He is not only *holy humanity* but also *glorified humanity*. The writer of Hebrews informs us that Christ presently sits at the right hand of God (Heb. 1:3) and is ever occupied with making intercession on our behalf – He is our Great High Priest (Heb. 2:17, 4:15). Having a distorted or deficient view of Christ's humanity ensures a degraded view of His priestly operations and sympathies. We are *fallen humanity* and it is our natural tendency to approach Christ for help and comfort concerning the depraved outworking of our own flesh, but with these failings He cannot directly relate. However, Christ in His perfection can sympathize with the weakness of humanity which is suffering as a result of sin. This latter aspect is depicted in Leviticus 15. J. N. Darby's literal translation of Hebrews 4:15-16, without the translator's additional words in verse 15, *"we are, yet,"* affirms this understanding of Christ's priesthood:

> *For we have not a high priest not able to sympathize with our infirmities, but tempted in all things in like manner, **sin apart**. Let us approach therefore with boldness to the throne of grace, that we may receive mercy, and find grace for seasonable help* (Heb. 4:15-16; New Translation – Darby).

The latter portion of Hebrews 4:15 has been used to teach that Christ was tested and did not sin. Though this is true, it is not what the writer is declaring. The passage is not highlighting the sinless perfection of Christ but His inherent impeccability. Christ was tested in every way you and I are, except in our sin – every aspect of his humanity was completely uninfluenced by sin. Jeremiah bluntly summarizes our internal spiritual condition: *"The heart is deceitful above all things, and desperately wicked"* (Jer. 17:9; KJV). We are prone to sin because we are rotten to the core! Modern-day Christianity has generally accepted this passage to mean what it does not say, but this was not the case of believers before our time; they understood that Christ was both sinless and impeccable in character.

William Newell clarifies the meaning of Hebrews 4:15 in relationship to Christ's humanity and priesthood:

> The word "yet" inserted in both the Authorized and the Revised versions here, "yet without sin," is an utter hindrance, instead of a true translation. The Greek reads, "tempted like as we, without sin," or, "sin apart." The Greek word for without, *choris*, signifies having no connection with, no relationship to. Temptation does not involve sin.[3]

With this understanding one might ask: "If Christ had no connection with or relationship to sin within Himself, how does He as our High Priest, feel our infirmities?" F. W. Bruce answers this question:

> How great an encouragement to know that upon the throne of God there is One who can be "touched by the feelings of our infirmities, but was in all things tempted like as we are, sin apart." Sin was to Him no temptation: there was nothing within that answered to it, except in suffering. There was and could be with Him no sinful infirmity; but He was true Man, His divine nature taking nothing from the verity of His manhood, living a dependent life as we, and, with no callousness such as the flesh in us produces, in a world everywhere racked with suffering through sin, and out of joint, the trial of which He knew as no other could.[4]

Christ, as a man, sustained the harsh living conditions of a cursed planet, the contradiction of sinners, the opposition of Satan, and the hatred of the World. As High Priest, Christ sympathizes, not in any way with sin or forbidden desires, but with the suffering saints of God as they endure what He already has on this earth (but not near to the extent that He did). He knows all about living for God in a wicked world. In this we find a solace and comfort for our distressed souls. But there is no pity at the Throne of Grace for the lusting of our flesh and the active sin of our members, for these must be dealt a deadly blow from the sword of the Spirit. Christ does not weep at the funeral of vile and rotten flesh. If it were our lusts and sins He sympathized with, He would be sympathetic with all men and not just believers. Yet, only the redeemed are invited to *"come boldly,"* and only the redeemed *"obtain mercy, and find grace to help in time of need"* (Heb. 4:16; KJV).

Beloved of the Lord, let us not degrade Him in character or priestly office by thinking of Him in some way tolerant, considerate, or sympathetic to matters that are foreign to His being and are repulsive to His holy nature! He experientially understands the consequences of our sin but not our propensity to embrace it. In this respect, Leviticus 15 reminds us of our inherent human frailty and our need for the Lord's compassionate grace to overcome our infirmities and to empower us to suffer in a sin-cursed world with righteous spiritual dignity.

Meditation

> Yet Lord, alas! What weakness within myself I find;
> No infant's changing pleasure is like my wandering mind.
>
> And yet Thy love's unchanging, and doth recall my heart,
> To joy in all its brightness, the peace its beams impart.
>
> Oh guard my soul, then, Jesus, abiding still with Thee;
> And, if I wander, teach me soon back to Thee to flee.
>
> — J. N. Darby

The Day of Atonement
Leviticus 16

The Laws of Cleanliness and Holiness, the third major section of Leviticus, conclude with chapter 15. Leviticus is the worship manual for the priests, and at the heart of this revelation are the instructions pertaining to the Day of Atonement in chapter 16. All that was discussed before this – the ritualistic offerings (Lev. 1-7), the religious officials (Lev. 8-10), and the indications and rationales for various sacrifices (Lev. 11-15) – has its crescendo in Leviticus 16: the annual day of repentance and restoration. On this day, the tenth day of the seventh month, blood atonement would be offered by the high priest for all the sins of the nation committed during the previous year (vv. 29-34).

After the death of Nadab and Abihu, the Lord spoke to Moses: *"Tell Aaron your brother not to come at just any time into the Holy Place inside the veil, before the mercy seat which is on the ark, lest he die; for I will appear in the cloud above the mercy seat"* (Lev. 16:2). Jehovah dwelled above the Mercy Seat, which was the lid of the Ark of the Covenant, located in the Most Holy Place of the tabernacle. God was now limiting access to this fifteen by fifteen foot area, the most holy ground on earth. There would be only three occasions in which the priests would be permitted to venture into the Most Holy Place: on the Day of Atonement each year, to place the most holy incense before the Lord, likely in a gold vessel (Ex. 30:34-38), and to cover the Ark of the Covenant when necessary to relocate the tabernacle. The Kohathites would then enter the Most Holy Place to carry the Ark to its new location (Num. 4:15).

The Altar of Incense, although located in the Holy Place, was really associated with the Ark of the Covenant; thus, the altar is often spoken of as being *"before the Lord"* (Lev. 16:12-14; 1 Kgs. 6:22; Ps. 141:2). However, the Golden Altar had to be separated from the Most Holy Place by a veil so that the priests could burn special incense upon it twice a day (Ex. 30:34-38), and also so they could apply the blood of the sin offerings upon its horns to link it with the work of atonement accomplished on the Bronze Altar (Lev. 4:7, 18). But on the Day of Atonement, the blood of a bull and a goat was not only applied to the Alter of Incense, but also taken beyond it and directly applied to the Mercy Seat on the Ark of the Covenant. The writer of Hebrews explains why this annual atonement was necessary and what it foreshadowed:

> *For the law, having a shadow of the good things to come, and not the very image of the things, can never with these same sacrifices, which they offer continually year by year, make those who approach perfect. For then would they not have ceased to be offered? For the worshipers, once purified, would have had no more consciousness of sins. But in those sacrifices there is a reminder of sins every year. For it is not possible that the blood of bulls and goats could take away sins* (Heb. 10:1-4).

The Day of Atonement was an annual reminder of human sin and that the blood of animals did not satisfy God's anger over sin or purge the sinner's guilty conscience. Rather, the entire feast pointed the Jewish nation to God's ultimate provision in Christ, who would accomplish both.

The limited access to the Holy Place also reminded the Jews that God was intrinsically holy and man was inherently corrupt. At other times, the high priest could carry his basin of animal blood as far as the Golden Altar of Incense which was directly in front of the veil, but no further, lest he died. Given the solemn and sacred nature of the Day of Atonement, there was a lot of preparatory effort on behalf of the priests to do everything just right. Alfred Edersheim summarizes the rabbinical tradition that developed through the following centuries:

> Seven days before the Day of Atonement the high priest left his own house in Jerusalem, and took up his abode in his chambers in the Temple. A substitute was appointed for him, in case he should die or become Levitically unfit for his duties. Rabbinical punctiliousness went so far as to have him twice sprinkled with the ashes of the red heifer – on the 3rd and the 7th day of his week of separation – in case he had, unwittingly to himself, been defiled by a dead body (Num. 19:13). During the whole of that week, also, he had to practice the various

priestly rites, such as sprinkling the blood, burning the incense, lighting the lamp, offering the daily sacrifice, etc. For, as already stated, every part of that day's services devolved on the high priest, and he must not commit any mistake.[1]

The sprinkling of the ashes of the red heifer for purification purposes is explained in Numbers 19 and referenced in Hebrews 9:13. At the time of Christ's coming, this rite was evidently performed for the high priest twice before the Day of Atonement, just in case the high priest had unwittingly been ceremonially defiled (e.g., touched something dead, that is, which had not been properly prepared to eat). What God had instituted to foreshadow His Son's future sacrifice for sins had developed into a dead religion of ritualistic affairs performed by people oblivious to their own desperate need to be reconciled with God.

On the Day of Atonement, after completing the usual morning sacrifice of a lamb as a burnt offering, Aaron put off his normal priestly attire in the tabernacle and bathed. He then dressed in a simple white linen outfit with a white sash and white turban (or "miter"); he was also to wear trousers underneath it all (v. 4; Ex. 39:27-29). Including the morning and evening sacrifices, Alfred Edersheim notes that during the course of this day the high priest would change his raiment and wash his whole body five times, and his hands and feet ten times.[2] To enter the Most Holy Place and to collect and apply the blood of the sin offerings, the high priest wore the white linen garment, but to offer the morning and evening sacrifices, the burnt offerings (the rams), and to bless the people, he wore his normal beautiful priestly attire.

The two sets of sin and burnt offerings were to be performed in a precise order. Aaron was to offer a bull as a sin offering to atone for his own sins and those of his household before offering the goat on behalf of the nation (v. 6, 11). After laying his hands upon the bull and confessing his own sins and those of his household (which included the priesthood), Aaron was to kill the bull and collect its blood in a basin. Next, he was to take a censer containing burning coals from the Bronze Altar beyond the veil into the Most Holy Place. Having securely positioned the censer there, he was to put as much finely-beaten sweet incense as his hands could hold on the censer. He exited the Most Holy Place to retrieve the basin of bull's blood and then reentered the Most Holy Place a second time.

While standing on the east side of the Ark of the Covenant, Aaron used his forefinger to sprinkle the blood of the bull once upon the Mercy Seat and then seven times downward in front of it (v. 14). The now smoke-filled room would limit Aaron's exposure to God's Shekinah glory, the brilliant cloud above the Mercy Seat (v. 2). To gaze directly on the Shekinah cloud would result in death (v. 13). After exiting the Most Holy Place, Aaron placed the basin of bull's blood near the veil.

Aaron then presented two goats, which formed one sin offering, before the Lord at the Bronze Altar (v. 7). The efficacy of Christ's sacrifice as God's sin offering for mankind cannot be adequately foreshadowed in one atoning sacrifice; thus, two goats were required. This type of dual imagery is utilized elsewhere as well: in the ministries of Moses and Aaron, for example. The former represents Christ as an Apostle, and the later as a Priest; both men working together harmoniously prefigured these offices of the Lord Jesus.

Aaron cast two lots. The goat that received the *Lord's lot* would be sacrificed, while the goat that received *la-Azaze* lot would be "the scapegoat" and released in the wilderness never to be seen again (v. 8). C. H. Mackintosh expounds on how the Lord Jesus Christ is typified in the goat on which the *"Lord's lot"* fell:

> "The Lord's lot" fell upon one, and the people's lot fell upon the other. In the case of the former, it was not a question of the persons or the sins which were to be forgiven, [rather] ... this typifies the death of Christ as that wherein God has been perfectly glorified, with respect to sin in general. This great truth is fully set forth in the remarkable expression, "the Lord's lot." God has a peculiar portion in the death of Christ – a portion quite distinct – a portion which would hold eternally good even though no sinner were ever to be saved. In order to see the force of this, it is needful to bear in mind how God has been dishonored in this world. His truth has been despised. His authority has been condemned. His majesty has been slighted. His law has been broken. His claims have been disregarded. His name has been blasphemed. His character has been traduced.
>
> Now, the death of Christ has made provision for all this. It has perfectly glorified God in the very place where all these things have been done. It has perfectly vindicated the majesty, the truth, the holiness, the character of God. It has divinely met all the claims of His throne. It has

atoned for *sin*. It has furnished a divine remedy for all the mischief which sin introduced into the universe. It affords a ground on which the blessed God can act in grace, mercy, and forbearance toward all.[3]

By virtue of the cross, a sovereign God can display the matchless glories of His character and majestic attributes of His nature; this was all made possible because the Lord's lot fell on Christ. The bull was offered for the sins of Aaron and his house, but the goat was sacrificed for all the sins of the people; it therefore held great significance in the mind of God because of all it signified in relationship to Calvary.

Aaron killed the first goat, collecting its blood in a basin. He then entered the Most Holy Place a third time and repeated the application of blood on and in front of the Mercy Seat (vv. 15-16). After departing from the Most Holy Place, Aaron placed the basin of goat's blood before the veil and picked up the basin with the bull's blood, which was then sprinkled once upward on the veil and seven times downward before the veil.

This procedure was repeated with the goat's blood. The blood of the bull and of the goat was then mixed by pouring the basin of bull's blood into the basin of goat's blood and then pouring a portion of the mixture back into the just-emptied basin. In accordance with the instructions for the sin offering, Aaron sprinkled the mixed blood on the horns of the Golden Altar of Incense (4:7, 18), and seven times upon the altar itself (v. 19). In all he would sprinkle the expiatory blood forty-three times, taking care that his own clothing should not become spotted with the sin-laden blood.[4] This completed, Aaron was to exit the tabernacle and with his finger apply some blood to the horns of the Bronze Altar and then pour out the remaining blood at its base (4:25, 30, 34).

It is noted that the reference to "the altar" in verse 18 is not specific and some commentators believe it speaks of the Bronze Altar. Verses 20 and 33 indicate that atonement and purification were made for the "Most Holy Place" (the blood on and before the Mercy Seat), "the tabernacle" (the blood on and before the veil, and on the Golden Altar), and "the altar" (the blood on the horns and poured out at the base of the Bronze Altar). Given the detailed instructions of the sin offering in Leviticus 4, which required the blood of the bull to be put on the horns of the Golden Altar, it seems more likely that "the altar" referenced in verse 18 refers specifically to the Altar of Incense, for the blood of a sin offering was always applied to the Bronze Altar.

Hence, on the Day of Atonement the blood of a bull and of a goat connected the Mercy Seat on the Ark of the Covenant with the Golden Altar of Incense and the Bronze Altar. Atonement for the sins of the nation was achieved and all that pertained to the tabernacle was cleansed and purified by blood. Likewise, through the shed blood of Christ, a repentant sinner not only receives forgiveness of sins (figuratively accomplished at the Bronze Altar), but is positionally cleansed and justified in Christ to offer acceptable praise and worship (as shown in the Golden Altar), and to do so personally before God in the throne room of heaven (symbolized by the Ark of the Covenant). The way into God's presence is completely secured through the redemptive work of Christ: *"Jesus said to him, 'I am the way, the truth, and the life. No one comes to the Father except through Me'"* (John 14:6). Ironically, the priests later referred to the path of entrance between the Holy Place and Most Holy Place in the tabernacle as "the way." Indeed, only through Christ can a sinner be redeemed and enter into God's presence.

After atonement had been made and the sanctuary had been cleansed from defilement, Aaron confessed the sins of the people on the living goat, which was then to be taken by a ceremonially clean man to be released in the wilderness (vv. 20-21). After completing this task, this man was to bathe himself and wash his clothes before reentering the camp (v. 26). This cleansing was also required of the man who took the carcasses and skins of the sin offerings to a clean place to be burned (vv. 27-28).

The scapegoat completes the picture of divine substitution before us: one goat died in the place of the people; this allowed the sins of the people to be transferred to the other goat, who symbolically carried these away from the camp (v. 22). According to the Talmud, scarlet cord or a piece of cloth was placed around the scapegoat's neck; this cord was said to turn white as the goat was being led into the wilderness to show that Jehovah had forgiven the nation's sins. While this anecdote is not biblically confirmed as factual, the symbolism of the story holds true. Isaiah reflected this thought when he pled with the Northern Kingdom of Israel, promising that faithful obedience to Jehovah would be rewarded with forgiveness and blessing:

> *"Come now, and let us reason together," says the Lord, "though your sins are like scarlet, they shall be as white as snow; though they are red like crimson, they shall be as wool"* (Isa. 1:18).

According to rabbinical tradition, the cord did not change color after 30 AD, the year Christ was crucified (Talmud Bavli; Yoma 39:b). The Jews believed their sins were only forgiven if the scarlet cord turned white; if it failed to do so, this indicated Jehovah had rejected the atonement offered for their sins. Clearly, both biblical and rabbinical sources indicate that what was foreshadowed in the Day of Atonement has been fulfilled by the sacrifice of God's Son at Calvary. About two years prior to the destruction of the temple in 70 AD, the writer of Hebrews confirmed God had replaced the Levitical system of offerings by a new and eternal covenant that accomplished what the Law could not (Heb. 7:19) – the propitiation of sins:

> *In that He says, "A new covenant," He has made the first obsolete. Now what is becoming obsolete and growing old is ready to vanish away* (Heb. 8:13).

In 70 AD, that system of sacrifices did vanish and it has not reappeared over the course of two thousand years. Prophetically speaking, we know the religious form of this system will be briefly revived during the Tribulation Period before the Antichrist puts an end to it (Matt. 24:15; 2 Thess. 2:4-6). Nonetheless, God's New Covenant with the houses of Judah and Israel was prophesied by several Old Testament prophets and has been now sealed with the blood of Christ (Isa. 45:17; Jer. 31:31; Ezek. 34:25; Heb. 8:8). This means that no Jew today can receive forgiveness of sins apart from coming to Jesus Christ, their resurrected Messiah.

God was demonstrating through the Day of Atonement that He could righteously deal with human sin and all of its consequences by judging an innocent substitute. Atoning blood throughout the Old Testament period allowed Jehovah to forebear the transgressions of those who exercised faith in His word and to continue in fellowship with them. At Calvary, Christ suffered for all these previously atoned sins as well as all the future sins of humanity (Rom. 3:25).

After the scapegoat was sent away with its escort, Aaron was to enter into the tabernacle and remove the white linen garment he had previously put on there (v. 23). He was to wash his entire body, don the normal holy garments of the high priest, and return to the Bronze Altar to sacrifice the two rams for a burnt offering: one for himself and the other for the nation (v. 24). Aaron then reentered the tabernacle, washed, and put on his white linen garment again in order to reenter the Most Holy Place to retrieve the censor. Afterwards, he again washed and, enrobed in his normal priestly attire, left the white linen robe in the Holy Place. The high priest would then offer the evening sacrifice and, according to Jewish tradition, closed the day with a lamp-lighting ritual in the courtyard in conjunction with an offering of incense (Yoma 7:4).

"That Day"

The Law did not require the Jews to "afflict your souls," except on the Day of Atonement (v. 31). Because of this unique distinction, the Jews in New Testament times commonly referred to the Day of Atonement as *"the fast"* (Acts 27:9). *Yom Kippur*, as it is formally referred to today, was the most important day on the Hebrew calendar. Hence, sometimes the Day of Atonement was simply referred to as "that Day" or "the Day" (v. 30). Because of its significance, it would be a day of rest (as a Sabbath day), a day of fasting and of serious reflection and repentance before the Lord. As *"afflicting your souls"* (Lev. 23:27) is a vague term, the rabbinical writings set forth how the Jews were to observe the Day of Atonement. These call for a twenty-five hour fast (from food and fluids), and a cessation of work, bathing, and marital relationships. The Day of Atonement was to be a day devoted to prayer and confession and, as previously mentioned, there was no other day like it on the Jewish calendar.

The Hebrew word *yowm*, normally translated "day," appears frequently in the Old Testament; however, only about twenty times is it used in the Hebrew expression that correlates to the English phrase, "on that day." This expression first appears in Leviticus 16:30 in reference to the Day of Atonement. The phrase "on that day" is then found twice in Numbers 9:6. Here it describes the unusual situation of a Jew who wanted to keep the Passover Feast, but had been defiled by a dead body. God informed Moses that those who were defiled should keep the Passover, not "on that day," but rather on the fourteenth day of the following month. On the first Passover, a lamb took the place of the firstborn in each family. God used this event also to emphasize the importance of substitutional death as the only means of justifying sinners (i.e., the innocent must take the place of the guilty). The same truth is observed in the next occurrence of "on that day" in Joshua 4 when the Ark of the Lord, carried by the priests, conducted the Israelites through the Jordan, picturing what was accomplished positionally for the believer through the death, burial and resurrection of Christ.

This day had been marked on God's calendar before the foundations of the world were laid – the day propitiation was offered by His own Son for all humanity's sins (Heb. 2:9; 1 Jn. 2:2). It was the day redeeming blood flowed from Immanuel's veins to ensure the redemption of all those who exercise faith in God's message of salvation and are justified in Christ. The psalmist wrote of this spectacular day and, like him, we too can rejoice in it:

> *The stone which the builders rejected has become the chief cornerstone. This was the Lord's doing; it is marvelous in our eyes. This is the day the Lord has made; we will rejoice and be glad in it* (Ps. 118:22-24).

The Church often sings the latter portion of this Psalm as a praise chorus, without regarding its proper context. In other words, we have taken a text out of its proper context and are proclaiming it in a different way than what the Spirit of God intended. While it is true that the Lord is sovereign over each of our days, the focus of our joy is not *our day*, but *the day* Christ was rejected of men and judged by God for our sins. May we treasure the full value God breathed into the text of Psalm 118 three thousand years ago. This day, the day our sins were paid for in full, is the one which was shadowed in the Day of Atonement; like the psalmist, we can certainly rejoice and be glad in it!

Contrasting Garments

In this passage, it is what Aaron does faithfully on behalf of the people, not who he is personally, which distinguishes him as a picture of Christ's future priesthood. What Aaron was personally in the Levitical priesthood is contrasted with the personal excellence of Christ as the eternal High Priest in Hebrews 5 and 7. For example, Aaron derived his *"glory and beauty"* from the garments he wore, but the glory of the Lord Jesus emanates from His very person (Ex. 28:2). Aaron's beauty and glory only lasted as long as he lived and wore the priestly garments, but the Lord Jesus is the *"Lord of Glory"* (1 Cor. 2:9) from eternity past and will be forevermore (John 1:1, 17:1-5).

Aaron had two sets of priestly garments, but he was to exchange his garments of *"glory and beauty"* for the simple white linen outfit and miter only once a year on the Day of Atonement (v. 4). Jewish tradition records that the high priest, after removing these clothes in the tabernacle, did not wear this same white linen outfit again. Although this raiment is referred to as *"holy"* (v. 4), there was neither glory nor beauty in the work that needed to be accomplished to atone for the sins of the people. Clearly, this pictures the Holy One (Luke 1:35, 4:34) who willingly put aside His glorious appearance, left heaven, and came to earth to become holy humanity for the express purpose of suffering death to provide propitiation for human sin:

> *Christ Jesus, who, being in the form of God, did not consider it robbery to be equal with God, but made Himself of no reputation, taking the form of a bondservant, and coming in the likeness of men. And being found in appearance as a man, He humbled Himself and became obedient to the point of death, even the death of the cross* (Phil. 2:5-9).

On the Day of Atonement, Aaron wore his simple white linen coat and miter and was permitted to sprinkle the blood of a bullock and a goat on and before the Mercy Seat to atone for the nation of Israel's sin that year; this means of making atonement had to be repeated every year. But at Calvary, the Lord Jesus was stripped bare and shed His own blood to seal the New Covenant forever. His loud cry, *"It is finished!"* (John 19:30), uttered just before He relinquished His life, was an eternal declaration of what He had accomplished on our behalf. God's judicial wrath for human sin was appeased through His Son's sacrifice:

> *But Christ came as High Priest of the good things to come, with the greater and more perfect tabernacle not made with hands, that is, not of this creation. Not with the blood of goats and calves, but with His own blood He entered the Most Holy Place once for all, having obtained eternal redemption. For if the blood of bulls and goats and the ashes of a heifer, sprinkling the unclean, sanctifies for the purifying of the flesh,*

> how much more shall the blood of Christ, who through the eternal Spirit offered Himself without spot to God, cleanse your conscience from dead works to serve the living God? And for this reason He is the Mediator of the new covenant, by means of death, for the redemption of the transgressions under the first covenant, that those who are called may receive the promise of the eternal inheritance (Heb. 9:11-15).

Aaron had to repeat the blood sacrifices day by day and year by year because the blood of bulls and goats could only cover sin temporarily until the revelation of what these sacrifices pictured: the ultimate solution for human sin. Through Christ's sacrifice, righteous justice for sin was answered, and by His blood those who trust Him for salvation are purged from filth and guilt and become clean vessels fit for God's use. Christ has opened a way (the only way) for man to pass within the heavenly veil and enter the very place from where Christ originally came (Heb. 6:18-20).

Application

During Old Testament times, Jehovah dwelt in a tabernacle or temple among His covenant people. Because of national idolatry, this ended at the time of the Babylonian invasion and the subsequent destruction of the temple (Ezek. 10). After Christ's death and resurrection, the entire Levitical system was replaced and put away to ensure that the type did not compete with the antitype, that is, the New Covenant seal in Christ's blood (Heb. 8:13). Unfortunately, many Christians today still place an emphasis on an earthly sanctuary that does not exist. This results in using wrong terminology which introduces an alternative and unbiblical idea of what the Church is or where the real sanctuary is. The Church is not a lifeless building; it is a living spiritual body (Eph. 2:19-22). "The house of God" is not a building in which Christians gather; rather, it is the Church itself (1 Tim. 3:15). The only door of entrance into the true Church is the Lord Jesus (John 10:1, 14:6). Thus, there is a stark difference in how the term "house of God" is used in the Old Testament to refer to the tabernacle or a physical temple, and how it is used in the New Testament after Pentecost to designate the Church.

Additionally, the term "sanctuary" in the Old Testament referred to a location within the temple or the tabernacle where the priests officiated worship on behalf of the nation of Israel. In the Old Testament, as we have just seen, access to God was limited. Only the high priest on the Day of Atonement could gain entry into the Most Holy Place (God's sanctuary), and he did so in trepidation and not without the blood of a goat and bullock.

In the New Testament, the term "sanctuary" is never applied to a physical room in which the Church gathers for worship, but to the abode of God, either in heaven or in the believer. In the Church Age, God dwells within those who have been born again (1 Cor. 6:19), and is therefore among His people when the local assembly comes together (1 Cor. 3:16-17). No bricks and mortar can contain Him, but those who have responded to His invitation to be saved have His abiding presence forever. If we had been Aaron on the Day of Atonement, what fear and apprehension would we have felt standing before the mercy seat of the holiest place on earth with blood dripping off our fingers? Beloved, that is how much reverence you and I should have for His sacred dwelling place now! Paul pleads with the believers at Corinth on this matter:

> *Flee sexual immorality. Every sin that a man does is outside the body, but he who commits sexual immorality sins against his own body. Or do you not know that your body is the temple of the Holy Spirit who is in you, whom you have from God, and you are not your own? For you were bought at a price; therefore glorify God in your body and in your spirit, which are God's* (1 Cor. 6:18-20).

The earthly sanctuary of the Old Testament was purified by animal blood, which allowed man limited access to God. In the New Testament, God's earthly sanctuary is those who have been redeemed and cleansed by His Son's blood. This allows every individual who trusts Christ for salvation to enjoy complete and full access to God. Let each believer keep short accounts with God by confessing and forsaking sin, and after Christ's blood has again fully cleansed and purified what was defiled, let us work to keep God's sanctuary glorious and untainted.

In the Church Age we have the great privilege of coming in the Spirit directly into the heavenly sanctuary to pray and to praise God. Moreover, while sojourning on earth, believers have the honor of representing God in His holy living temple – the Church. Today, no physical earthly structure will bring honor to His name; rather, this privilege is reserved

Be Holy and Come Near

for believers willingly living in purity. These believer-priests dedicate themselves to keep God's sacred temple holy.

Meditation

> In your hearts enthrone Him; there let Him subdue
> All that is not holy, all that is not true;
> Crown Him as your Captain in temptation's hour;
> Let His will enfold you in its light and power.
>
> — Caroline M. Noel

The Place of Worship
Leviticus 17:1-9

The Lord addresses two matters of grand importance to Him in this chapter. The first is the location He should be worshipped by His people. At this point, this was the tabernacle, though later, after the Israelites conquered and settled Canaan, Jerusalem would be designated as the permanent site where all sacrifices would be offered to the Lord. The tent of meeting would be replaced by a magnificent temple which King Solomon would build some five centuries later. The second topic of this chapter is the significance that God ascribes to blood – it is considered the life of the flesh, and therefore the power of atonement was in the blood. Accordingly, several regulations and prohibitions concerning blood are contained within Leviticus 17 (these are addressed in the following devotion).

Concerning the first subject matter, the Lord specifically stated all animals destined as sacrifices were to be slaughtered at the tabernacle. This would ensure no sacrifices were offered to Him outside the manner He had dictated. Moses was to deliver the following command to Aaron:

> *"Whatever man of the house of Israel who kills an ox or lamb or goat in the camp, or who kills it outside the camp, and does not bring it to the door of the tabernacle of meeting to offer an offering to the Lord before the tabernacle of the Lord, the guilt of bloodshed shall be imputed to that man. He has shed blood; and that man shall be cut off from among his people, to the end that the children of Israel may bring their sacrifices which they offer in the open field, that they may bring them to the Lord at the door of the tabernacle of meeting, to the priest, and offer them as peace offerings to the Lord. And the priest shall sprinkle the blood on the altar of the Lord at the door of the tabernacle of meeting, and burn the fat for a sweet aroma to the Lord. They shall no more offer their sacrifices to demons, after whom they have played*

> the harlot. This shall be a statute forever for them throughout their generations."
>
> Also you shall say to them: "Whatever man of the house of Israel, or of the strangers who dwell among you, who offers a burnt offering or sacrifice, and does not bring it to the door of the tabernacle of meeting, to offer it to the Lord, that man shall be cut off from among his people" (vv. 3-9).

This law was modified at the end of their forty-year pilgrimage in the wilderness to permit the slaughter of clean animals deemed fit for sacrifice elsewhere besides the tabernacle, if the animals were not to be offered as blood sacrifices to the Lord (e.g. burnt offerings; Deut. 12:20-28). The tabernacle was first pitched at Shiloh (Josh. 18:1). Later, David brought the Ark of the Covenant to Jerusalem and fabricated a tabernacle for it (2 Sam. 6:17). Logistically speaking, this commandment would have been nearly impossible in Canaan. How could a Jew in the far northwestern corner of Canaan, for example, bring a cow sixty miles to be slaughtered at the tabernacle; the meat would have little value by the time it was transported back to its point of origin. However, while dwelling in the wilderness this commandment was a practical one: First, it ensured no one would offer sacrifices to Jehovah anywhere else than the tabernacle and at any other's hand than a priest's. Second, if someone wanted to slaughter a clean animal for food, they would have to bring the animal to the tabernacle and offer it as a peace offering, which gave the priests a constant supply of meat.

The command was the same for Jew or sojourning stranger; all clean animals which could be sacrificed were to be brought to the priests at the tabernacle and slaughtered there (v. 8). If someone disobeyed this commandment and butchered an animal on their own elsewhere, it was considered an offering to demons and that person was to be cut off from the commonwealth of the nation. If the incident was actually one of idolatry, the offender would be severely judged by God (Ex. 20:4; Deut. 4:27). C. H. Mackintosh explains why the consequences for offering a sacrifice at a non-tabernacle location were so severe:

> This was a most solemn matter; and we may ask what was involved in offering a sacrifice otherwise than in the manner here prescribed? It was nothing less than robbing Jehovah of His rights, and presenting to

Satan that which was due to God. A man might say, "Can I not offer a sacrifice in one place as well as another?" The answer is, "Life belongs to God, and His claim thereto must be recognized in the place which He has appointed – before the tabernacle of the Lord." That was the only meeting place between God and man. To offer elsewhere proved that the heart did not want God. The moral of this is plain. There is one place where God has appointed to meet the sinner, and that is the cross – the antitype of the brazen altar. There and there alone has God's claim upon the life been duly recognized. To reject this meeting place is to bring down judgment upon oneself – it is to trample underfoot the just claims of God, and to arrogate to oneself a right to life which all have forfeited. It is important to see this.[1]

Certainly one could argue that an animal could be slaughtered more easily at its owner's location, rather than leading or driving it all the way to the tabernacle and then hauling the meat home again. While this may be logistically true, this conclusion is one of human reasoning that defies God's command. It is a necessary component of all divine tests for man to push beyond the realm of what seems logical; if obedience was always easy and reasonable, our devotion would remain unproven. The command was a matter of importance to God, for His people must understand that there was only one means and one location in which a sinner could approach Him – it had to be His way and His place. Later, more revelation of *"The Way"* (John 14:6) would come to humanity as the eternal and living Word of God, the Lord Jesus Christ (John 1:1). He would be both the Messenger and Message to be obeyed.

Throughout the Old Testament there are various distinct economies of truth God reveals to mankind. These serve as a test – will man righteously hold to this divine revelation? If people choose to obey what is revealed through faith, they will be justified before God (Gen. 15:6). If not, they will receive the wrath of God, as Paul explains: *"For the wrath of God is revealed from heaven against all ungodliness and unrighteousness of men, who suppress the truth in unrighteousness, because what may be known of God is manifest in them, for God has shown it to them"* (Rom. 1:18-19). Through scientific processes we only grasp a small portion of truth concerning God's order in creation. This limitation prompts us to ponder the vast unknown beyond our knowledge. He has constructed a cosmic stage, has set something in motion which is bigger than we can comprehend, and, at the same time, put before every conscious individual an unavoidable test. Everyone has some revelation of God, whether it is creation that proclaims its Creator (Rom. 1:19-20), or the feelings of guilt from our offended conscience that indicate a moral order over the universe (Rom. 2:15), or by hearing a Christian testimony of a changed life, or by being exposed to God's written Word. In some measure God has expressed Himself and a standard of righteous truth to everyone. This poses a test of obedience: will we exercise faith in this revealed truth, though we do not fully understand it?

On the other hand, biblical faith is not blind belief as some skeptics claim. On the contrary, the Bible challenges its readers to test and reason out Scripture: *"Test all things; hold fast what is good"* (1 Thess. 5:21). This testing is not to prove that Scripture is true, but to personally affirm that it is true. Paul complimented the Bereans because *"they received the word with all readiness of mind, and searched the Scriptures daily, whether those things were so"* (Acts 17:11; KJV). Biblical Christianity has this distinction over the religious movements of the world – the seeker is challenged to test the Scripture to validate its truthfulness. Religion imposes propaganda without permitting an opportunity to validate truthfulness against itself and available evidence. God knows man will live out faithfully only that which he has first proven to be true. The fear and scare tactics of the world's religions effectively strangle the heart from ever exercising love that is anchored in truth.

God does not want us to respond to Him in this way. He does not want robotic followers or those who blindly associate with Him out of fear. Concerning what prompts good behavior, He knows that love is a more powerful motivator than fear (1 Jn. 4:18). Accordingly, He wants us to understand the expressions of His love towards us so we might experience His love and then freely return it to Him (1 John 4:19). The Lord confirmed that our love for Him is shown through our obedience: *"If you love Me, keep My commandments"* (John 14:15). So, God has revealed much truth for us to test and verify, but there will always be a test of faith for that part which we cannot reason out. God's message to us in simplified form is this: You must trust Me for what you do not understand. If you do, I will justify you, bless you, have fellowship with you, and open your understanding of deeper truths – will you trust Me? This is what former atheist C. S. Lewis came to realize: "I believe in God as I believe that the Sun has risen, not only because I see it, but because by it I see everything else."² In Leviticus 17 the Jews are presented with a test in the form of a command. Would they demonstrate love for Jehovah by obeying it? Unfortunately, rampant idolatry has characterized much of their history and the cost of their disobedience has been devastating.

Jerusalem

Before King David's death, he installed his son Solomon as the new king of Israel. David instructed Solomon to build a temple in Jerusalem for the Lord God of Israel (1 Chron. 22:6). As the tabernacle would no longer be moved and would soon be replaced by a temple, David revised the duties of the Levites and confirmed that the place of worship would now be Jerusalem (1 Chron. 23:24-32). Some have referred to the Bible as being "The Tale of Two Cities," but not London and Paris as in Charles Dickens's classic story: rather, the reference is to Jerusalem and Babylon. Throughout Scripture, Babylon represents the evil pagan world under Satan's control, whereas Jerusalem is the holy city connected with God's name.

Jerusalem is first mentioned in Genesis 14 where we find Melchizedek, a godly king-priest, representing God there. He ruled in righteousness and brought peace to the city. The next reference of Jerusalem is associated with Abraham's test of faith in the land of Moriah (Gen. 22:1-3). God told Abraham to go to a specific mountain in the land of Moriah (near Jerusalem) and to offer his *"only son"* whom he loved as a burnt sacrifice. No reason was given, and Abraham asked no questions. It is worth noting the narrative emphasizes three times that Isaac was his *"only"* son. Though Ishmael was also Abraham's son, he was a product of the flesh, and therefore not the son of divine promise (Heb. 11:17). God completely understood the gravity of the sacrifice and consequential agony to Abraham's soul. Abraham was in such intimate communion with God that God allowed Abraham to feel, at least in a measure, the anguish God would feel in giving His own Son for the suffering of death for mankind. God commanded Abraham to offer Isaac as a burnt offering on a mount in the land that He would show him. Abraham proved his love for the Lord, and the Lord intervened to stop the sacrifice and to provide a ram to be offered in Isaac's place. Abraham offered the ram *"instead of his son"* (Gen. 22:13). Accordingly, *"Abraham called the name of the place, The-Lord-Will-Provide; as it is said to this day, 'In the Mount of the Lord it shall be provided'"* (Gen. 22:14). This prophecy would be fulfilled over two thousand years in the future, when God provided His own Son as a sacrifice for human sin just outside of Jerusalem.

A millennium after Abraham's test, David offered a burnt sacrifice to God on a mountain in Moriah to stay a judgment of pestilence against Israel (1 Chron. 21). Pride had lured David to number the men of Israel, and God responded with a disciplinary plague. A generation later, Solomon built a spectacular temple on Mount Moriah, the same location that the Lord had appeared unto David when he offered the sacrifice to avert the plague (2 Chron. 3:1). Another millennium later, the Lord Jesus Christ was tried and crucified on or near the same location. In a future millennium, the Lord Jesus will reign from Jerusalem, which will then be honored as the religious capital of the world (Zech. 14:16-17).

From Genesis to Revelation, Scripture indicates that Mount Moriah (Jerusalem) is a special location to the Lord. After the Israelites settled in Canaan, Jerusalem would be formally recognized as the only place that worship was to be offered to Jehovah for as long as the earth exists, except during the Church Age. Presently, all believer-priests (Christians) become the temple of God and lift up worship and living sacrifices heavenward unto God wherever and whenever they desire (1 Pet. 2:5, 9; Rev. 1:6; Rom. 12:1).

The pattern of God's plan for human redemption was first revealed to us in Genesis 22. Abraham's saga is so traumatic, yet so awe-inspiring, that our finite minds are captivated to ponder Calvary from a heavenly perspective of divine anguish. God would judge His innocent and only begotten Son at Calvary, near Jerusalem, for our sin. Only by embracing the Savior's cross at Jerusalem would man find forgiveness and a solace to comfort his grieving soul. To the Jew, God declares, *"Zion, you who bring good tidings, get up into the high mountain; O Jerusalem, you who bring good tidings, lift up your voice with strength, lift it up, be not afraid; say to the cities of Judah, 'Behold your God!'"* (Isa. 40:9). Concerning the Gentiles, it was the Lord's will for evangelism to begin at Jerusalem and then spread to the uttermost parts of the world (Matt. 28:19-20; Acts 1:8).

During the Millennium Kingdom, the message to the world shall be *"And it shall come to pass that everyone who is left of all the nations which came against Jerusalem shall go up from year to year to worship the King, the Lord of hosts, and to keep the Feast of Tabernacles"* (Zech. 14:16). The Lord ascended into heaven from Jerusalem, and He will return to Jerusalem to establish His earthly kingdom (Acts 1; Zech. 14). From Isaiah 2:1-5 and 66:20 we learn that Jerusalem shall then be the religious center of the world. Christ will reign from there, and from there all the nations will come to praise, worship, and learn (Zech. 14:16-21). There will be no war or violence, only peace. All the earth shall see the glory of the Lord Jesus. So great will be the glory of the Lord upon the earth that there will be no need for the sun or moon to illuminate it (Isa. 60:18-20). Though due to Jewish disobedience God permitted its destruction several times in its history, Jerusalem is the location where God chose to tie His name. The Lord wept over the city, suffered in the city, and chastened its inhabitants, but there is a coming day when it will be full of joy and shine forth the glory of God to all nations!

Application

In the opening chapter of the book of Nehemiah we are introduced to a Jewish man named Nehemiah who, though he was living in Babylon, was keenly interested in the affairs at Jerusalem. A group of Jews, Nehemiah's brother Hanani being among them, had just returned from visiting Jerusalem. A concerned Nehemiah immediately inquired about two things: the welfare of God's people and the location where God had chosen to place His name – Jerusalem. The report was not favorable; 140 years after Nebuchadnezzar's successful invasion, the wall around Jerusalem and, indeed, much of the city lay in ruins, and the burned gates of the city had not been replaced. Though the temple had been built, and sacrifices were being offered to Jehovah, the people themselves were *"in great distress and reproach"* (v. 3).

We read of Nehemiah's response to this report: *"So it was, when I heard these words, that I sat down and wept, and mourned for many days; I was fasting and praying before the God of heaven"* (v. 4). As previously mentioned, the Law did not require the Jews to fast, except on the Day of Atonement, but Nehemiah was deeply affected by the dismal report and immediately petitioned the Lord for help while fasting *"day and night"* (v. 6).

Nehemiah enjoyed a position of prominence and social security within the Babylonian government, but his heart was with his people and he was zealous for God's testimony in the world. Jerusalem should be a city of glory and praise, rather than a reproach to God's name. Nehemiah knew that a wall around Jerusalem would serve both for protection and for exclusion. Once erected, the wall would provide defense against their enemy and also bind the Jews in a spiritual safe haven, exclusive of heathen ways. Thus, Nehemiah poured out his heart in prayer before the Lord.

Nehemiah's reaction was evidence of his great concern for the Lord's work and His people. Do we feel the same sense of desperation today that Nehemiah felt long ago? In the Church Age, the Church is the temple of God and is to directly display His character and declare His offer of salvation among the nations. Do we mourn over the Church's indifference, moral failures, and lack of commitment to the Lord Jesus Christ and His Word? What might God do today, if believers, like Nehemiah, were broken over the Church's ruined testimony of Christ, and in prayer and fasting pleaded with the Lord to revive His Church?

Meditation

> Oh! men and brethren, what would this heart feel if I could but believe that there were some among you who would go home and pray for a revival – men whose faith is large enough, and their love fiery enough to lead them from this moment to exercise unceasing intercessions that God would appear among us and do wondrous things here, as in the times of former generations.
>
> — C. H. Spurgeon

The Life of the Flesh
Leviticus 17:10-16

The second main topic addressed in Leviticus 17 is the significance God ascribes to blood – it is *"the life of the flesh."* In sacrificial substitution, an innocent life is exchanged for the one deserving judgment; therefore, the power of atonement and redemption is in the blood of the substitute. In Old Testament times the substitute was an animal, whose sacrifice typified the ultimate and final Substitute for the judgment of human sin – the Lord Jesus Christ. Because of blood's significance, Jehovah instituted certain regulations concerning the shedding of blood and a prohibition against eating blood in this chapter.

The Prohibition Against Eating Blood (vv. 10-12)

The Jews were commanded not to consume blood seven times throughout the Pentateuch (e.g., Lev. 3:17, 7:26-27), but the limitation is most clearly explained in this chapter. God first delivered this command to Noah and his family as they exited the ark. The command had not been needed previously, as it was not until after this deluge that God gave mankind permission to kill animals for meat (Gen. 9:3).

Verse 11 supplies two reasons for abstaining from eating blood: *"For the life of the flesh is in the blood, and I have given it to you upon the altar to make atonement for your souls; for it is the blood that makes atonement for the soul."* First, the life of the creature is in the blood. Without blood circulating through the miles of veins and arteries in our bodies, we would quickly die. Blood not only provides the billions of cells in our bodies with the oxygen, nutrients, hormones, etc. needed to function properly, but it also takes the waste products of metabolism to where these can be removed from the body. Accordingly, blood is identified with life – without it we cannot live. To shed blood ends a life God created. Hence, to refrain from eating blood was to demonstrate respect for the sanctity of the life.

The second reason for avoiding blood in food is related to the significance God had imputed to blood as the visible means of atoning for sins. The writer of Hebrews explains the spiritual meaning of verse 11: *"And according to the Law almost all things are purified with blood, and without shedding of blood there is no remission"* (Heb. 9:22). For the priest to apply the blood of a sin offering on the Bronze Altar or the Mercy Seat meant that an innocent life had been forfeited to cover the transgression of another. It was not that blood was inherently efficacious, but rather God, for man's sake, had decreed blood was His symbol for atonement and forgiveness. If no life was given and no blood applied, there was no forgiveness of sins. The prohibition against eating blood fostered a proper regard for the manner in which sin could be covered, and thus the penalty for ignoring this command was severe: the offender was to be cut off from his people, that is, put out of the Jewish social economy altogether.

The Slaughter of Game (vv. 13-16)

Having previously addressed where domesticated clean animals that were suitable for sacrifice should be slaughtered, Moses turns to the matter of killing wild animals that were still considered clean under the Mosaic Law. These might be caught in a snare or trap, or shot while hunting. Because these animals could not be offered as a sacrifice, there was no requirement to bring them to the tabernacle; indeed, this would have been extremely difficult. One can only imagine the bizarre complications of herding a wild animal to the tabernacle to be slaughtered. For example, a hunter would only be able to wound an animal and then somehow get it to the priests before he could properly kill it. Thankfully, there was no such restriction. However, the stipulation of properly draining out the blood before consuming the meat still applied (vv. 13-14). The life of the animal, its blood, had been shed and man was to have respect for the life that had been taken to provide for his needs. Therefore, the blood of game animals was to be drained out on the ground and not eaten.

If anyone did eat the meat from the carcass of a clean domesticated animal that had not been killed at the tabernacle, that individual was to wash his clothes and bathe and wait until evening to become ceremonially clean again (vv. 15-16). This caveat did not allow for the intentional out-of-place slaughter of those animals which could be sacrificed, but rather for the butchering of animals that died of natural causes or were attacked and killed by a wild beast. The reason eating off such a carcass resulted in uncleanness is twofold. First, the blood of the clean animal had not been drained properly, which meant that as one ate the meat, he or she was also consuming the blood. Second, as previously mentioned, an individual became unclean after any contact with a carcass, unless it had just been appropriately killed at the tabernacle (Lev. 11:39-40). This restriction was later lifted for Gentiles sojourning with the Israelites (Deut. 14:21), but Jews were not to eat animals that were found dead; such carcasses were to be *"thrown to the dogs"* (Ex. 22:31).

Application

As Christians, Leviticus reminds us that the blood of Christ is the foundation of our faith and our acceptance with God. Through the blood of Christ, God can righteously justify condemned sinners who believe on His Son's name for salvation (Rom. 3:22-24). Likewise, the applied blood of Christ is the basis of the sinner's confidence that he or she can draw near to a holy God, who is a consuming fire of perfection, without fear. Paul explains this precious truth in his epistle to the Romans:

> *But God demonstrates His own love toward us, in that while we were still sinners, Christ died for us. Much more then,* **having now been justified by His blood***, we shall be saved from wrath through Him. For if when we were enemies we were reconciled to God through the death of His Son, much more, having been reconciled, we shall be saved by His life. And not only that, but we also rejoice in God through our Lord Jesus Christ, through whom we have now received the reconciliation* (Rom. 5:8-11).

The righteousness of God beyond what was revealed in the Law was fully displayed at Calvary; it was here God judged His Son for all the offenses humanity had committed against Him (Rom. 3:21). This means that He can, through the blood of Christ, extend forgiveness to those who were dead in trespasses and sins. Through this righteous transaction, God is demonstrating the harmony of all aspects of His holy character in the matter of saving sinners: He is just, righteous, merciful, gracious, loving, compassionate, longsuffering, sovereign, all-knowing, all-powerful, unchanging, etc. C. H. Mackintosh warns believers not to let this fundamental truth – justification through Christ's blood alone – slip from our doctrinal foundation:

> *It is all through the blood of Jesus* — nothing less — nothing more — nothing different. *"It is the blood that makes an atonement for the soul."* This is conclusive. This is God's simple plan of justification. Man's plan is much more cumbrous, much more roundabout. And not only is it cumbrous and roundabout, but it attributes righteousness to something quite different from what I find in the word. If I look from Genesis 3 down to the close of Revelation, I find the blood of Christ put forward as the alone ground of righteousness. We get pardon, peace, life, righteousness, all by the blood, and nothing but the blood. The entire book of Leviticus, and particularly the chapter upon which we have just been meditating, is a commentary upon the doctrine of the blood.[1]

If it were not for the cross and the shed blood of Christ, God would be constrained by His holy character to commit the guilty (that is, the entire human race) to the judgment of eternal death. May the believer never forget the tremendous significance God the Father ascribes to His own Son's blood – we are redeemed and cleansed by the blood of Christ alone! On this matter, the hymn writer Robert Lowry poetically answers his own question: "What can wash away my sin? Nothing but the blood of Jesus. What can make me whole again? Nothing but the blood of Jesus." Amen and Amen!

Meditation

> Though our nature's fall in Adam shut us wholly out from God,
> Thine eternal counsel brought us nearer still, through Jesus' blood.
> For in Him we found redemption, grace and glory in Thy Son;
> Oh, the height and depth of mercy! Christ and His redeemed are one.
>
> — Robert Hawker

I Am the Lord Your God
Leviticus 18

Chapters 18 through 22 compose the next major section of Leviticus. The central topic of this text is God's laws governing personal conduct, but the common tie between immorality and idolatry is also emphasized. Most of us will find portions of these chapters somewhat disgusting to read, but as F. B. Hole remarks, such legislation is necessary because the heart of man is desperately wicked:

> Three chapters follow – 18, 19, and 20 – which in many respects make terrible reading, but which, if read quietly as in the presence of God, are calculated to have a wholesome effect upon us. We are brought face to face, especially in chapters 18 and 20, with great depths of depravity, and it is a solemn and soul-searching thing to realize that we have within us that fallen, fleshly nature which is capable of such things as these. The sins prohibited have largely to do with the sexual nature of mankind, and it is today perfectly obvious that sins of that nature underlie a vast amount of the depravity and crime that fill every land.[1]

Without divine intervention, any of us is capable of committing the gross sins listed in these chapters, and more.

Chapter 18 supplies instructions as to what constituted a lawful marriage between a Jewish man and a woman, and also a stern warning against idolatry. Their time in Egypt had exposed the Israelites to many immoral and corrupt customs (v. 3). The Israelites were headed to Canaan and it too was full of many deplorable practices of which Jehovah did not approve (Gen. 19).

The chapter commences with the Lord instructing Moses to remind the Israelites that He alone was their God: *"I am the Lord your God"* (v. 2). This statement serves as a preamble for the covenant treaty formed in this chapter. The phrase is only found once prior to this point in Leviticus, but beginning with verse 2, it occurs twenty-three times in the remainder of the book. This expression occurs three times in this chapter (vv. 2, 4, 30), while the shortened phrase *"I am the Lord"* is found three additional times (vv. 5, 6, 21). The repeated assertion is to motivate the Jews to obey Jehovah's laws – they were accountable to Him to do so: *"You shall therefore keep My statutes and My judgments, which if a man does, he shall live by them: I am the Lord"* (v. 5). The verse implies that those who choose to live by Jehovah's commandments will also enjoy an abundant life through them. F. Duane Lindsey summarizes the practical outcome of obedience inferred by this verse.

> Obedience to God's laws produces in His people happy and fulfilled lives (26:3-13; Deut. 28:1-4). For example, the marital and sexual restrictions in Leviticus 18 constitute the basis for a stable and happy family life.[2]

Having asserted His sovereign rule and authority, Jehovah sets forth laws to govern permissible marriages among them. Although the word "marriage" is not specifically stated in this passage, it is implied by the phrase *"to uncover the nakedness"* which speaks of the legitimate sexual union between a husband and wife. Fornication (sexual intercourse with someone other than one's legal spouse) was strictly forbidden and punishable by death in nearly all cases (Lev. 20:10-15). Thus, Moses is not speaking here of casual sexual affairs, as the Law did not permit these at all; rather, the regulations given concern marriages among close kinfolk (v. 6).

It was prohibited to marry your: mother (v. 7), stepmother (v. 8), sibling – even if a half-sibling (v. 9), granddaughter (v. 10), stepmother's daughter (v. 11), aunt (vv. 12-13), and uncle (v. 14). Today we speak of these family relationships in degrees of genetic association. First-degree relatives, such as siblings (including non-identical twins), parents, and children have half their genetic information in common. Second-degree relatives, such as half-siblings, aunts and uncles, nephews and nieces, and grandparents, share one-fourth of the same genetic information. Third-degree relatives share one-eighth of their genetic material, i.e., first cousins, half-uncles and half-aunts, half-nephews and half-nieces. Note: These genetic commonality portions are generalized based on probability.

Two things can be observed from the marital prohibitions in this chapter. First, marriages among first-degree and second-degree relations were forbidden; however, marriages between third-degree relatives (e.g., first cousins) were not. Marriage unions, after the death or divorce of a spouse, were forbidden among in-laws (vv. 14-16). Although there may not have been a substantial genetic link with these individuals, the marriage was still forbidden. This is likely due to the fact that a husband and wife, in creating an intimate and permanent family unit, were considered "one flesh" (Gen. 2:24). Consequently, any sexual relationships among family members united by marriage (i.e., in-laws) would be considered incest. For this reason, a man could not marry his daughter in-law or step-granddaughter (v. 17). And perhaps it is for this same reason a man could not marry his wife's sister as a rival to her (v. 18). Marrying two sisters certainly caused much turmoil in Jacob's house. At this point we pause to note God never endorses polygamy in Scripture; in fact, His pattern for marriage is beautifully displayed in Genesis 2 and affirmed by Christ in Matthew 19 – one man and one woman until death separates them.

One might ask why these boundaries for marriage are issued now, when it is obvious that some of the Hebrew patriarchs married close family members? For example, Abraham married his half-sister Sarah, and Isaac married Rebekah (his first cousin once removed). The reason for the timing of these commands is not given in Leviticus 18, so we can only speculate. What is evident is that there is no apology for the past, *"for where there is no law there is no transgression"* (Rom. 4:15); however, now that the Law was stated, infractions would be promptly addressed.

Medically speaking, we now know that the closer the genetic tie between the parents, the greater the risk of birth defects for their children. For example, a child of unrelated parents has a risk around two to three percent of being born with a serious birth defect or some type of genetic disorder. This risk doubles for children whose parents are first cousins and do not have a family history of genetic disorders. However, the risk of birth defects or death for children of first-degree relatives is about thirty percent.[3] It is noted that today about one in five couples worldwide are first cousins.[4]

A brief review of genetics will demonstrate how recessive defects are more likely to be expressed in such situations. Humans have 46 paired chromosomes (23 autosomals), with about 23,000 genes. If two parents each have a copy of the same recessive defect (which is more likely if the parents themselves are closely related), they may both pass their copy of this altered gene on to a child, so the child receives both flawed copies. As the child then does not have a normal, functioning copy of the gene, the child will develop a disorder. Though the parents in such a case are "carriers" of the genetic condition, they may not be affected by it. Autosomal recessive genetic disorders are more likely if two parents are related.

It would have been normal for siblings and cousins to marry each other in the days following Eden and after the flood. However, because the human genome was relatively pure at that time, there was little risk of birth defects among their offspring. Several millennia later, mutated human genes would have become more numerous, and perhaps for this reason Jehovah chose at this time to institute this set of laws to reduce birth defects among His people. Or, He may have simply desired to preserve the sanctity of the family from inappropriate lusting or from being degraded by worldly thinking and behavior.

The remainder of the chapter is devoted to rebuking particular worldly and heathen practices. The first two directives pertain to unlawful lusting; sexual intercourse with a menstruating woman was forbidden (v. 19), and adultery would not be tolerated among God's people (v. 20). In Jewish society, the latter command would have been clearly understood to include betrothed couples (i.e., those under a marriage covenant, see Deut. 22:22-25). In this chapter, Moses reaffirms the seventh of the Ten Commandments, which had been previously delivered to him on Mount Sinai.

Furthermore, the idolatrous practice of placing one's firstborn child alive in the white-hot arms of the false god Molech as a burnt offering would not be tolerated (v. 21). However, we read that some Jews were practicing this pagan ritual over eight centuries later in the days of Jeremiah (Jer. 32:35). Finally, homosexuality and sexual relations with beasts are both described as an abomination to the Lord; these are acts of rebellion against God's creation order and design for heterosexual marriage (vv. 22-23).

The first thirty verses of Leviticus 18 declare what the Israelites should not do; the remainder of the chapter tells them why they should not do it. The nations who dwelled in Canaan had defiled it with their pagan and immoral behavior; consequently, God was ready to spew them out of that land (vv. 24-25). Likewise, God warned His people they had better obey His commandments after He settled them in Canaan, or else He would spew them out of the land in the same way (vv. 26-28). This eventually happened with the exile of the Northern Kingdom in 722 B.C. after it fell to Assyria, and with the Babylonian conquest of the Southern Kingdom in 605 B.C. The Jews were not to defile themselves in their new homeland by engaging in the immoral and heathen customs of the Canaanites. Anyone who did was to be promptly removed from the commonwealth of the nation (v. 29). William MacDonald notes the common connection between immorality and idolatry highlighted in this text:

> It is no accident that impurity and idolatry are found together in the same chapter (see also chap. 20). A person's morality is the fruit of his theology, his concept of God. The Canaanites were a graphic illustration of the degradation that idolatry produces (vv. 24-27). When the children of Israel took possession of the land, they killed thousands of these people at Jehovah's command. When we consider the moral degradation of the Canaanites, as described in verses 24-30, we can understand why God dealt so harshly with them.[5]

Unfortunately, the pleas of Moses for the moral and spiritual purity of the Israelites in Canaan did not make a lasting impression. Not much more than half a decade later and only some ten to twenty years after the Jews entered Canaan, secret idolatry was already rampant among the people. Joshua voiced a passionate appeal to the people to put away their false gods (Josh. 24). He reminded them that Abraham left the idols of his family in Ur to have communion with the God of Glory in a land promised to him, and that the Israelites must do the same. The Jews did not repent that day; this ushered in centuries of divine chastening as recorded in the book of Judges.

Leviticus 18 concludes in the same way it began, with an affirmation of God's divine position; *"I am the Lord your God"* (v. 30). Obedience to the Lord's edicts of this chapter would have precluded centuries of His disciplinary judgments. Jehovah was their God and He loved His people too much to leave them in rebellion.

Application

We might be foolish enough to think that these sorts of pagan temptations pertain only to Old Testament days, but the apostle John echoed the same warning to Christians not long before his death, saying, *"keep yourselves from idols"* (1 Jn. 5:21). The bottom line is that fornication and idolatry walk together. Those who do not fear God will not obey His commands for holy living. This is why John sternly admonished Christians to be idol-free; misplaced affection leads to unchecked lust and eventually immorality. Anything in this world that robs God of our love is an idol and will inevitably steal our time, resources, and purity. If we want God's blessing, we must trust and obey Him.

Meditation

> The true man of God is heartsick, grieved at the worldliness of the Church, grieved at the toleration of sin in the Church, grieved at the prayerlessness in the Church. He is disturbed that the corporate prayer of the Church no longer pulls down the strongholds of the devil.
>
> — Leonard Ravenhill

Be Holy
Leviticus 19

The diversity of subjects addressed in this chapter illustrates that the matter of practical holiness is to extend into every aspect of our lives. The Jews were to learn that holiness is not merely correct behavior, but it extends to one's attitude: loving what God deems good and hating what He calls evil. Israel was to stand with God (and against themselves) on every point of the Law, and to do so with loyal earnestness.

All human affairs in life are subject to God's laws and judgments (Rom. 2:1-4; Rom. 14:10-12). This divine accountability is punctuated by the frequent phrases *"I am the Lord,"* and *"I am the Lord your God,"* found some fifteen times in Leviticus 19. In fact, no chapter in the entire Bible has more occurrences of these phrases. The predominant theme of the chapter is expressed in verse 2: *"You shall be holy, for I the Lord your God am holy."* God is holy and desires His people to live holy lives also. With this understanding, F. Duane Lindsey summarizes Jehovah's objective in this chapter:

> The holiness of God (v. 2) is the bedrock supporting the practical holiness promoted by these laws. Though the specific rationale behind some of the commands (e.g., v. 19) may not be clear to a modern interpreter, the ethical commands of this chapter are not arbitrary but are based on the just, humane, and sensitive treatment of the aged, the handicapped, the poor, the resident alien, the laborer, and others. These commands even reach behind mere outward behavior to inward motivation (vv. 17-18). It is also noteworthy that the basic principles of the Ten Commandments are incorporated into chapter 19, though not in the same order and not always with the same emphasis.[1]

Scripture and our conscience explicitly tie our morality to the unchanging holy nature of God. Many in our post-modern society will reject the accountability of this statement, but Paul shows it to be true in

Romans 1 through 3; he thoroughly proves that all of humanity has fallen short of God's perfection, that is, His standard of holiness (Rom. 3:23). When Scripture speaks of God's character, there is an implied admonition to imitate Him – *"be holy."*

Honor Your Father and Mother (v. 3)

Moses commenced this set of warnings by affirming that children are to honor and obey their parents and that the Sabbath day was to be kept holy. Ultimately, the reverence for both commandments will be taught and observed in the home. If parents do not teach their children to respect God-ordained authority, they will, as adults, have little regard for law and order. Those who do not respect authority go their own way in life and suffer the harsh reality of an insubordinate spirit. Paul also quotes the fifth of the Ten Commandments in his epistle to the Ephesians and notes the promise associated with it:

> *Children, obey your parents in the Lord, for this is right. "Honor your father and mother," which is the first commandment with promise: "that it may be well with you and you may live long on the earth"* (Eph. 6:1-3).

A child not corrected would be socially miserable and a nuisance to society. His sinful ways and rebellious manner would probably lead him into an early grave. Samson, Absalom, and Eli's sons are examples of such. However, a child who practices obedience is much more likely to live a happy and prosperous life.

The Greek word translated "children" in Ephesians 6:1 is *teknon,* which means "that which is derived of another" (i.e., children are derived from their parents). Age is not implied, meaning that the application of the word is not limited to small children. A different Greek word, *paidion,* is used to speak of infants and small children. Therefore, children should always respect and honor their parents regardless of how old they are. Of course, when children marry and have children of their own, the new parents become accountable to do what is God-honoring and best for their own family. The stipulative phrase, *"in the Lord,"* implies children are to serve their parents as unto the Lord in matters of righteousness, but not in matters of sin. In the case of Korah, some of his sons refused to follow their father into rebellion and thus escaped the divine judgment which completely wiped out the rebels. They disobeyed their father in order to follow God's expressed will, which had been clearly shown to them.

Keep the Sabbath Day Holy (vv. 3-4)

Moses reiterates the second and fourth of the Ten Commandments in verse 4; idolatry was prohibited among God's people and the Jews were to keep the Sabbath day holy. This principle dates back to the creation of the world. God labored six days to create the heavens and the earth and then rested on the seventh day (Gen. 1:1-2:3). The key words in Genesis 2:1-3, the passage speaking of God's rest, are "seven" and "sanctified." The number seven is God's number and a fundamental building block throughout Scripture. God speaks of completeness or perfection through the number seven. The word "sanctified" means "set apart" or "holy." The week of creation ended with a day of rest for the Lord. This was a divine response, not to weariness, but to satisfaction (Isa. 40:28). Although God did not command mankind to keep the Sabbath at this time, He taught, through example, the principle of resting one day in seven.

The Mosaic Law decreed that the children of Israel "set apart" the seventh day as a day to rest and to worship God (Ex. 20:8-11, 23:10-12, 31:13-17). While Christ was ministering on earth, He reaffirmed nine of the Ten Commandments, but not the fourth one concerning keeping the Sabbath day holy. Neither did the apostles issue such a command to the Church. In fact, the early Church did not gather corporately on Saturday, but on Sunday: the first day of the week, Christ's resurrection day (1 Cor. 16:2; Acts 20:7). The believers gathered then to worship their Savior, not to keep the Law. This is why John refers to Sunday as the "Lord's day" (Rev. 1:10). Christians should regularly gather as a local church on Sunday for worship, prayer, mutual encouragement, and teaching (Acts 2:42; Heb. 13:10).

Peace Offerings (vv. 5-8)

Some of the regulations governing the peace offering, which were previously stated in Leviticus 3 and 17:3-9, are mentioned here again. Peace offerings were freewill offerings, but could not be eaten after the second day.

Loving Your Neighbor (vv. 9-14)

Landowners were to leave standing grain in the corners of their fields and the fallen clusters of grapes in their vineyards to be a provision for the poor (vv. 9-10). There was no spirit of entitlement in this edict; those who were in need would be required to glean fields and beat out the grain, and to scavenge for grapes to press into wine. Moreover, the eighth and ninth of Ten Commandments are referred to in verse 11: stealing, cheating, and lying against one's neighbor were forbidden. God's people were to show their reverence for Jehovah by demonstrating love and respect for each other, especially in their care for the blind, the deaf, and the handicapped (v. 14). Laborers were to be paid a fair and timely wage for their work (v. 13).

The offense of swearing by the name of Jehovah and rendering a false statement was particularly offensive to God (v. 12), as it brought disdain upon His name and broke the third of the Ten Commandments. The Jewish judicial system was to be impartial; both the poor and the mighty were to receive the same justice (v. 15). Slandering one's neighbor or plotting his demise was prohibited (v. 16); God's people were not to hold grudges or harbor hatred in their hearts towards each other (vv. 17-18). Rather, all exchanges between neighbors should be guided by a general rule: *"Love your neighbor as yourself"* (v. 18). This verse supplies a summation of the whole Law as it pertains to our interactions with others (Gal. 5:14). We should act towards others in the same way we would want to be treated by them. This meant that in some cases, the Jews should rebuke each other for matters of sin, but they were in no way to avenge themselves for personal offenses committed against them (i.e., they were not to take the Law into their own hands). Personal vendettas and mob action were an affront to God's justice.

While most of us do not live in a commune composed solely of God's people, as was the case with the Jewish nation when Moses delivered these commands, Paul does provide similar counsel to the believers at Rome in how to interact daily with humanity in general:

> *Repay no one evil for evil. Have regard for good things in the sight of all men. If it is possible, as much as depends on you, live peaceably with all men. Beloved, do not avenge yourselves, but rather give place to wrath; for it is written, "Vengeance is Mine, I will repay," says the Lord. Therefore "If your enemy is hungry, feed him; if he is thirsty,*

give him a drink." ... Do not be overcome by evil, but overcome evil with good (Rom. 12:17-21).

How should Christians treat their neighbors? In short, Christians are to be a giving and forgiving people (Matt. 18:21-22). We are to recall that, *"Love thinks no evil"* (1 Cor. 13:5). God is slow to anger, but quick to forgive and we should follow His example (Ps. 145:8).

Separation Demanded (v. 19)

Three examples of proper separation are given in verse 19. First, interbreeding among livestock was forbidden. For example, the Jews were not to breed a stud donkey with a mare horse to obtain a mule – this would add confusion to God's created order. Second, different kinds of seeds were not to be sown in the same field to prevent cross-pollination. Third, the Jewish garments were not to be made of a mix of wool and linen. Additionally, men and women were not to wear the same type of clothing (Deut. 22:5); however, everyone was to wear a fringe of blue as a badge of their identification with Jehovah (Num. 15:38). Obviously, this was not a moral issue, but it would serve as a daily reminder that holy Jehovah was a God of separation and the Jews were to be separate from other nations in their conduct and appearance.

In the spiritual sense, Paul conveys a similar message of holiness and separation to the believers at Corinth:

> *Do not be unequally yoked together with unbelievers. For what fellowship has righteousness with lawlessness? And what communion has light with darkness? And what accord has Christ with Belial? Or what part has a believer with an unbeliever? And what agreement has the temple of God with idols? For you are the temple of the living God. As God has said: "I will dwell in them and walk among them. I will be their God, and they shall be My people." Therefore "Come out from among them and be separate, says the Lord. Do not touch what is unclean, and I will receive you." "I will be a Father to you, and you shall be My sons and daughters, says the Lord Almighty"* (2 Cor. 6:14-18).

Being God's temple on earth should motivate every believer to depart from sin. To do so secures the Lord's blessed fellowship and care.

In summary, the appearance and customs of the Israelites were to mark them as a unique people. Their attire (which included a blue fringe), their food, their farming methods, their slaughtering of animals, their family structure, and their system of worship all declared that they were a peculiar people among the nations.

While the Church is not under such distinct particulars, the concepts of separation from evil and worldliness and maintaining a distinction between the genders are again upheld in the New Testament. James proclaims that worldliness is enmity with God (Jas. 4:4), and Paul reminds Christians to refrain from anything that even has the appearance of evil (1 Thess. 5:22).

In regards to the differences between men and women, the New Testament affirms it is natural for women to have longer hair than men (1 Cor. 11:14-15). Women are to cover their heads during times of spiritual exercise, such as prayer and teaching, while the men remain uncovered (1 Cor. 11:4-7). While women are attending to the visual ministry of the Church, men are to lead and engage in the audible ministry (1 Cor. 14:33-35; 1 Tim. 2:8, 11-12).

Through philosophy and deception, Satan works to confuse our minds as to the order that God has decreed for us. Just as the Israelites were not told all the "whys" for these unusual practices, neither is the Church; God just expects us to yield to and obey what He commands – thus marking us as the most peculiar people on earth!

Righteous Behavior Demanded (vv. 20-37)

The remaining portion of this chapter contains an assortment of regulations governing righteous behavior among God's people. If a man and a female slave betrothed to another man had sexual relations, both were to be scourged and the man was to pay damages to her owner and bring a trespass offering to the tabernacle (vv. 20-22). If the woman had been of free status, both the man and woman would have been put to death (20:10), unless it was a case of rape; then, only the man would be executed (Deut. 22:25).

Once in Canaan, the Jews were not to pick the fruit of the trees for three years. The fruit of the fourth year was dedicated to the Lord (and perhaps devoted to the Levites). The fruit of the fifth year could be harvested and eaten by all (vv. 23-25).

Other specific practices forbidden among God's covenant people included:

- Eating flesh in which the blood had not been properly drained (v. 26)
- Practicing witchcraft (v. 26)
- Men trimming their beards in accordance with pagan practices (v. 27)
- Cutting one's flesh as an expression of mourning; this was a pagan practice (v. 28)
- Marking one's body with tattoos, also a heathen burial custom (v. 28)
- Prostituting one's daughter (v. 29)
- Breaking the Sabbath day (v. 30)
- Consulting mediums or those with familiar spirits (v. 31)
- Dishonoring the elderly (v. 32)
- Not being kind to strangers or offering them hospitality (vv. 33-34)
- Dishonest business practices (vv. 35-37)

The reaffirmation of previously delivered commandments along with the administration of all these new statutes was for the purpose of denoting the Jews as a separated people. They were Jehovah's people and He was their God. He was holy and He demanded that they be holy also: *"You shall be holy, for I the Lord your God am holy"* (v. 2). The Jews should have gladly conformed to God's instructions, not just because it was the Law, but because they knew and loved the Lord. It is the same with Christians today! We should not merely obey the Lord to avoid being hurt by Him through chastening, but rather, our desire should be not to hurt the heart of God through willful disobedience.

Application

Jehovah is a holy God. To be associated with Him, His people must be holy too – as this chapter shows, the Law posed rigid stipulations for their worldly separation. Regardless of the various dispensational differences presented in Scripture, God's people in all ages have the same opportunity to demonstrate love for the Lord through obedience to

His commands and their willful consecration from the world. To do so may be inconvenient or uncomfortable, but it pleases the Lord and the benefits of His presence and communion are amply worth it! For example, consecrated believers are invited to *"come boldly to the throne of grace, that we may obtain mercy and find grace to help in time of need"* (Heb. 4:16). And James reminds us that *"the effective, fervent prayer of a **righteous** man avails much"* (Jas. 5:16). A powerful effectual prayer life is one of the rewards of living a consecrated life of faith.

Paul knew that real spiritual power was supplied through answered prayers; consequently, he instructed the saints at Thessalonica to *"pray without ceasing"* (1 Thess. 5:17) and the believers at Ephesus to pray always *"with all prayer and supplication in the Spirit, being watchful to this end with all perseverance and supplication for all the saints"* (Eph. 6:18). To his spiritual son Timothy, he exhorted that *"men pray everywhere, lifting up **holy hands**, without wrath and doubting"* (1 Tim. 2:8). God's people have the opportunity to lift their hands to God in prayer anytime and anywhere to ask for wisdom and grace for anybody in any situation. But our lifted hands must be holy (i.e. reflecting a pure heart), and we must pray without doubting and without wrath (no works of the flesh can be present). It is evident from the weak condition of the Church that much of our praying does not comply with these criteria. In the practical sense, unconfessed sin, wrong motives, or carnal intentions (Jas. 4:1-3) stagnate the flow of God's blessings into our lives.

Meditation

> Consecration is the narrow, lonely way to overflowing love. We are not called upon to live long on this planet, but we are called upon to be holy at any and every cost. If obedience costs you your life, then pay it.
>
> — Oswald Chambers

Condemned Behavior
Leviticus 20

This chapter levies harsh penalties for many of the prohibitions listed in the previous two chapters. Once guilt had been thoroughly established, the appropriate penalty for the crime was to be executed immediately. As Solomon notes, when justice is not swiftly enacted on the guilty, the idea of "free sin" gains a grip in the carnal nature of man: *"Because the sentence against an evil work is not executed speedily, therefore the heart of the sons of men is fully set in them to do evil"* (Eccl. 8:11). If people begin to think they will escape punishment for their crimes, they will sin more. When this ideology gains ground, the tenuous moral foundation of our society will speedily crumble away. Civil order, in every righteous sense, will eventually be lost. Accordingly, the Jewish judicial system was to be marked by impartiality, true testimonies, uncorrupted evidence, an appropriate retribution for the crime, and prompt punishment. There were to be no judicial appeals, no delays, no retrials, etc.

Anyone who sacrificed a child as a burnt offering to Molech was to be stoned (vv. 1-3). If the Jewish community failed to execute the lawbreaker, God would destroy not only the guilty, but also all those connected with him in the offense, including his family (vv. 4-5). Other crimes which demanded the death penalty included:

- Those who consulted mediums and familiar spirits (vv. 6, 27)
- Anyone who cursed his/her parents (v. 9)
- Anyone who committed adultery (v. 10)
- A man who committed incest with his father's wife or his daughter-in-law, and the woman in question – this was not a situation of rape (vv. 11-12)
- Those who engaged in homosexual activities (v. 13)

- A man who married both a woman and her mother – all three were to be burned (v. 14)
- Anyone who had sexual perversions with animals – the animal was to be destroyed as well (vv. 15-16)

Other sexual perversions carried a lesser penalty:
- If a man had intercourse with his sister or half-sister they were to be excommunicated (v. 17).
- If a man *knowingly* had intercourse with a menstruating woman, they were to be excommunicated (v. 18).
- If a man had sexual relations with his aunt, it is stated that God would judge them, but no specifics are given (v. 19).
- If a man had sexual relations with his uncle's wife or his sister-in-law, they would die childless (vv. 20-21).

For the last situation, it is noted that this law only applied as long as the brother was alive. If he died without a son, his brother was bound to marry his sister-in-law (the widow) and name their first son after the deceased (Deut. 25:5). Such marital unions were called levirate marriages and were necessary to ensure that family inheritances, such as land, were passed down to the next generation.

An Exhortation to Holiness

Twice in this chapter, which pronounces judgment on sexual perversions and religious sins, God exhorts His people to holiness (vv. 7-8, 22-26). God had chosen the Jews to be a distinct people living among the nations and, thus, the Jews were not to follow the world's pattern of life (vv. 23-24). Even what the Jews touched and ate marked them as a peculiar people (v. 25). They were to be holy people because their God was, and is, holy (v. 26).

Egypt and Canaan each had their pagan practices and opinions, but Israel was to think as God did on every issue of life – their opinions and practices must conform to God's Word:

You shall observe My judgments and keep My ordinances, to walk in them: I am the Lord your God (Lev. 18:4).

Therefore you shall keep My ordinance, so that you do not commit any of these abominable customs which were committed before you, and that you do not defile yourselves by them: I am the LORD your God (Lev. 18:30).

There are occasions in life in which our flesh either yearns for that which is prohibited by God's Word or that it loathes to do something God's Word commands us to do. Dear believer, at such times just yield to the Lord; it may not make sense to do so and it may cost you to do so, but it will be best for you to do so. God is honored in such a decision and we will reap His blessing in accordance with His sovereign plan. C. H. Mackintosh encourages us to get a clear and practical sense of this truth:

> The word of God must settle every question and govern every conscience. There must be no appeal from its solemn and weighty decision. When God speaks, every heart must bow. Men may form and hold their opinions; they may adopt and defend their practices; but one of the finest traits in the character of "the Israel of God" is profound reverence for, and implicit subjection to, "every word that proceeds out of the mouth of the Lord." The exhibition of this valuable feature may, perhaps, lay them open to the charge of dogmatism, superciliousness, and self-sufficiency, on the part of those who have never duly weighed the matter; but, in truth, nothing can be more unlike dogmatism than simple subjection to the plain truth of God; nothing more unlike superciliousness than reverence for the statements of inspiration; nothing more unlike self-sufficiency than subjection to the divine authority of holy Scripture.[1]

If God's Word requires us to do something – just do it! If God's Word prohibits us from doing something – do not do it! The human nature longs for wiggle-room to assert itself against God's revealed will for our lives. We should not be guilty of searching for loopholes around God's expressed prohibitions or even probing the outer boundaries of what might be permissible, just to see if God loves us enough to lift His chastening hand. It should be the desire of every true believer to be in the center of His will: only there does our conscience enjoy peace and we obtain God's full blessing.

Application

The exhortations to godly living and the severe consequences for failing to do so contained in this section of Leviticus prove to us that there is no deception, no secret sin, no immoral act, no impurity of any kind that is compatible with God's character: *"God is light, and in Him is no darkness at all"* (1 Jn. 1:5). The Lord will not, in fact cannot, have any part in our sin. John continues: *"If we say that we have fellowship with Him, and walk in darkness, we lie and do not practice the truth. But if we walk in the light as He is in the light, we have fellowship with one another, and the blood of Jesus Christ His Son cleanses us from all sin"* (1 Jn. 1:6-7). If we want to enjoy communion with God, we must choose the lighted pathway of holiness to reverently venture into the wonders of His presence. He cannot defy His pure character by entering the darkness of sin when we choose to reside there – we must through repentance come out and stand again in the light of His righteousness.

The child of God is to constantly discern between what is holy and what is evil, between what is wise and what is foolish. That which is holy and wise should be obeyed, and that which is evil and foolish should be shunned. As a believer relies on God's grace to accomplish holy living, the victory is won through Christ, and the devices of Satan are spoiled. God's will for the believer is that he or she should refrain from doing sin, and that he or she should indeed practice a sin-free life altogether (1 Jn. 2:1). However, on this side of glory, sinless perfection is a pursuit, not a reality – thank God our salvation is not based on our doings, but upon His grace. And praise be to God, our new nature received at conversion cannot sin and enables us to pursue after righteousness rather than to be controlled by our old nature (1 Jn. 3:9). Let us all pursue holiness, for in holiness we find not the inability to sin, but the ability not to sin.

Meditation

Believers compose the household of God, His living temple on earth to shine forth His virtue; God forbid that we disdain His name before the nations. Charles Spurgeon forcibly conveys this point as he addresses professing Christians:

> Professor! Is sin subdued in you? If your life is unholy, your heart is unchanged, and if your heart is unchanged, you are an unsaved person.

If the Savior has not sanctified you, renewed you, given you a hatred of sin and a love of holiness, He has done nothing in you of a saving character. The grace which does not make a man better than others is a worthless counterfeit. Christ saves His people, not in their sins, but from them. "Without holiness no man shall see the Lord." *"Let everyone that names the name of Christ depart from iniquity."* If not saved from sin, how shall we hope to be counted among His people? Lord, save me now from all evil, and enable me to honor my Saviour.[2]

Priestly Regulations
Leviticus 21-22

Leviticus 21 and 22, along with chapters 16 and 17, are directly addressed to Aaron and his sons, the priests. The high priest was the sole person anointed to represent the people to God and effect atonement for the nation, though all of the priests offered worship on behalf of the nation. It was of the utmost importance, then, that the priests be fit for the office and remain ceremonially clean to the greatest extent feasibly possible.

According to the Law, anyone who touched something dead became ritually defiled until that evening (11:24-40). Anyone who touched a dead *person*, or even entered the tent of the dead, would be ceremonially unclean for seven days (Num. 19:14-16). If a priest, he would be disqualified from serving in the tabernacle during this time. Hence, criteria were needed for when contact with a corpse of a deceased person was permissible (21:1-6). In short, the priests were only allowed to be defiled for the death of a close relative. This meant they could not personally grieve with or comfort the families of friends who had suffered the loss of a loved one. The priests (and all Israelites, for that matter) were also to refrain from the heathen practice of cutting or marring one's body to express grief while mourning the dead (21:5). Leviticus 21:6 explains why these restrictions were necessary for the priests:

> *They shall be holy to their God and not profane the name of their God, for they offer the offerings of the Lord made by fire, and the bread of their God; therefore they shall be holy.*

They had a special office and a ministry to perform; therefore, it was crucial for them to remain undefiled in order to perform it. Their high office required holiness and ceremonial cleanliness to the fullest extent possible. Paul's charge to the Corinthians captures the same sense of urgency: *"Dearly beloved, let us cleanse ourselves from all filthiness of the flesh and spirit, perfecting holiness in the fear of God"* (2 Cor. 7:1). As believer-priests in the Church Age, we should desire to be as holy as a redeemed sinner can be.

The prominent duties of the priestly office also necessitated high morality in his home life. A priest was not to marry a harlot or a divorced woman, but he could marry a widow (21:6-7). If a priest's daughter engaged in harlotry (which was a common practice in pagan societies), she was to be burned to death (21:9). The requirement for a priest to be blameless in his household is paralleled in the New Testament requirements for church leadership (1 Tim. 3; Tit. 1). Priests, of Old and New Testament times, were to represent the Lord's character not only in their ministry, but in all aspects of their lives.

It is for this reason an even more restrictive standard of conduct was imposed on the high priest. For example, he was not permitted to depart from his ministry to show respect for the dead or to leave his ministry to mourn with the grieving, even if the deceased were his own parents (21:11). He was also not permitted to tear his priestly clothes or uncover his head, which were customary practices to show remorse for the dead (21:10). He was only permitted to marry a virgin, whereas an ordinary priest could marry a widow (21:13). This was a necessary restriction because the son of the high priest could potentially be the next high priest. Thus, any child his wife bore to him must be unquestionably his, and not that of her previous husband. This precaution protected the priestly lineage which must extend down from Aaron (21:15). Because the high priest was anointed with holy oil, his home and married life were to be above reproach and a holy example for others to follow (21:12).

The remaining portion of chapter 21 confirms that not only did a man need to be a descendant of Aaron to qualify for priestly ministry, but he must also be physically fit for service (21:21). This meant he could not have abnormalities in his features such as blindness, lameness, or deafness; even a disfigured nose, a crooked back, and unusual shortness were disqualifications (21:18, 20). Some disqualifications might be short term versus absolute disqualifications, such as a broken foot or hand, scurvy, an icy scab, or injured testicles (21:19-20). Such an intricate scrutiny of each priest reminds us of Paul's warning for believers to examine themselves before eating the bread and drinking the wine at the Lord's Supper (1 Cor. 11:27-28), lest they suffer God's chastening hand. L. M Grant suggests if one has a question about being defiled, it is best not to partake in the obligations of a spiritual person, but rather to get right with the Lord first:

> Often now a person may intuitively realize that his moral or spiritual condition is such that he ought to avoid any handling of spiritual things. If we are in an unclean moral state, how much better is this avoidance than any hypocritical pretense of religious observance! At least the person will realize the need of being cleansed.[1]

While this is true, obviously the best course of action would be to confess what is known to be sin, to be cleansed of it, and then to participate in the Lord's Supper as commanded – *"so let him eat."* The Levitical priests who were disqualified for physical reasons were still permitted to eat the food of the priests (e.g., the holy bread), but were not to perform any official functions in the tabernacle (21:22-23).

Chapter 22 is an addendum to the previous chapter. If a priest did become ceremonially unclean for any reason (e.g., contact with something dead or a leper), he was not permitted to partake of the holy food in the tabernacle. No unclean person was permitted in the tabernacle at any time. A defiled priest was to follow the law of separation and perform what was necessary to become clean again; in most cases this only required him to bathe, wash his clothes, and wait until evening (22:1-9).

Strangers, visitors, and hired servants were not permitted to eat the holy food of the priest; it was only for them and their families. However, a slave purchased by a priest and the slave's family were also permitted to eat of it. If a daughter of a priest married a man who was not from the tribe of Levi, she was not allowed to eat of the priest's food. A daughter who was widowed or divorced and did not have children and resided in her father's house could share in the holy food (22:10-13).

Anyone who unintentionally ate the holy food designated for priests could make restitution by replacing what had been eaten plus a fifth (22:14-16). This was consistent with the regulations of the trespass offering previously mentioned in Leviticus 5 and 6.

Not only were the offering priests required to be without blemish, but all animals brought to the tabernacle for sacrifice had to be acceptable also (22:17-21). No disfigured, disabled, or diseased animal was suitable for sacrifice (22:22). The following disqualified animals from being offered, even if presented by strangers as a gift (22:25): overgrown or stunted limbs (22:23); damaged or removed reproductive organs (22:24); extreme immaturity – an animal less than eight days old (22:26-27). Also, a mother and her young could not be sacrificed on the same day (22:28).

Next, the Jews were again reminded that the meat from a peace offering (a sacrifice given in thanksgiving) had to be eaten on the same day it was sacrificed (22:29-30). In the final verses of chapter 22, the Lord explains the motivation for the priests to perform all these commandments:

You shall not profane My holy name, but I will be hallowed among the children of Israel. I am the Lord who sanctifies you, who brought you out of the land of Egypt, to be your God: I am the Lord (Lev. 22:32-33).

As believer-priests in the Body of Christ, we too do not want to profane God's name and we should ever be mindful of the ministry that we have been sanctified in Christ to perform. C. H. Mackintosh reminds us that this priestly ministry of praise and worship was not obtained by our choosing, but rather was an outcome of our spiritual birth. Thus, to honor the Lord is our priestly duty and privilege:

[Believers] are members of the true priestly house over which our Great High Priest presides, and to which all true believers belong (Heb. 3:6). Every child of God is a priest. He is enrolled as a member of Christ's priestly house. He may be very ignorant; but his position, as a priest, is not founded upon knowledge, but upon life. His experience may be very shallow; but his place as a priest does not depend upon experience, but upon life. His capacity may be very limited; but his relationship as a priest does not rest upon an enlarged capacity, but upon life. He was born into the position and relationship of a priest. He did not work himself thereunto. It was not by any efforts of his own that he became a priest. He became a priest by birth. The spiritual priesthood, together with all the spiritual functions attaching thereunto, is the necessary appendage to spiritual birth. The capacity to enjoy the privileges and to discharge the functions of a position must not be confounded with the position itself. They must ever be kept distinct. Relationship is one thing; capacity is quite another.[2]

May believers never forget who they are in Christ, and the important priestly ministry in which they are to joyfully and faithfully engage. Let us also remember that whatever we do for Christ does not define our value to Him or to each other – all true believers are "beloved brethren" and fully accepted in the Lord (Matt. 23:8; Eph. 1:6)!

Application

As previously discussed, some commandments of God we know are morally right, while other decrees are right solely because they are divinely commanded. Much, if not all, of the content of these two chapters corresponds with the latter category. For these and similar ordinances, the practical application for us is to learn submission through obedience to what we do not fully understand. Often God presents us with something that is significant to Him through a command which we do not perceive as valuable. God does not need to explain Himself to be obeyed; in fact, the lack of exposition imposes a grander test of our faithfulness.

If we truly believe God is holy and His ways are above our ways, then it stands to reason we will not fully understand all He commands. If we did understand the reasons for such things, there would be no room for biblical faith to be exercised, that is, *"the substance of things hoped for, the evidence of things not seen"* (Heb. 11:1). And we can only please God by expressing that kind of faith, that is, faith that reaches beyond the power of senses and reason to firmly grip God's Word (Heb. 11:6). Nurturing this kind of personal faith will enable the believer to endure persecution and trials with enduring hope, especially when life's affairs are disorienting. Having a predetermined disposition to trust what is eternal and unchangeable, namely, God's faithfulness, will deliver us from the grip of despair.

Meditation

Faith for my deliverance is not faith in God. Faith means, whether I am visibly delivered or not, I will stick to my belief that God is love. There are some things only learned in a fiery furnace. ... Faith is deliberate confidence in the character of God whose ways you cannot understand at the time.

— Oswald Chambers

The Spring Feasts of Jehovah
Leviticus 23:1-22

We are not told why the Lord instituted His feasts. Certainly, routine observances such as annual feasts, the redemption of the firstborn (of man and beast), annual tithes, and the Sabbath day would remind the Jews of God's goodness to them. Perhaps such regular observances were to protect them from wandering affections. All of these regulations are first introduced in Exodus, but further expounded here in Leviticus. For example, instructions concerning the Feasts of Jehovah (v. 2) were initially provided in Exodus 34, but more detail on the subject matter is given in this chapter.

Every Jewish male was required to present himself before Jehovah three times a year at The Feast of Unleavened Bread, The Feast of Weeks, and The Feast of Ingathering (Ex. 34:18-23). In all, seven feasts were to be observed: Passover, Unleavened Bread, Firstfruits, Weeks (Pentecost), Trumpets, Day of Atonement, and Tabernacles. The first three feasts ran together in the spring, Pentecost followed fifty days afterwards, and the three remaining feasts were separated by only a few days in the fall. Each feast was to be a *"holy convocation"* or, literally, a "sacred calling together" before the Lord. Like the Sabbath day, these feast days were set aside solely for Jehovah; it was a time for worship and reflection, not for labor (vv. 2-3).

The feasts were to be observed *"before the Lord,"* which initially meant at the tabernacle, but later at the temple in Jerusalem. Each of the three seasons of festivals was tied to the Jewish agricultural calendar. The Feast of Unleavened Bread occurred in the March and April timeframe and related to the barley harvest. The Feast of Weeks occurred during the wheat harvest (about seven weeks after the barley was reaped) and marked the end of the spring harvest time. The Feast of Weeks is also referred to as Pentecost (Acts 2:1, 20:16), the Day of Firstfruits (Num. 28:26), and The Feast of Harvest (Ex. 23:16). The Feast of

Ingathering, also known as The Feast of Tabernacles, occurred at the end of the agricultural year in September or October.

Summary of the Spring Feasts

These feasts were celebrations of the Lord's goodness, and each provided the Jews with the opportunity to offer back to God a portion of what they had received from Him. In keeping the feasts, the Jews would acknowledge both their dependence upon God and that He was their source of blessing. Thus, they would reaffirm year by year, feast by feast, that they belonged to the Lord. Not only would the feasts of Jehovah continually remind the Jews of God's faithfulness to bless them, but from an eschatological standpoint these seven feasts provide a prophetic outline of God's future dealings with the nation of Israel.

Passover

The Passover Feast and The Feast of Unleavened Bread were both instituted in Exodus 12. The annual Passover Feast was to remind the Israelites of their deliverance from Egypt and their restoration to Jehovah through redemption. Through the sacrifice of an innocent substitute (a yearly male lamb without blemish) and the application of its blood, the firstborn of each house was saved from the tenth plague. But beyond this, the entire Jewish nation obtained a new beginning and a new life with God at this time. The Hebrew calendar was to align itself with this event marking *"the beginning of months"* (Ex. 12:2); Passover was held on the fourteenth day of the first month in the Jewish calendar.

Though a lamb would be sacrificed for each household during Passover, the language throughout Exodus 12 specifically states that from God's perspective, there was one specific lamb that would be sacrificed by and for the entire nation: *"Then the whole assembly of the congregation of Israel shall **kill it** at twilight"* (Ex. 12:6). Though the Jews slaughtered thousands of lambs at twilight, the specific command was to kill the *Passover* – a single sacrifice was in view (Ex. 12:6, 11, 21, 27). The lamb was to be roasted with fire and whatever was not eaten was to be completely burned; it was completely consumed in judgment. Unmistakably, Jehovah was preparing the nation of Israel for the coming of the Lamb of God, whom they collectively would nail to a cross. While hanging from a cross, He, the sacrifice, completely consumed the fire (God's wrath) for human sin.

Besides the lamb, the Passover meal included unleavened bread and bitter herbs. The unleavened bread spoke of the urgency of the forthcoming journey out of Egypt; there was no time to properly prepare leavened bread. The imminent expectation of deliverance flavored the entire feast; its participants were to have their loins girded, their shoes on, and their staffs in hand. Everyone was to be ready to go! The bitter herbs represented the bitterness of Jewish bondage in Egypt. Bitterness on the earth resulted from the fall of humanity in the Garden of Eden.

The Passover meal year by year would serve as a memorial feast of what God had accomplished through blood redemption in Egypt; however, it has its culmination in the ultimate redemptive work of God at Calvary. The Lord Jesus instituted the Lord's Supper just hours before His death to commemorate in the hearts of believers for centuries to come what He would accomplish through the sacrifice of Himself (Luke 22:19-20). The Passover Feast then pictures Christ on the cross; this was the day the Passover lambs were slain and was also the day when the Lamb of God was slain for the sins of the world (1 Cor. 5:7).

Unleavened Bread

The Passover Feast was to be held the fourteenth of the first month, The Feast of Unleavened Bread on the fifteenth day, and The Feast of Firstfruits on the following day (v. 6). The Feast of Unleavened Bread was to last seven days, meaning the total duration of the first three spring feasts was to be eight days (v. 8). Only unleavened bread was eaten on the night of the Passover, but a further restriction was observed during the following seven days of The Feast of Unleavened Bread; there was not to be any leaven in any of the Jewish homes (Ex. 12:15, 19). Leaven is alive and as previously noted, in Scripture it speaks of sin, a corruptive influence, or evil doctrine (Matt. 13:33; 1 Cor. 5:8).

Though the Israelites had been immersed in a pagan culture when they were in Egypt and would find themselves in a similar circumstance in Canaan, its filth and corruption were not to be found in their homes. Though they were in the world, they were not to be of the world. In a later tradition, Jewish parents actually hid leaven in their homes so that their children could search it out and sweep it out of the house before The Feast of Unleavened Bread commenced. The Feast of Unleavened Bread speaks of Christ in the grave the day after Passover; like the unleavened bread,

Christ's body had neither life while in the grave nor had it been previously influenced by sin (i.e., Christ lived an unleavened life).

Firstfruits
The first fruit offering was to be presented before the Lord in baskets each spring. The first gleanings (the best part) of the barley harvest were to be brought to the temple. A priest would then wave a sheaf of it before the Lord as an acknowledgement that He was the Lord of the entire harvest (v. 10). This grain was for the priests who continually served in the temple. The wave sheaf ceremony was to occur on the sixteenth day of the first month; this was the day after The Feast of Unleavened Bread began (v. 11). It was to be accompanied by a burnt offering of a yearling male lamb without blemish, a double-portion meal offering, and a drink offering of wine (vv. 12-13). The Jews were not allowed to personally partake of the barley harvest until after these offerings were presented before the Lord (v. 14).

As in the meal offering of Leviticus 2, the fine flour of the offering speaks of the superb moral character of Christ, and its lack of leaven typifies Christ's sinless and impeccable nature. The oil on the bread pictures the infusing power and communion of the Holy Spirit during the Lord's earthly ministry. The wave sheaf, which represents the resurrected Lord Jesus, was not to be burned on the altar. Having completed the propitiatory work of Calvary, the Lord Jesus will never suffer the wrath of God again for human sin. In fact, the wave sheaf would become part of the leavened wave loaves presented before the Lord at The Feast of Pentecost. This symbolizes the union of the resurrected Christ with Jewish believers on the day of Pentecost to form that mysterious spiritual body called the Church (2:12, 23:9-14; Acts 2).

The Lord Jesus declared that He is *"the resurrection and the life"* (John 11:25). Paul proclaimed Christ was the firstfruits from the dead; He is the first man to have experienced glorification, but a harvest of faithful souls is yet to follow (1 Cor. 15:20). In this respect, Christ was the wave sheaf; the full harvest is yet to come. The hope of resurrection is the "blessed hope" for every true believer (Titus 2:13).

Pentecost

The Feast of Weeks occurred seven weeks and one day (i.e., 50 days) after the waving of the barley before the Lord. This celebration occurred towards the end of the wheat harvest in late spring or early summer.

The sacrifices for The Feast of Pentecost, in addition to the daily sacrifices, included: two young bullocks, one ram, and seven yearly lambs for a burnt offering, one kid of the goats for a sin offering, and two yearly lambs for a peace offering (vv. 18-19; Num. 28:26-31). These were to be accompanied by a meal offering, which will be explained momentarily, and a drink offering (v. 18).

Of these required offerings, the meal offering is the most unusual: two leavened loaves composed of ground grain from the recent wheat harvest (vv. 16-17). While portions of other unleavened meal offerings were burnt on the Bronze Altar, nothing with leaven could be offered to the Lord in this way (2:11). The two wave loaves were to be waved before the Lord and then eaten by the priests (v. 20).

This was the only time throughout the entire year that leavened bread was presented to the Lord. Although not specifically stated, it is assumed that oil was mixed into the leavened dough before baking, as all meal offerings were to be anointed with oil before being burned on the altar, or to have oil mixed within before they were baked (2:1-16). As discussed previously, the olive oil is a symbol of the Holy Spirit, but what is the significance of the leaven in the meal offering, especially since leaven represents an evil influence? Perhaps understanding more about how the dough was leavened before being baked will be helpful in answering this question. L. Duane Lindsey describes the process:

> The bread was leavened by placing in the dough a lump of leaven (i.e., sourdough) from bread of the preceding barley harvest, thus reemphasizing the close connection between the barley and the wheat harvest, and the festivals associated with them.[1]

Recall that the resurrected Lord Jesus was represented in the barley wave sheaf at The Feast of Firstfruits. The grain from this sheaf was later ground and used to create sourdough. Fifty days later, a lump of the barley sourdough was placed into the freshly ground wheat flour to create the two wave loaves, thus, the wave sheaf and the wheat harvest that followed are connected in the two loaves. Obviously there is no leaven in Christ, the Wave Sheaf, but believers united with Him (the Church) still have a leavened nature within them. L. M. Grant further explains the symbolism of this unique meal offering of the two loaves.

> The two wave loaves picture the acceptance of both Jewish and Gentile believers, who are seen in 1 Corinthians 12:13 to be joined together in one body by *"the baptism of the Spirit."* As the waving of the sheaf of firstfruits is typical of the ascension of the Lord Jesus to heaven, so the waving of the two loaves pictures the Church as being *"raised up together"* and made to *"sit together in the heavenly places in Christ"* (Eph. 2:6). This could not be applied to Israel, for Israel is God's earthly people, but the Church is identified today with Christ in heaven. Wonderful grace!

> These wave loaves are said to be "the firstfruits to the Lord." This does not contradict the fact that the wave sheaf (offered 50 days earlier) was the sheaf of firstfruits, typical only of Christ raised and glorified. From this viewpoint Christ stands alone. But when the people are considered, the firstfruits from among mankind focuses upon the Church, which is the first result of the work of Christ. So James 1:18 tells us, "Of His own will He brought us forth by the word of truth, that we might be a kind of firstfruits of His creatures." This has taken place before the general harvest which will involve Israel and the nations.[2]

C. H Mackintosh also affirms the two leavened loaves waved before the Lord symbolically represent the acceptance of all believers, that is, the Church, in Christ before God:

> Thus, on the day of Pentecost, the church was presented, in all the value and excellency of Christ, through the power of the Holy Ghost. Though having in itself the leaven of the old nature, that leaven was not reckoned, because the divine Sin Offering had perfectly answered for it. The power of the Holy Ghost did not remove the leaven, but the blood of the Lamb had atoned for it. This is a most interesting and important distinction. The work of the Spirit in the believer does not remove indwelling evil. It enables him to detect, judge, and subdue the evil; but no amount of spiritual power can do away with the fact that the evil is there — though, blessed be God, the conscience is at perfect ease, inasmuch as the blood of our Sin Offering has eternally settled the whole question; and, therefore, instead of our evil being under the eye of God, it has been put out of sight forever, and we are accepted in all

the acceptableness of Christ, who offered Himself to God as a sweet-smelling sacrifice, that He might perfectly glorify Him in all things, and be the food of His people forever.[3]

The two wave loaves represent the spiritual body of the Church composed of both Jews and Gentiles. The Law imposed a wall between these two groups, but the efficacious work of Christ has pulled down that barrier and eternally united them in the bonds of divine love and peace (Eph. 2:14-16). This explains why only burnt offerings were required at The Feast of Firstfruits, but a sin offering (one kid of the goats) and a peace offering (two yearling lambs) had to be presented at Pentecost. As this feast pictures the acceptance of all believers in Christ, a sin offering of the substitutionary goat was imperative. Since the peace offering typifies the fellowship of believers with God through the Lord Jesus Christ, the two lambs had to be offered also.

As The Feast of Firstfruits speaks of the Lord Jesus being alone in His resurrection and ascension, only a burnt offering was required to show God's acceptance of all that had been accomplished. But Pentecost, as seen in Acts 2, involves the blessing and acceptance of those whom the Lord calls His "beloved" and His "brethren" – His Church (2 Thess. 2:13; Heb. 2:1).

Application

Three points of application are suggested:

First, the fine flour of the wave sheaf (Christ), the oil (the Holy Spirit Himself), the grain from the wheat harvest (redeemed sinners), and the heat of the oven are all used to produce two wave loaves which are presented before the Lord. The invisible heat of the oven, which nullifies the influence of the leaven within the dough, corresponds to the power of the Holy Spirit to mortify our sinful impulses (Rom. 8:13). This allows believers to offer themselves as acceptable living sacrifices to God. Jehovah appreciated the loaves waved before Him, even though leaven was present within them – this reality should be encouraging to all God's children. Though we all are still in the flesh, positionally speaking, God does not see us that way (Rom. 8:9). The application is clear; as believer-priests in the Church Age are controlled by the Holy Spirit, the high moral character of Christ is exhibited and ascends to God as a living sacrifice (Rom. 12:1). May we be God-fearing, Christ-loving, Bible-believing, Spirit-controlled Christians who remind everyone of the Lord Jesus!

Second, the two leavened wave loaves picture Jew and Gentile becoming one in Christ, that is the Church (Eph. 2:11-22). The two leavened loaves then represent all redeemed sinners since Pentecost (i.e., all who have trusted the gospel message of Jesus Christ). Yet, all believers live with the presence of leaven, our nature inherited from Adam. Despite the corruption within, we, as believers, have been sanctified in Christ and enabled to glorify God in Christ through the power of the Holy Spirit. In practice, the Church has many spots, but positionally speaking, She will never suffer the flames of the altar – God's wrath. Rather, Christ in His Church is waved before and presented to God unto the praise of His Glory! This is one of many pictures of a Pre-tribulation rapture of the Church in the Old Testament. Believers have a "blessed hope" in Christ; let us therefore press on with watchful endurance; today may be the day of His return and our eternal gathering unto Him (1 Thess. 4:13-18; Tit. 2:13; 1 Jn. 3:2-3).

Third, when Christ walked upon the earth, the Jews had been without their own king for more than six centuries. Four different Gentile empires had ruled over them during that time, most of them cruelly. The Jews longed to be liberated from Roman oppression and to be a self-governing nation again. The prophesied Messiah was desired as a means to fulfill this political ideology, but in a spiritual sense the heart of the people had drifted far from God through the centuries. The *"feasts of Jehovah"* had become the *"feasts of the Jews"* (John 5:1, 6:4). The legalistic traditions of the Pharisees harshly controlled the people and perverted the teachings of the Mosaic Law. For example, their oral laws deemed it wrong to serve others or to do good deeds on the Sabbath day, and upheld that it was more honorable to give money to God than to use it for the proper care of aged parents. So, when their long-awaited Jewish Messiah did arrive, His message of repentance and spiritual transformation was not only unwelcome but also flatly rejected – it was not what the Jews wanted, though it was exactly what they needed. In this darkened spiritual state, they even loathed the works of mercy the Lord performed on the Sabbath.

As a final point of application, may the Church, who is waiting for the coming of the Lord Jesus Christ, not repeat the error of the Jewish nation who removed their coming Messiah from their plans and inserted a religious ideology, legalism, in His place! The writer of Hebrews reminds us: *"For yet a little while, and He who is coming will come and will not tarry. Now the just shall live by faith; but if anyone draws back, My soul has no pleasure in him"* (Heb. 10:37-38). The world is evil and growing more so as the number of unregenerate sinners inhabiting this planet increases each day. Many of God's people are suffering terribly worldwide, but yet the Lord has not returned for His Church. Beloved, He is coming and His return is imminent. The Church must suffer the heat of the oven to be honorably represented before the Lord, but she will never be burned on the altar; She will never experience the flaming judgment of God's wrath that will come upon the entire world during the Tribulation Period (1 Thess. 1:10, 5:9; Rev. 3:10). Let us watch and wait for Him with patience – He is coming!

Meditation

O child of God, there is for thee
A hope that shines amid the gloom,
A gladsome hope that thou shalt see
Thy Lord, for He will surely come.

Exalted now to Heaven's throne,
The Savior there of sinful men;
His loving heart yearns over His own,
And for them He will come again.

Then joy unmingled will be thine,
Earth's tears and trials all forgot;
So cheer thy heart, no more repine,
His word is sure: He'll tarry not.

— Thomas D. W. Muir

The Fall Feasts of Jehovah
Leviticus 23:23-44

Seven annual feasts were to be observed by the Jews: Passover, Unleavened Bread, Firstfruits, Harvest (Pentecost), Trumpets, Day of Atonement, and Tabernacles. The first three feasts ran together in early springtime, Pentecost occurred fifty days after the Firstfruits observance, and the three remaining feasts were separated by only a few days in the beginning of autumn (this would normally correspond to our month of September). This created a long interim between these and the spring feasts, which typify Christ's death (Passover), burial (Unleavened Bread), resurrection (Firstfruits), and the creation of the Church (Pentecost).

From a prophetic viewpoint, the gap between the spring and fall festivals pictures the Church Age, and the fall feasts themselves God's future dealings to restore a remnant of Israel to Himself. These include The Feast of Trumpets, The Day of Atonement, and The Feast of Tabernacles, and collectively these became known as "the High Holy Days," and mark the conclusion of the religious year (i.e., there were no more biblical feasts until Passover the following spring).

Moses directed that The Feast of Trumpets should be observed on the first day of the seventh month; however, sometime after the Babylonian exile the Jews began to commemorate this feast on the first day of Tishri; Tishri is the first month of the Babylonian calendar. Over time the Jews adopted the Babylonian calendar, including the Babylonian names for the months of the year in association with the Feasts of Jehovah. Thus, the first day of the seventh month became known as the first day of Tishri and The Feasts of Trumpets soon was referred to as *Rosh Hashanah*, which literally means "the head of the months." In fact, today the Jews continue to celebrate The Feast of Trumpets as a New Year festival; this means Passover no long marks the start of the Jewish calendar as God intended. It is noted the ancient rabbis believed God initiated the creation of the world on this very day. This celebration began a period of time known as the "Ten Days of Repentance," a time of personal reflection, leading up to *Yom Kippur*, the Day of Atonement.

Summary of the Fall Feasts

Trumpets

The feast is not specifically titled in Scripture, but is identified by the phrases *"a memorial of blowing of trumpets"* (v. 24) and *"a day of blowing the trumpets"* (Num. 29:1). Since the blowing of the trumpets became the distinguishing characteristic of the day, it became known as The Feast of the Trumpets. Scriptural reasons were provided for the other feasts, but not so for this one. Other than that a memorial sounding of the trumpets was to occur and that it was a holy convocation, no details are provided in Leviticus 23, and even the types of burnt offerings are not specified. However, Numbers 29:1-3 provides more information about the offerings to be sacrificed at this feast: a young bullock, a ram, and seven young lambs were to be offered as burnt offerings; each group of animals was to be presented on the altar with a meal offering and drink offering. A kid from the goats was also to be offered as a sin offering. Jewish tradition considered this feast to be a preparatory call of the people to stand before God in judgment, which would occur ten days later on the Day of Atonement.

Another mysterious aspect of this feast is that the text does not specifically state what is to pierce the silence of this special day. The Hebrew word *teruah* is translated "blowing of trumpets" in both Leviticus 23:24 (where *teruah* first appears in Scripture) and Numbers 29:1. *Teruah* literally means "a clamor" and by implication "an acclamation of joy," "a loud noise," or "an alarm." The word is tied with the sounding of a silver trumpet as an alarm in Numbers 10:5-6, and the blowing of a ram's horn, the *showphar,* in the year of Jubilee (Lev. 25:9). It is also used to speak of "a shout of joy" by people (Ezra 3:11-13), the noise of musical instruments (Ps. 33:3), and even the clang of a cymbal (Ps. 105:5). In summary, the exact meaning of *teruah* is indeed indefinite and what was to initiate the joyful clamor unknown.

The Septuagint attempts to clarify what was blown by adding the Greek word *salpiggon* or "of trumpets" to Leviticus 23:24. When combined with *keratine*, which means "made of horn," the Septuagint always refers to the *shophar*, the ram's horn. The other horn referred to in Scripture is the *hacocerah* (i.e., "metal kind"), which was a long, straight, slender, silver trumpet (clarion). It was used by the priests in several applications: to assemble the congregation, to orderly move the Israelite encampment, to sound an alarm, to signal warfare, and to blow over offerings and newly anointed kings (Num. 10:1-10; 1 Kgs. 1:34). All this to say, we are not told the specifics of "the clamoring" that was heard on this feast day. Jewish tradition favors the *shophar,* but in reality, all that is practiced presently during The Feasts of Trumps is developed tradition.

Today, a series of one hundred *shophar* blasts, consisting of four different types of tones and various repetitions, is sounded to announce the convening of God's courtroom of judgment. The final blast is a longer and louder unbroken sound, *Tekiah Gedolah*, which supposedly signals a final invitation before *Yom Kippur* to receive repentance and atonement from the King who sits on the heavenly throne. We must understand this long-standing Jewish tradition, which was practiced in New Testament times, to appreciate what Paul probably had in mind when he referred to "the last trump" as the moment the Church will be raptured from the earth and be glorified with Christ (1 Cor. 15:51-52).

With this understanding, let us consider the eschatological ramifications of the "last trump" terminology, which some Christians connect with both the event and the timing of the rapture of the Church. Those who hold a Mid-Tribulation view of the rapture have identified "the last trump" with the seventh of the seven trump judgments recorded in Revelation 8-11. However, the seventh trumpet judgment is not the last trumpet blast to be heard during the Tribulation; there is another at the end of this period which announces the re-gathering of all Jews back to Israel (Matt. 24:31). The meaning of this particular trumpet call is established in Exodus 19, which relates to assembling the Jewish nation together before the Lord on the earth, not the rapture of the Church to heaven. Thus, the seventh trumpet judgment in Revelation is not the last trumpet blast of the Tribulation period, but rather, the one in Matthew 24:3, which occurs at the Second Advent of Christ. Then, the Lord will call His covenant people (those who have survived the holocaust of the antichrist) back to the land of Israel. This divinely refined Jewish nation will receive the Holy Spirit and be with Christ during His Millennial Kingdom on earth (Ezek. 39:28-29). From a symbolic standpoint, The

Feast of Trumpets pictures the future calling of the Jewish people back to Israel.

With this understanding, let us consider an important application for the Church. There is a loss of imminence if one adopts a Mid-Tribulation rapture view. The view is forged chiefly by equating the seventh trumpet judgment in Revelation with the last trumpet referenced in 1 Corinthians 15:51-52, which clearly indicates the rapture of the Church. But as just shown, the seventh trumpet in Revelation is not the last trumpet blast to occur during the Tribulation Period, thus, there is no connection pertaining to the Church in these references – thus no Mid-Tribulation rapture view can be supported. The prophetic emphasis for the midpoint of the Tribulation Period is not the rapture of the Church, but the Abomination of Desolation (i.e., when the Antichrist breaks his covenant with Israel and demands to be worshipped as God).

Any understanding of the rapture other than a Pre-Tribulation view has the Church looking for two things: first, preparatory signs given to the nation of Israel to announce *Jacob's Time of Trouble* and, second, the coming of the Antichrist. However, the Lord never told the Church to be looking for the Antichrist, but rather to be intently watching and waiting for His unannounced return to the air to rapture the Church. This is called "the Day of Christ" (1 Cor. 1:7-8; Phil. 1:6, 10; 1 Thess. 4:13-19), and precedes God's wrath upon the wicked which is known as "the Day of the Lord." The latter day is said to come upon the wicked as an unexpected thief in the night, but "the Day of Christ" is greatly longed for and anticipated by the Church! In conclusion, The Feast of Trumpets pertains to Christ's calling the Jewish nation back to Israel after the end of the Church Age, not the rapture of the Church.

The Day of Atonement

The Day of Atonement had special significance among the seven feasts of Jehovah and took place on the tenth day of the seventh month (v. 27). As we discussed the details of this feast during our review of Leviticus 16, it suffices here to merely summarize. As referenced three times in this chapter, this feast day was actually a day for afflicting one's soul (vv. 27, 29, 32); the Jews understood this to mean a time of fasting and reflection. As with all the feasts, this was a "holy convocation," meaning there was to be no normal work done this day; in fact, God promises destruction upon anyone who did (v. 30).

Only on the Day of Atonement was the high priest permitted to enter the Most Holy Place of the tabernacle, and apply the blood of a bull and of a goat on and before the Mercy Seat. This atoned for (covered) all the sins the nation committed the previous year. It was also a unique occasion because the high priest put off his normal glorious attire and wore a plain white linen garment while applying the blood of atonement. This feast was an annual reminder of the ongoing problem of sin and that the blood of animals did not satisfy God's anger over sin or purge the sinner's guilty conscience. Rather, the entire feast pointed the Jewish nation to God's ultimate provision in Christ. From an eschatological viewpoint, this feast represents a future day during the latter part of the Tribulation Period when the Jewish nation accepts Jesus Christ as their Messiah and receives the Holy Spirit (Zech. 12:10).

Tabernacles
Five days after The Day of Atonement came The Feast of Tabernacles, falling on the fifteenth day of the seventh month in the Hebrew calendar (v. 34). The feast lasted a total of eight days; the first and the eighth days (vv. 35-36) were declared a "holy convocation," a high Sabbath day (v. 39). In contrast to the "affliction of souls" that took place on The Day of Atonement, this feast was a time of thanksgiving and rejoicing. With harvest season complete, and the barns and storehouses full, it was time for everyone to gather and express their gratitude to Jehovah. Hence, this festival was sometimes referred to as "The Feast of Ingathering" (v. 39).

Each Jewish family was to cut down branches from various leafy trees, such as willows and palms, and to erect makeshift booths to dwell in for the seven nights and eight days of the festival (vv. 40-42). This activity was to remind the Jews of how God delivered them from bondage in Egypt and that they dwelled with Jehovah in the wilderness while residing in tents (v. 43). The booths, then, were a memorial of what God had accomplished for His people. Jehovah did not want them to forget that He was their beginning. For this reason, The Feast of Tabernacles was to be an annual event throughout their generations (v. 43).

This feast pictures the glory of the Jewish nation after they are purified and restored to Jehovah at the end of the Tribulation Period (Rom. 9:27, 11:25-27). During the Millennial Kingdom, the Jewish nation will come into all the fullness of the Abrahamic covenant; thus, The Feast of Tabernacles forms a lovely and fitting close to the entire series of Jehovah's feasts. In recognition of its prophetic meaning, William Kelly notes the significance of the eight-day duration of The Feast of Tabernacles:

> The feast was the shadow of coming glory. God thus shows us, by this remarkable introduction of the eighth day here, the connection of the earthly blessing with the heavenly glory of resurrection. Resurrection points to heaven, and can never satisfy itself except in heavenly places; and therefore a link is here intimated with glory on high, whilst there is the fullest possible recognition of a day of rest and blessedness for the earth and the Jewish people. As we are told here in the latter part of it, they were all to keep this feast with gladness and joy. The eighth day is evidently brought in in a mysterious way – not now pointing to those who may be a testimony for God where all seemed to be removed from the earth, as we saw in the notice of the harvest at the end; but now, when we have the fullness of the witness of glory here below, this finger, so to speak, points upward, showing that in some way not developed in this chapter there will be the connection of the resurrection and heavenly glory with the day of Jehovah for the earth.[1]

Recall that the number eight is tied with new beginnings in Christ. For example, the Lord Jesus was raised up from the dead on the first, or eighth, day of the week – Sunday. The Jewish nation will experience the fullness of joy, peace, and blessing after being infused with the resurrected life of Christ. At the Lord's Second Coming to the earth, He will identify with His covenant people again and they will accept Him, the One they previously crucified, as their Messiah (Zech. 12:10). Spiritual fruit such as joy, peace, and love can only be produced through spiritual rebirth which coincides with the Holy Spirit being poured out upon the Jewish nation at the end of the Tribulation Period. From that day forth, the Jewish nation will enjoy a wondrous new beginning with Jesus Christ, their Messiah (Joel 2:25-3:21; Zech. 12:10-13:1).

Had the Jews understood the prophetic meaning of The Feast of Tabernacles, it is doubtful they would have been so careless as to its observance through the centuries. In the days of Nehemiah, the Jews knew nothing about it until the Law of Moses was read to them (Neh. 8:14-17), even though the nation observed this feast some eighty years earlier under Zerubbabel's leadership. This is one of many historical examples that illustrates man's natural propensity to forget those things which are important to the Lord.

Unfortunately, Jewish history shows a stubborn negligence in keeping the Feasts of Jehovah. What is observed today by modern Judaism is but a shadowy form of what was required in Scripture. But this is always the expected outcome of human traditions. This is especially true when man commercializes and socializes a biblical event or idea that God has not commanded to be observed, especially if it no longer has significance because what it symbolized has been fulfilled. Christ has come and put away the Old Covenant, which could not save, to establish an eternal one which can. While the prophetic fulfillment of the last three feasts still lies in the future, there is no need for the Jews (or the Church for that matter; Col. 2:16-17) to keep the feasts of Jehovah today; their Messiah has already come and offered them eternal life.

Summary

Each of the Feasts of Jehovah was a holy convocation for the entire nation. Not only were the sacrifices for the feasts to be executed precisely per the Mosaic Law, but all the normal activities of the tabernacle were to continue through the festivals. These include: burnt offerings, meal offerings, drink offerings, Sabbath observances, free-will gifts, and vow offerings (vv. 37-38). The seven Feasts of Jehovah provide an exceptional prophetical blueprint of God's means of reconciling the nation of Israel to Himself forever. Every aspect of this blueprint centers in the work of Christ. Within this prophetic framework is also a clear picture of a Pre-Tribulation rapture of the Church:

Passover (1st month, 14th day): This pictures Christ on the cross on Friday; this was the day the Passover lambs were slain and was also the day when the Lamb of God was slain for the sins of the world (1 Cor. 5:7).

Unleavened Bread (1st month, 15th day): This speaks of Christ in the grave on Saturday; like the bread, Christ's body had neither life while in the grave nor had it been previously influenced by sin (i.e., Christ lived an unleavened life).

Be Holy and Come Near

Firstfruits (1st month, 16th day): This typifies Christ's resurrection on Sunday; He was the firstfruits from the dead (1 Cor. 15:20).

Pentecost (fifty days after Firstfruits): This pictures the formation of the Church (Christ's body of believers), fifty days after Christ's resurrection. The events at Pentecost conveyed a final ultimatum to Israel (Acts 2).

Note: The Church Age is represented by the gap between the spring and autumn feasts (this also relates to the interval between Daniel's 69th and 70th weeks; Dan. 9:24-27). The autumn feasts speak of Israel's future acknowledgement of Christ as Messiah, their restoration to Him, and the blessings of His Millennial Kingdom.

Trumpets (7th month, 1st day): This refers to the time when Christ will gather all the Jews back to Israel and under His rule (Matt. 24:29-31; Ezek. 39:28-29). The Church will be with Christ in heaven prior to this event.

The Day of Atonement (7th month, 10th day): This pictures the future event when the Jews will repent and receive Jesus Christ as their Messiah (Heb. 9:28; Zech. 12:10).

Tabernacles (7th month, 15th day): This announces the future release of the Jews from the Antichrist's rule during the Tribulation Period, and the blessings of Christ's rule during His Millennial Kingdom.

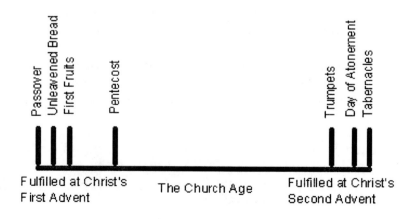

God indeed has a wonderful plan for the nation of Israel. Prophetically speaking, the spring feasts have been completed, while the fall feasts are yet to be fulfilled, though certainly the current ingathering of Jews back to the land of Israel is a preface to the fulfillment of the Feast of Trumpets. When the last trumpet of the Tribulation Period is heard, every Jew will be gathered from out of the nations back to the land of Israel; this refined remnant will then receive the Holy Spirit (Ezek. 39:28-29). Each feast prophetically presents a portion of God's plan to fully restore the Jewish nation to Himself once and for all during Christ's Millennial Kingdom. This ultimate restoration is pictured in the feasts of Leviticus 23.

Application

The message for the Church contained within this festival pattern is an exciting one, as the Church will be translated into the clouds to be with Christ prior to the restoration of the Jewish nation (Rom. 11:25-26; 1 Thess. 4:13-18). At that moment all believers will receive a Christ-like, glorified body. Paul says our present bodies are perishable, weak, and temporal; however, our glorified bodies will never perish, but be powerful and spiritual (1 Cor. 15:51-53). The former often dishonors the Lord, while that will be impossible with the latter – there is no flesh nature within it to cause the glorified body to rebel against the Lord.

John states believers will have a body like the Lord Jesus' body, which obviously cannot commit sin: *"Beloved, now we are children of God; and it has not yet been revealed what we shall be, but we know that when He is revealed, we shall be like Him, for we shall see Him as He is"* (1 Jn. 3:2). Paul describes the same truth: *"For our citizenship is in heaven, from which we also eagerly wait for the Savior, the Lord Jesus Christ, who will transform our lowly body that it may be conformed to His glorious body, according to the working by which He is able even to subdue all things to Himself"* (Phil. 3:20-21). Having a Christ-like body in heaven means everyone will morally act like God forever. There will be no ill thoughts about other people, no crippling bents, no temptations, nor will there be any addictions with which to grapple. God is a holy God, and to dwell in His presence we will have to be holy too – and we will be!

Paul states the appearing of the Lord Jesus is the blessed hope of the Church (Tit. 2:11), and those who love the Lord's appearing (i.e., live as if the Lord could come back at any moment) will be rewarded for doing so (2 Tim. 4:8). John says those who live expectant of Christ's return will live purely, because the Lord is pure and because a believer would not want to be ashamed when He does suddenly come for His people (1 Jn. 2:28, 3:3). So, although believers have not received their resurrection bodies yet, they are to live as though they have!

As the believer's flesh nature will be eradicated, the present needs and desires of our bodies will cease to exist. There will be no need for air, water, food, rest, sleep, or reproduction. The upshot is that perfect bodies will not need eyeglasses, wheelchairs, hearing aids, pacemakers, dentures, pain medications, sleep aids, etc. Doesn't heaven sound great?

Meditation

It may be at morn, when the day is awaking,
When sunlight through darkness and shadow is breaking,
That Jesus will come in the fullness of glory
To receive from the world His own.

It may be at midday, it may be at twilight,
It may be, perchance, that the blackness of midnight
Will burst into light in the blaze of His glory,
When Jesus receives His own.

Oh, joy! Oh, delight, should we go without dying;
No sickness, no sadness, no dread and no crying.
Caught up through the clouds with our Lord into glory,
When Jesus receives His own.

— H. L. Turner

The Oil and the Bread
Leviticus 24:1-7

This chapter commences the final section of Leviticus, which deals with miscellaneous laws, warnings, and promises. Leviticus 24 particularly warns against blasphemy and murder. However, before getting into this, we are given a series of directives pertaining to the oil for the Lampstand in the tabernacle and for the showbread presented before the Lord in the Holy Place. The construction of the Lampstand and Table of Showbread had already been discussed in Exodus 25, but this chapter provides further instructions for the oil and for the bread associated with these articles.

The Oil for the Lampstand

As the priests entered the Holy Place of the tabernacle from the east, the first piece of furniture they would notice would be the glowing golden Lampstand on the left side of the fifteen-by-thirty-foot room. Across from it stood the Table of Showbread, and on the far western side of the room was the Altar of Incense, just in front of the veil that divided the tabernacle into the Holy and Most Holy Places. While God's holy presence above the Mercy Seat prevented man from communing with God in the Most Holy Place, every aspect of the Holy Place (including the Lampstand and the Table of Showbread), portrays Christ's ongoing work to enable believers to have fellowship with God.

The Lampstand was formed from one solid piece of pure gold that weighed one talent (about 75 pounds). This candelabrum consisted of a central stem with three branches springing up and out from each side. At the top of the stem and each branch was a cup made in the form of an open almond flower. This open cup held the lamp's reservoir of olive oil into which the wick was inserted.

The light of the Lampstand was not to be extinguished (except when the tabernacle was being moved); consequently, the use of consumable candles was prohibited. Accordingly, the light of the Lampstand was produced by seven ever-burning wicks; each wick drew a constant supply of fine olive oil from its own reservoir. The priests entered into the Holy Place twice a day for the morning and evening offerings. Besides placing hot coals and specially prepared incense upon the Golden Altar, the priests also trimmed the seven wicks of the Lampstand and, as needed, filled each reservoir with oil (vv. 3-4).

The number seven is God's number and represents perfection, completeness, and holiness. The usage of this number in association with the light of the Lampstand symbolizes Christ's divine testimony of truth. Likewise, the resource that enabled the seven flames to illuminate the tabernacle (the oil) is also a symbol of divinity; pure oil is often used in Scripture to represent the person and work of the Holy Spirit. Another place this can be seen is in Zechariah's vision of two olive trees supplying oil to a lampstand. Speaking of the oil, the Lord told Zechariah how His work would be accomplished: *"Not by might nor by power, but by My Spirit"* (Zech. 4:6). God was confirming that it would be His Spirit working in Joshua and Zerubbabel (the two trees) to accomplish His will and provide a testimony of Himself in Jerusalem. The Lampstand in the tabernacle, then, speaks of God's perfect revelation of truth in Christ through the power of the Holy Spirit.

Types of Christ and of the Holy Spirit are combined in the imagery of the Lampstand. Christ is depicted as God's light to a lost world – the One who exposes the darkness of sin: *"Then Jesus spoke to them again, saying, 'I am the light of the world. He who follows Me shall not walk in darkness, but have the light of life'"* (John 8:12). The Lord Jesus was the evidence of God's truth in visible flesh, but the Holy Spirit was also working to enable the ministry of Christ to prosper. In fact, the Lord did not begin His public ministry until He had been anointed by the Holy Spirit (John 1:32; Acts 10:38). Clearly, the work of the Holy Spirit cannot be separated from the public testimony of the Lord Jesus Christ. While on earth Christ was God's Lampstand to show sinners the way to God, and the Holy Spirit worked many miracles to testify that Christ was telling the truth. While it is true that Christ is the light of the world, the Lampstand pertains more specifically to His revelation of truth to the believer; that is, the light in which the believer must continue to walk in order to maintain fellowship with God.

The priests in the tabernacle had the wonderful opportunity to preview *"the copy and shadow of the heavenly things"* (Heb. 8:5), but as believers in Christ, we presently walk amid the heavenly things themselves (Eph. 2:6; Heb. 9:23). May the Spirit of God illuminate our understanding concerning such glorious riches; these are things too precious, too vast, and too astonishing to keep to ourselves.

The Showbread

The Table of Showbread with its twelve cakes identifies Christ as the Bread of Life, the One we must continually feed upon; He is the substance of our fellowship with God. The twelve loaves of unleavened bread, the *"bread of the presence,"* upon the table served as a constant reminder of God's continual blessings and presence among His people. Initially, it was Moses who set the bread in order on the table: *"He put the table in the tabernacle of meeting, on the north side of the tabernacle, outside the veil; and he set the bread in order upon it before the Lord, as the Lord had commanded Moses"* (Ex. 40:22-23). Further instructions concerning the showbread itself are recorded in this chapter:

> *And you shall take fine flour and bake twelve cakes with it: two-tenths of an ephah shall be in each cake. You shall set them in two rows, six in a row, on the pure gold table before the Lord. And you shall put pure frankincense on each row, that it may be on the bread for a memorial, an offering made by fire to the Lord* (vv. 5-7).

The loaves symbolize the humanity of the Lord Jesus Christ as "the Bread of Life." They were to be made of fine flour to picture His moral fitness, and without leaven to portray His sinless perfection. The sweet-smelling frankincense that was placed upon the loaves spoke of the Lord's complete devotion to His Father.

Each Sabbath day twelve new cakes of showbread were to be placed before the Lord, and Aaron and his sons were to eat the original cakes in the Holy Place (vv. 8-9). The fact that the bread was presented every seven days (seven is the number of perfection) and then consumed by the priests typifies the perfection of the believer's enjoyment of Christ's fellowship. Although the showbread pictures Christ, the number of loaves (twelve) clearly ties it to the twelve tribes. Throughout the Bible *twelve* is the number that pertains to *governmental perfection*; there is no doubt that here it represents the twelve tribes of Israel under God's leadership.

As a nation, Israel, in a future day, will enjoy full fellowship with Christ and will freely partake of His goodness. During the first part of the Tribulation Period, there will be 144,000 Jews (12,000 Jews from each tribe) who are sealed to be witnesses for the Lord: *"And I heard the number of those who were sealed: one hundred and forty-four thousand of all the tribes of the children of Israel were sealed"* (Rev. 7:4). After these faithful Jews have completed their ministry in the Tribulation Period, we read:

> *Then I looked, and behold, a Lamb standing on Mount Zion, and with Him one hundred and forty-four thousand, having His Father's name written on their foreheads… They sang as it were a new song before the throne, before the four living creatures, and the elders; and no one could learn that song except the hundred and forty-four thousand who were redeemed from the earth. These are the ones who were not defiled with women, for they are virgins.* ***These are the ones who follow the Lamb wherever He goes.*** *These were redeemed from among men, being firstfruits to God and to the Lamb. And in their mouth was found no deceit,* ***for they are without fault before the throne of God*** (Rev. 14:1-5).

The twelve cakes of unleavened bread upon the Table of Showbread give a prophetic foretaste of the time when Israel will be completely restored to the Lord Jesus Christ, the Lamb of power, and will ever be with Him and before Him. This will be the culmination of God's provision for His ancient covenant people to be blessed and have fellowship with Him.

Application

The Golden Lampstand was the only source of light and the Table of Showbread the only source of food for the priests in the Holy Place. This reminds us that God's people need divine light as well as divine food to remain in fellowship with Him and to be able to serve Him properly.

The Lampstand was adorned with gold almond blossoms (Ex. 25 and 37). Blossoms normally occur in springtime, after the deadness of winter has passed; thus, the blossom represents new life, or, more specifically, resurrection life. This symbol of new life would reappear later when God indicated His endorsement of Aaron as His high priest by causing his staff (a dead rod) to bud, shoot forth blossoms, and then yield almonds (Num. 17:8). Thus, light and life are inseparably connected in the message of the Lampstand.

What application does the Lampstand have for the believer today? From New Testament revelation we understand what symbolically is represented in the Lampstand: that the resurrection life of Christ, the truth of Christ, and the Holy Spirit all reside in the believer today. Consequently, as the believer remains in fellowship with Christ and chooses to live for Him, a world filled with satanic darkness becomes illuminated with divine truth. The life of Christ must be lived out, and this is only possible by yielding to divine truth. Not living according to divine truth grieves the Holy Spirit and thus diminishes His supernatural enablement in our lives. Each believer is called to be a living lampstand for Christ.

Scripture affixes lampstand responsibility on both individual believers (Matt. 5:14) and local churches (Rev. 1:20). Light testifies of divine truth and of divine power in action; thus, the Lord Jesus exhorted His disciples:

> *You are the light of the world. A city that is set on a hill cannot be hidden. Nor do they light a lamp and put it under a basket, but on a lampstand, and it gives light to all who are in the house. Let your light so shine before men, that they may see your good works and glorify your Father in heaven* (Matt. 5:14-16).

Good works that glorify God cannot be conjured up by the doings of the flesh; only as a believer is enabled by the Holy Spirit can he or she *shine out* a testimony of Christ's life within him or her. The same is true of a local assembly. The Holy Spirit unifies and empowers believers to work together to be a testimony of Christ to their associated communities. Are you shining for Him? Is your local assembly a brilliant testimony of Christ's splendor to your community? The seven wicks of the Lampstand were to burn *"before the Lord continually"* in the tabernacle (Lev. 24:4). As believers continue to abide in Christ, the lost cannot avoid seeing the brilliance of Christ shining out from them. What this dark world needs is a true testimony of Christ.

The Table of Showbread also conveys a powerful lesson for the believer to consider. As foreshadowed in the manna (Ex. 16), the Lord

Jesus is the living bread which came down from heaven; anyone who partakes of Him receives eternal life and enjoys His abiding presence forever (John 6:35, 48). One "eats" of the Bread of Life by trusting Christ alone for salvation and then the believer continues to eat of Him (that is, to feed upon His word) to grow in Him. George Rodgers explains why it is important for believers to continually feed on Christ:

> Christ is the food of our love. I could never have loved God had I not seen Him in Christ. Christ is the proof and the expression of God's great love to man; and when I see this, my faith works by love and draws me to God, and I exclaim, *"I love Him because He first loved me!"* The more I meditate on Christ the warmer and purer is my love to God. I cannot love God by trying to love Him, but when I see and feel that God loves me, sinful as I am, and that, as seen in Christ, He is the most lovely and loveable being in the universe, I feel love, joy, and peace spring up in my heart, and I enter at once into rest. No one can be healthy and strong who does not get good food; and no soul can be truly healthy that does not feed on Jesus Christ.[1]

In the spiritual sense, trusting in Christ is likened to eating and internalizing His word (John 6:35, 40-50). These two qualities of God's blessing and fellowship are symbolized in the twelve cakes of unleavened bread. We have the privilege of enjoying these privileges now; the nation of Israel will in a future day! May we feed on God's Word and, as the Holy Spirit enables us, shine out what we have enjoyed and internalized.

Meditation

> Sweet feast of love divine, 'tis grace that makes us free,
> To feed upon this bread and wine, in memory, Lord, of Thee.
> Here conscience ends its strife, and faith delights to prove,
> The sweetness of the Bread of Life, the fullness of Thy love.
>
> — Edward Denny

Blasphemy
Leviticus 24:10-23

At first glance it seems that the narrative of "dos" and "don't dos" is abruptly interrupted with the account of two men striving together; in the process one of the two men, a son of a Hebrew woman and Egyptian man, blasphemed the name of Jehovah (vv. 10-11). The blasphemer was put into prison until the mind of the Lord might be declared to Moses on the matter (vv. 12-13). There was no ambiguity about Jehovah's ruling: *"Whoever curses his God shall bear his sin. And whoever blasphemes the name of the Lord shall surely be put to death"* (Lev. 24:15-16). Jehovah's name is holy and anyone cursing the almighty God, the Creator of all things, deserved capital punishment.

Moses was instructed to remove the accused man from the camp. Those who heard him blaspheme were to lay their hands upon his head to publicly testify of the offense and to identify the one who had committed it. The entire congregation was then to stone the blasphemer (v. 13), which they immediately did (v. 23). One might wonder why the Levitical instruction was interrupted in order to record the judgment of a single blasphemer, but the event illustrated God's holiness and, therefore, is not at all a disruption in the account. God was to be reverenced in the land, and not even "strangers" were to blaspheme the name of the God of Israel. Warren Wiersbe explains:

> The basis for obedience to the law is the fear of the Lord, and people who blaspheme His holy name have no fear of God in their hearts. Every Jew knew the third commandment: *"You shall not take the name of the Lord your God in vain, for the Lord will not hold him guiltless who takes His name in vain"* (Ex. 20:7). So fearful were the Jews of breaking this commandment that they substituted the name "Adonai" for "Jehovah" when they read the Scriptures, thus never speaking God's name at all. To respect a name is to respect the person who bears that name, and our highest respect belongs to the Lord.[1]

To degrade Jehovah's name is to attack His holy character and authority. Not only did Moses convey Jehovah's ruling concerning the blasphemer, but he also reminded the nation of other important judicial matters:

- Murderers were to be put to death (vv. 17, 21).
- Anyone who killed another's animal needed to pay restitution (vv. 18, 21).
- Anyone who maliciously disfigured or injured his neighbor was to receive the same privation as punishment (v. 20).

Moses informed his countrymen that there was to be only one law in the land where the Lord would settle them. Both Jews and sojourners were under the same set of statutes. No sentencing compromises or impartial judgments would be tolerated. The Law was rigid and only in rare situations did it offer grace. This dispensational reality would be in stark contrast with the message of Jesus Christ, who offered the Jews forgiveness for their sins solely by grace through faith. Yet, the Jewish nation rejected the Lord's kind offer, and instead blasphemed and crucified Him (Luke 22:65, 23:33).

This sin of blasphemy relates to violating God's commandment: *"You shall not take the name of the Lord your God in vain, for the Lord will not hold him guiltless who takes His name in vain"* (Ex. 20:7). The psalmist reminds us God's name is *"holy and awesome"* (Ps. 111:9). Accordingly, God Himself is blasphemed when dishonor is affixed to His name. This can be accomplished in two ways, either by exalting what is ordinary to a high and holy status, or by reckoning what is lofty and divine, such as God's name, as of common value.

Practically speaking, what does obedience to the third of the Ten Commandments entail? How is this commandment violated today? Charles Hodge clarifies the matter for us:

> The third commandment, therefore, specially forbids not only perjury, but also all profane, or unnecessary oaths, all careless appeals to God, and all irreverent use of His name. All literature, whether profane or Christian, shows how strong is the tendency in human nature to introduce the name of God even on the most trivial occasions. Not only are those formulas ... constantly used without any recognition of their true import, but even persons professing to fear God often allow

themselves to use His name as a mere expression of surprise. God is everywhere present. He hears all we say. He is worthy of the highest reverence; and He will not hold him guiltless who on any occasion uses His name irreverently.[2]

In the New Testament, the word "blasphemy" appears in both a noun form *blasphemia*, occurring nineteen times, and in a verb form *blasphemeo*, found thirty-five times. *Blasphemia* is translated "blasphemy," "evil speaking," and "railing." It denotes slander or speech injurious to another's good name (Matt. 12:31) or irreverent speech disdaining divine majesty (Matt. 26:65). *Blasphemeo* is rendered "blasphemer," "defame," "rail on," "revile," and "speak evil."

When an individual rails, slanders, or speaks irreverently of or evil against God, that individual has blasphemed God. Specifically applied, the sin of blasphemy involves showing disdain or a lack of reverence for God or for what He deems as sacred (Matt. 26:65), or attributing divine characteristics to something or someone other than God (Mark 14:64). The psalmist sums the matter up concisely – only fools blaspheme the name of God! *"Remember this, that the enemy has reproached, O Lord, and that a foolish people has blasphemed Your name"* (Ps. 74:18). The foolishness of man is never more obvious than when he maligns his Creator. The "mystery of iniquity" will run its due course. Man scoffed at God's impending judgment during the days of Noah, man blasphemed God as Paul preached the gospel message (Acts 26:11), and blasphemy of God will be unchecked during the future Tribulation Period. Thus, the increase of mankind's blasphemy against God is a sign of the end of the Church Age (2 Tim. 3:1-2).

Application

Believers should not take part in the desecration of God's name – Holy is His name! For many Christians, a relearning of righteous speech patterns and proper conduct to honor God's name are required. That the unsaved will lack reverence for the Lord's name is somewhat understandable, but why do Christians debase God's name in speech or in conduct? Often they are unconscious of doing so. You may be thinking to yourself, "I do not blaspheme the Lord or show disrespect to His name!" However, this reflects a human understanding of blasphemy, not a biblical one. In actuality, in one form or another, we often unconsciously demean God's name. For example, how often have you heard someone say, "Holy ------"? This is a form of blasphemy, that is, taking what is high and holy and associating it with something earthly, whatever the other word may be (often something putrid).

The problem of believers unconsciously debasing God's name seems to have been present even in the early church, for Paul exhorts believers more than once to put away all evil speech and blasphemies (Eph. 4:31; Col. 3:8). Because Hymenaeus and Alexander had abandoned a good conscience and shipwrecked their faith, Paul committed them to the Lord in prayer, and unto Satan for buffeting. The end goal was *"that they may learn not to blaspheme"* (1 Tim. 1:20). William MacDonald comments on this passage:

> In the New Testament, *blaspheme* does not always mean to speak evil of God.... It might be used to describe the lives of these men as well as the words of their lips. By making shipwreck of the faith, they had undoubtedly caused others to speak evil of the way of truth, and thus their lives were living blasphemies.[3]

The Bible contains examples of individuals who blasphemed God and reveals that this sin will continue through the Church Age and into the Tribulation Period. God's exhortation to all believers is *"Be holy, for I am holy"* (1 Pet. 1:16). Not only are Christians not to speak blasphemy, but they must strive not to live blasphemously either (Jas. 2:7). God's will for the believer is that he or she should refrain from doing sin, and indeed, that he or she practice a sin-free life to the extent possible (1 Jn. 2:1, 3:4-10). However, on this side of glory, sinless perfection is a pursuit, not a reality – thank God our salvation is not based on our doings, but upon His grace. And, praise be to God, our new nature received at conversion cannot sin (1 Jn. 3:9). Let us all pursue holiness, for in holiness we find not the inability to sin, but the ability not to sin.

So, are you a blasphemer? Unfortunately, the answer is "yes," in the sense that we all are guilty of tarnishing the name of the Lord in one way or another – in this way Christians often unknowingly honor the devil. Either in word or deed, we have all communicated disdain for God's name and caused others to do the same. The more mindful we are of honoring God's name, the less likely we will be to possess carefree attitudes which predictably lead to offending God. Paul exhorted the believers at Colosse not to walk as they once did: *"But now you yourselves are to put off all these: anger, wrath, malice, blasphemy, filthy language out of your mouth"* (Col. 3:8). It is natural for an unsaved sinner to blaspheme God, for his or her fallen nature is at enmity with God; nothing in it can please God (Rom. 7:18, 8:8). However, a true believer has received a new nature and a new life (Gal. 2:20), and that nature seeks to exalt God, which requires putting to death continually the improper lusting of the flesh.

In short, we are natural rebels against God and, regrettably, none of us walks as perfectly as he or she should. The reality of the matter is that we blaspheme the name of the Lord in a variety of ways. The tongue is the tail of the heart that wags out of the mouth: our rebellious nature and the depravity within our hearts eventually spews out of our mouths (Matt. 12:34-35).

It has already been shown that one can communicate blasphemy against the Lord through speech or other ungodly conduct. The following sins are some specific examples of the different forms of blasphemy noted in Scripture, that is, behavior which disdains the name of the Lord and thus honors Satan: teaching false doctrine (1 Tim. 6:3-4), swearing falsely (Lev. 19:12; Matt. 5:3; Jas. 5:12), stealing (Prov. 30:9; Eph. 4:28), demoting the character of God (Job 8:1-7; Matt. 26:74), and having an impudent heart (Matt. 23:16-22; Col. 1:18).

If the unsaved masses are to be reached for Christ in this present day, the Church must rethink its careless attitudes regarding how it represents and proclaims the name of Christ. Deliberate disregard for the Word of God, complacency over sin, and loss of reverence for the Lord's name have degraded the name of Christ throughout the world. The Church desperately needs revival! May we all repent and again esteem Christ above all things, *"that in all things He may have the preeminence"* (Col. 1:18), and may we fervently pray as Solomon did so long ago: *"That all peoples of the earth may know Your name and fear You, as do Your people"* (2 Chron. 6:33).

Be Holy and Come Near

Meditation

Holy, holy, holy! Lord God Almighty!
Early in the morning our song shall rise to Thee;
Holy, holy, holy, merciful and mighty!
God in three Persons, blessed Trinity!
Holy, holy, holy! though the darkness hide Thee,
Though the eye of sinful man Thy glory may not see;
Only Thou art holy; there is none beside Thee,
Perfect in power, in love, and purity.

— Reginald Heber

The Law of the Land
Leviticus 25

Laws governing the land are contained in this chapter. Commandments pertaining to the Sabbatical year and the year of Jubilee are stated, as well as instructions governing the redemption of both land and people sold because of economic hardship.

The Sabbatical Year

The Jews were already familiar with the concept of working six days and consecrating the seventh day, the Sabbath, to the Lord. The Jews, their slaves, and their beasts of burden were all to rest on the Sabbath Day. The Lord now imposed the same restriction on the land; it was to be worked six years followed by an entire year of rest (v. 3). This meant no sowing, pruning, reaping, or harvesting would be permitted during the seventh year; the fields, the olive groves, and the vineyards were to receive a full year's inactivity (vv. 4-5). Whatever grew naturally during this time could be freely gleaned by anyone, especially the poor, and anything left would be God's provision for the beasts of the field. However, there was to be no organized harvest or sale of what the land did produce that year (vv. 6-7).

The Sabbath year ensured that one year in seven all Jews would share the same equality; they must live off the land, or rather, live by faith that Jehovah would provide for their needs that year. Certainly, this agricultural prohibition would remind the Jews that God owned the land on which they lived and that they were merely stewards of it (v. 23). Apparently, the Sabbatical year was also the appropriate time for the canceling of debts (Deut. 15:1-11) and the freeing of Jewish slaves (Deut. 15:12-18).

Unfortunately, biblical evidence confirms the Jews did not follow this law before or after their seventy-year Babylonian exile. Jeremiah confirmed the duration of their captivity and the associated rest for the land in Israel (Jer. 25:11). One may wonder why the Lord would determine a seventy-year cessation from agricultural work. 2 Chronicles 35:14-21 informs us of the reason for this specific length of time: the Jews had not been honoring the Sabbath year for 490 years and exactly seventy years were due the Lord and He collected them all at once.

To validate the fulfillment of Jeremiah's seventy-year agricultural prophecy, God caused Ezekiel to record the exact starting date and Haggai the precise ending date of this judgment. This period began on March 14, 589 B.C. (Ezek. 24:2) and ended when the foundation of the temple was laid on its previously-completed base (Hag. 2:18). Haggai confirmed that Jehovah would again bless the land with fruitfulness from that day forward (Hag. 2:19). God has infinite memory and is a precise counter, so whenever people think that they can somehow escape divine justice by outsmarting or out-maneuvering God, they will inevitably, in God's sovereign timing, learn their foolishness.

The Year of Jubilee

Before the Israelites set foot into the Promised Land, the Lord asserted His ownership of that land; His people were merely tenants (v. 23). The land was for the good of all of the Jews; it was not to be exploited to gain an advantage over the poor or those suffering hardship (v. 24). There were primarily two ways in which a Jewish man might be temporarily separated from his territorial inheritance: he sold (i.e., leased) the land (vv. 14-17), or he sold himself into slavery to pay off a debt (vv. 39-55). In both cases, the land transaction and the debt were to be forgiven in the year of Jubilee. The land went back to its rightful owner and the Jewish slave was given the option of full release. This chapter also supplies methods in which the land (vv. 23-28) and the slave (vv. 41, 48-55) could be redeemed prior to the year of Jubilee.

The year following the seventh sabbatical year was to be the year of Jubilee. Every fifty years on the Day of Atonement, a blast of the trumpet would signal the release of debts, slaves, and property. The sound of liberty was proclaimed throughout the land. The objective of this festive occasion was to ensure all family property (outside walled cities) was restored per the original inheritance and family members who had been temporarily sold into slavery could return home (vv. 10, 13). Jehovah knew strong families are the building blocks of a robust nation, and the year of Jubilee promoted this ideology. Lastly, as in the previous

Sabbatical year, the land was to enjoy a second year of agricultural rest (vv. 11-12).

Although selling one's land was not ideal, it was permitted with the understanding that the original owner was really leasing the land to a tenant until the year of Jubilee. Thus, the price of the land sold varied depending on how many years' crops could be grown on the land up until the year of Jubilee. Or, as Duane Lindsey puts it, "In other words, what one was really selling was the number of crops, a limited lease on the land paid in full in advance."[1]

If the Jews heeded His "Laws of the Land," then Jehovah promised His blessings on them in the land: there would be neither want nor war (v. 19). To alleviate the Jews' anxiety about not sowing or harvesting crops for two years, the Lord promised an abundant harvest in the sixth year preceding the Sabbath year and the year of Jubilee to hold them over for those two years (vv. 20-22). Regrettably, there is no biblical evidence to indicate the Jews ever obeyed the year of Jubilee statute; in fact, it is not mentioned outside the Pentateuch. Because of their clear violation of seventy straight Sabbath years prior to the Babylonian exile (2 Chron. 36:20-21), it is doubtful that the Jews ever consistently honored the year of Jubilee command.

Redemption of an Inheritance

After the Israelites conquered Canaan, that land would be divided by lot among the various tribes and clans. This inheritance would then be passed down from generation to generation to ensure tribal allotments were never lost. However, the Jews were to understand that the Lord owned the land and they were mere tenants, meaning that they could be evicted if they did not obey His laws for the land (v. 23).

If for economic hardship a Jew was forced to sell his property, his nearest relatives were to assist him in redeeming back that land (v. 25). For example, while Jeremiah was in prison, the Lord informed him his cousin Hanamel would visit him. God also revealed the purpose of the visit: Hanamel would request that Jeremiah purchase some property, a field in Anathoth, from him. The Babylonian occupation had put Hanamel and his family in a desperate situation, and he was looking for funds to sustain them through the crisis. Hanamel was following the very law before us, which allowed a kinsmen to redeem (purchase) property to ensure that it remained in the family (vv. 25-28). Although Anathoth was already under Babylonian control, meaning the field had little value, the Lord told Jeremiah to purchase the property and he did. Two copies of the deed were signed and preserved in a clay jar; this would allow for their retrieval when God brought the Jews back to their homeland seventy years later (Jer. 32:7-12).

If the financial situation of the Jew who sold his land improved, he had the option of redeeming the land back himself at any time (v. 26). The land's value was determined in reference to how many years remained until the year of Jubilee (vv. 27, 50-53). Two exceptions to this general code are noted. First, the release of property in the year of Jubilee did not apply to homes within walled cities (vv. 28, 31). Second, property within a walled city could only be redeemed within the first year of being sold (vv. 29-34).

Because the Levities were to dwell in cities and would not be allotted a specific region of land, they would be able to redeem their homes anytime, not just in the first year (vv. 32-33). However, the pasture lands that surrounded their cities, which were also a Levite possession, could not be sold at any time in order to ensure their tribal possession was preserved (v. 34). Regardless of whether or not he was able to redeem it, the property of any Jewish man would return to his family in the year of Jubilee (vv. 28, 33). Again, this was to ensure tribal and clan inheritances were not lost over time.

Caring for the Poor

The Jews were to be a hospitable people, especially to their destitute brethren. Favoritism was discouraged; their homes were to be open not just to esteemed visitors but also to each other. God had been gracious in deeding them the Promised Land; likewise, they were to be generous in assisting their poor brethren. Although the Jews were not forbidden to exact interest from foreigners (Deut. 23:20), there was to be no charging of interest to worsen the plight of their fellow countrymen (vv. 36-37). Moses exhorted his brethren: *"You shall not oppress one another, but you shall fear your God; for I am the Lord your God"* (Lev. 25:17). Besides our care for fellow believers in need, David and Solomon remind us to also attend to the necessities of the poor:

> *Blessed is he who considers the poor; the Lord will deliver him in time of trouble* (Ps. 41:1).

He who has pity on the poor lends to the Lord, and He will pay back what he has given (Prov. 19:17).

He who gives to the poor will not lack, but he who hides his eyes will have many curses (Prov. 28:27).

The Lord rewards those who attend to the needy. In the Church Age, through the power of the Holy Spirit, believers are able to fulfill God's fuller intention of the Law – to demonstrate divine love for each other (Rom. 13:10). One kept the Law by not stealing, but to fulfill the Law goes beyond this to selflessly giving to another. Therefore, Paul exhorts believers not only to care for each other and the poor, but also to extend compassion to those who oppose us. If they are hungry and thirsty, we are to provide them food and drink (Rom. 12:20). He explains that such kindhearted acts *"overcome evil by doing good"* (Rom. 12:21). Such conduct is a tangible and lasting testimony of Christ in our communities.

Redeeming Slaves

Reason would dictate that a new nation composed of liberated slaves would strongly disdain the practice of slavery; hence, it was doubtful any Jewish slaves were among the Israelites at the time Leviticus was written. However, given the depravity of the human heart, it would only be a matter of time before slavery existed among God's people. Indeed, not only slavery but many of the hideous crimes already mentioned in Leviticus did not exist among the children of Israel at the time the Law was given. But the fact that God was imposing severe penalties for gross and putrid behavior, yet unfamiliar to them, showed the Jews that God knew more about the depravity of their hearts than they did. In time, they would violate every dictate of the Law, despite being forewarned of God and despite, in many cases, the threat of the death penalty.

The Bible does not promote or condemn slavery, but it does acknowledge its existence, and provides regulations to limit its abuses. Similarly, divorce was never God's plan for marriage – He hates it (Mal. 2:16) – but the Law allowed for it and issued rules to limit its abuses. Such behaviors spring up from the same fountainhead – the depraved human heart (Matt. 19:8).

Hebrew history shows that there were two main reasons Jews would become slaves to other Jews (vv. 39-43) or resident aliens (vv. 47-53):

they might sell themselves into slavery in order to pay off a debt (such as a bride's dowry or a general economic hardship) or they could be forced into slavery as a result of a punitive judgment (e.g., as a recompense for a crime committed). In any case, God did not desire His people to be forced to serve others as slaves, but rather to be a liberated people who would freely serve Him (Neh. 5:1-13). Consequently, no Jew was to be held in slavery against his or her will for more than six years, no matter what circumstances caused the servitude or who owned him or her.

Jehovah did not want His people to suffer the oppression of slavery again. With that said, it was understood that sorrowful situations would arise, where it might be necessary to sell oneself or one's children into slavery, but this was not to be a long-term reality. A Hebrew slave was to be treated with respect, like a hired servant (vv. 40, 43).

Leviticus 25 extends protection to Jewish, not Gentile, slaves. Gentile slaves were to observe the Sabbath day rest (Deut. 5:14) and were not to be mistreated (Ex. 21:20-21), but beyond that they had no privileges. They were considered property for life and could be bought and sold at will (vv. 44-46).

On the other hand, Jews who were sold into slavery (whether to Gentile or Jewish owners) could be assured that their regrettable situation would last no more than six years (Ex. 21:1-6), and less if the year of Jubilee was a nearer event. A fortunate slave might be able to pay his or her own redemption price (vv. 39-43), or be liberated by a close relative (i.e., a kinsman redeemer; vv. 48-50). Redemption of a Jewish slave was permitted at any time and the amount would be proportional to the remaining years of service (vv. 48-49).

Probably the most notable kinsman redeemer in the Old Testament is Boaz, who not only redeemed Naomi's dead husband's property, but also married Naomi's widowed daughter-in-law Ruth, a Moabite (Ruth 4:4-9). This marriage was necessary to produce children in the family name, so that the property would be passed down to the next generation. Indeed, this marriage was fruitful and Ruth became the great-grandmother of King David (Ruth 4:17) and also a part of the lineage of the Jewish Messiah, the Lord Jesus Christ (Matt. 1:5).

As in the case of Boaz, a kinsman redeemer had to be next of kin, able to redeem, and willing to redeem. There was actually a closer relative to Ruth than Boaz, but, though this other man was able to redeem her, he was not willing to do so; in contrast, Boaz was and did

(Ruth 4:6). This story and its application remind us of the Lord Jesus, who became man (our kin, so to speak) in order to redeem us with His own blood. He was both willing and able to redeem what was lost to God (Gal. 4:5; Tit. 2:14). Like the gospel message to any sinner who longs to be redeemed, the option of redemption was always a possibility for a Jewish slave.

After six years of service or on the year of Jubilee, whichever occurred first (vv. 39-42), a Hebrew slave was to be released (with his family, if a man: v. 41), unless the slave desired to remain with his or her master for life. If this was the slave's choice (a man in this example), he was taken to a doorpost, his ear was placed next to the wood, and the master pushed or pounded an awl through the slave's ear (Ex. 21:1-6). The resulting hole marked him as a bondservant for life. In the Epistles, Paul often applies this term to himself to express his own love for the Lord Jesus Christ. The only reason a man would become a perpetual bondservant would be to express love for his master, or perhaps, if he had been given a wife while in slavery, love for his family (for his family would not be released if he chose to go free). Though not addressed in this passage, a female slave was given the same choice after six years of service (Deut. 15:17).

As love for the master is mentioned first, it seems to be the primary reason a slave would be willing to enter into a lifelong commitment to his or her master. Certainly, such a master must have demonstrated exceptional care for the slave over the previous years, otherwise the slave would not enter into this lifetime obligation; brutality would never cause a slave to make such a pledge. However, if we believe the slave in question had determined he or she could never be happier than in serving this master, the commitment becomes understandable.

Both David (Ps. 40:6-8) and the writer of Hebrews (Heb. 10:5-9) use the picture before us of the slave's love for his master to indicate the sacrificial love and pure devotion of the Lord Jesus for His Father:

> *Sacrifice and offering You did not desire;* ***My ears You have opened****. Burnt offering and sin offering You did not require. Then I said, "Behold, I come; in the scroll of the book it is written of Me. I delight to do Your will, O My God, and Your law is within My heart"* (Ps. 40:6-8).

The writer of Hebrews clarifies what it meant to the Lord Jesus to have His ears opened by the Father: *"Sacrifice and offering You did not desire, **but a body You have prepared for Me**"* (Heb. 10:5). In devotion to the Father the Lord Jesus told His disciples, *"I am the Good Shepherd; the Good Shepherd gives His **life** for the sheep"* (John 10:11). The Greek word translated "life" is *psuche,* which is sometimes translated "soul." However, the word does not refer to the human soul exclusively, but to the whole person or one's *total self.* That is what the Lord did at Calvary; in devotion to the Father, the Son gave all of Himself as a sin sacrifice on our behalf!

Application

God instituted slavery regulations to protect His people from abusing each other in future generations; however, His desire for them was that they assist one another in economic hardships, rather than take advantage of each other:

> *If one of your brethren becomes poor, and falls into poverty among you, then you shall help him, like a stranger or a sojourner, that he may live with you. Take no usury or interest from him; but fear your God, that your brother may live with you* (vv. 35-37).

Though Christians are not under the Law, this regulation highlights what God deems appropriate conduct for His people throughout all ages, that is, to rally around and help each other during times of distress: *"Bear one another's burdens, and so fulfill the law of Christ"* (Gal. 6:2). Indeed, this was the practice of the early Church. The poor, such as widows, were cared for (Acts 6:1; 1 Tim. 5:3-5). Christians did not value their possessions (of which they were merely stewards) more than each other (Acts 4:32). As a result of this loving and selfless mindset, all of the Lord's people were wonderfully sustained: *"nor was there anyone among them who lacked"* (Acts 4:34). God forbid that we, who have received so much goodness in Christ, should *"oppress one another"* by withholding back our temporal possessions from our brothers and sisters in need (vv. 14, 17).

God's covenant people of old were to understand that God owned everything and could dispossess them of their stewardship at any time: *"Indeed heaven and the highest heavens belong to the Lord your God, also the earth with all that is in it"* (Deut. 10:14-15). All that was bestowed on the Jewish nation was to ensure that all Jews prospered in the Promised Land. This attitude seems to have been resurrected after the coming of the Holy Spirit at Pentecost. Indeed, the testimony of the Church would be exemplary if such selfless, caring behavior was observed today.

Meditation

> Cast thy burden on the Lord,
> Only lean upon His Word;
> Thou wilt soon have cause to bless
> His eternal faithfulness.
>
> He sustains thee by His hand,
> He enables thee to stand;
> Those whom Jesus once hath loved
> From His grace are never moved.
>
> Human counsels come to naught;
> That shall stand which God hath brought;
> His compassion, love, and power,
> Are the same forevermore.
>
> — Rowland Hill

Blessing or Chastening
Leviticus 26

The message of this chapter is reminiscent of the scene which occurred at Marah a few months earlier. God had used Moses to deliver the Israelites from Egypt and now Moses was leading them to Mt. Sinai to meet their God, Jehovah. The Lord spoke of His statutes and commandments for the first time after transforming the bitter waters at Marah into satisfying, life-sustaining drink (Ex. 15). The principle Moses conveyed to the people was a simple one: obedience would be rewarded with God's blessing, but disobedience would be met with severe judgment, even with plagues like those used to punish Egypt. Moses reiterates the idea of retribution for rebellion in this chapter. The precise timing of the Marah declaration and the confirmation of it in Leviticus 26, as Arthur Pink explains, are important to understand:

> Nothing had been said to Israel about Jehovah's "statutes and commandments" while they were in Egypt. But now that they were redeemed, now that they had been purchased for Himself, God's governmental claims are pressed upon them. The Lord was dealing with them in wondrous grace. But grace is not lawlessness. Grace only makes us the more indebted to God. Our obligations of obedience can never be liquidated so long as God is God. Grace only establishes on a higher basis what we most emphatically and fully OWE to Him as His redeemed creatures.[1]

The truth presented to the children of Israel after their national redemption was a simple one; it represents the same reality parents must teach their children early in life: obedience brings blessing, but disobedience results in punishment. The variable of ignorance had been thoroughly removed by the giving of the Law. Now that the Jews had the Law, they knew exactly what God expected of them in their daily lives.

The first two verses summarize the entire chapter. If the Jews wanted God's blessing, they were to refrain from idolatry, to demonstrate their commitment to Him by observing the Sabbath (i.e., as a day of worship and rest), and to support the ministry and ministers of the sanctuary. The remainder of the chapter then identifies specific blessings for compliance and penalties for defiance.

Blessings for Obedience

Unlike the repeated warnings of divine judgment for disobedience (vv. 14, 18, 21, 23, 27), the condition for divine blessing, obedience, is only mentioned once: *"If you walk in My statutes and keep My commandments, and perform them ..."* (v. 3). This statement supplies the premise for all that follows in the form of blessings through verse 13. Apparently, knowing the stiffed-necked nature of His people, the Lord felt it was necessary to punctuate the aspects of His chastening hand, rather than elaborate on all the good that He longed to afford them. For their faithfulness, God's goodness could be expected in the following ways:

- Seasonal rainfall to ensure a bountiful harvest of fruits and grains (v. 4)
- Peace and safety in the land from wild beasts and from invasion (vv. 5-6)
- Invincibility in driving out the inhabitants of Canaan (vv. 7-8)
- Many children (v. 9)
- Fulfillment of the land covenant originally promised to Abraham (v. 9; Deut. 28-30)
- The Lord's abiding presence (vv. 11-12)

The Lord's promised abiding presence among those He freed from slavery was to permit them to freely walk with Him. This declaration is tenderly stated:

> *I will set My tabernacle among you, and My soul shall not abhor you. I will walk among you and be your God, and you shall be My people. I am the Lord your God, who brought you out of the land of Egypt, that you should not be their slaves; I have broken the bands of your yoke and made you walk upright* (vv. 11-13).

Oh that verse 13 would have closed the chapter, but the sound of the other shoe dropping begins in verse 14. God knew the heart of His people, and His stern warnings against their disobedience is no less a demonstration of His love for His people.

Chastening for Disobedience

The matter of disobedience is addressed in verses 14-39. There is a noticeable increase in the severity of divine judgments; five subsequent waves of chastening are promised for those who would persist in wrongdoing. Each new phase of retribution would be initiated after a call to repentance had been ignored. Increasing punishment for prolonged and profound rebellion could be expected, but the good news was God would provide a call to repentance before each escalation of discipline.

First Wave of Discipline – Distress: This would involve terror, disease, invasion, and diminished agricultural fruitfulness (vv. 16-17).

> *And after all this, if you do not obey Me, then I will punish you seven times more for your sins. I will break the pride of your power* (vv. 18-19).

Second Wave of Discipline – Drought: Severe drought would keep the land from producing as it should (v. 20).

> *Then, if you walk contrary to Me, and are not willing to obey Me, I will bring on you seven times more plagues, according to your sins* (v. 21).

Third Wave of Discipline – Wild Beasts: An invasion of wild beasts would kill their children, slaughter livestock, and make travel dangerous (v. 22).

> *And if by these things you are not reformed by Me, but walk contrary to Me, then I also will walk contrary to you, and I will punish you yet seven times for your sins* (vv. 23-24).

Fourth Wave of Discipline – Pervasive Disease: Pestilence and food shortages would occur; for example, ten women would be able to bake all their bread in a single oven (vv. 25-26).

And after all this, if you do not obey Me, but walk contrary to Me, then I also will walk contrary to you in fury; and I, even I, will chastise you seven times for your sins (vv. 27-28).

Fifth Wave of Discipline – Widespread Famine and Death, Invasion, and Dispersion: Their cities and idolatrous high places would be destroyed, and severe famine would result in cannibalism (vv. 29-31). The Jews, in fact, did resort to cannibalism during such extremities (2 Kgs. 6:29; Lam. 4:10). The final repercussions of chastening would desolate farmland, vineyards, and orchards while their cities would be destroyed by invading armies. Accordingly, God's people would be forcibly removed from the Promised Land and dispersed among the nations (vv. 32-39).

All of the five waves of discipline occurred just before and during the Babylonian invasion of the Southern Kingdom and its captivity which began in 605 B.C.

Repentance and Restoration

The various waves of judgment, separated by opportunities to repent, demonstrate God's measured approach to chastening His children in order to achieve the desired result of full repentance and of restoration (vv. 40-46). Gratefully, God's anger is tempered with mercy, and His longsuffering approach to chastening His rebel children is not overbearing, but rather gracious. It is not the Lord's objective to crush His people, but that they might be yielded before Him. This was the lesson Jacob, the father of the Jewish nation, learned at the brook Jabbok in Genesis 32 after wrestling with the Lord an entire night. Finally, the Lord had to hurt Jacob to cause him to yield to His will and cleave to Him. Unfortunately, Jacob's stubborn example would be the longstanding pattern for the Jewish nation for centuries to come.

The evidence of true repentance is a humble heart and acceptance of divine discipline for past sins (v. 41). Because of His unconditional covenant with Abraham to bless his descendants through Isaac, God could not abandon His people (v. 42). Despite all their failures, they were His covenant people and He loved them then, and still does. But He loves them too much to leave them the way they are. Ultimately, all of the Abrahamic promises to the Jews will be fulfilled during Christ's millennial kingdom (Luke 1:67-77); until that time "war" and "desolation" are determined against them for their rebellion (Dan. 9:26).

Application

The irresistible love of God can only be experienced by answering His invitation to know Him through His revealed Word. Our understanding of God's plan and our commitment to live it out will be directly proportional to the extent that we have known and experienced Him. The Lord Jesus said, *"He who has My commandments and keeps them, it is he who loves Me. And he who loves Me will be loved by My Father, and I will love him and manifest Myself to him"* (John 14:21). Continued submission to divine truth is the pathway to intimately experiencing and knowing God in deepening degrees. This is what Jehovah wanted for the Israelites, and it is what the Lord Jesus wants for His Church today.

The Lord Jesus promised that if we obey His commandments, He will manifest Himself to us in deeper fellowship (John 14:21). In order to walk with the Lord, we must be in agreement with Him on the matter of sin. For, *"can two walk together except they be agreed?"* (Amos 3:3). Surely, light has no communion with darkness; thus, may each of us walk with God according to divine truth and in moral integrity. We read in 1 John 1:5-7 that walking with God requires walking in the light of divine truth. A willingness to walk according to revealed truth brings happy fellowship with God and with other believers. We must have light to walk safely. When we choose to walk in the dark, we are inviting injury – the chastening hand of God.

Listen to Paul's medley of exhortations concerning the walk of the believer: we are not to walk as fools (Eph. 5:15), the way we formerly did (Eph. 5:8), or the way the Gentiles walk in the vanity of their minds (Eph. 4:17); but rather we are to walk as children of light (Eph. 5:8). In other words, do not be foolish; walk according to the truth, not in the darkness that you once did. Like the Jews, we also have no excuse; the element of ignorance has been taken away – we have God's Word which informs us of exactly how God expects us to behave.

Our choice is the same one Moses set before his countrymen in this chapter; will we, as children of God, receive His divine care (i.e. we practically enjoy the blessings we have in Christ) or the rod of His parental reproof? The apostles warn us: *"Be you therefore followers of*

God, as dear children" (Eph. 5:1); *"as obedient children, not fashioning yourselves according to the former lusts in your ignorance"* (1 Pet. 1:14); *"for whom the Lord loves He chastens"* (Heb. 12:6). Compliance prompts God's blessing, and defiance, His chastening hand. As witnessed in this chapter, the Lord's faithfulness to chasten and His balanced approach in doing so fully demonstrate that He knows how to deal with human rebellion.

Meditation

> Master, speak! Though least and lowest,
> Let me not unheard depart;
> Master, speak! For O, Thou knowest
> All the yearning of my heart,
> Knowest all its truest need:
> Speak! and make me blest indeed.
>
> Master, speak and make me ready,
> When Thy voice is truly heard,
> With obedience glad and steady
> Still to follow every word.
> I am listening, Lord, for Thee:
> Master, speak! O, speak to me!
>
> — Frances Havergal

Dedicated to the Lord
Leviticus 27

Vows of Dedication

In gratitude for some blessing received from the Lord, the Jews could offer Him a vow of dedication, which was made before the priests (Num. 18:14). The Lord provided the priests with instructions as how to both evaluate and to redeem what had been dedicated to the Lord by the people (vv. 1-25). People, animals, farmland, and personal property such as houses could all be committed to the Lord by vows. While each of these things had intrinsic value, much of what was dedicated to the Lord in this way was not directly usable by the priests. For example, there was no need of people or unclean animals at the tabernacle. For these cases, the priests were to assess the worth of the thing pledged, and then the individual who brought it was permitted to redeem with money what he or she had dedicated; in some situations, a twenty percent premium was added to the price.

If a person dedicated a slave to the Lord and then backed out of it, or dedicated with the idea of immediate redemption (i.e., donation of money instead), then the redemption price to be paid to the priest was as follows (vv. 3-7):

- A 20 to 60 year old male – 50 shekels
- A 20 to 60 year old female – 30 shekels
- A 5 to 20 year old male – 20 shekels
- A 5 to 20 year old female – 10 shekels
- A 1 month to 5 year old male – 5 shekels
- A 1 month to 5 year old female – 3 shekels
- A 60 year old or older male – 15 shekels
- A 60 year old or older female – 10 shekels

The reason that male slaves were valued more than female slaves was not related to his or her intrinsic worth as a person, but rather to the amount of labor which he or she could perform (e.g., men were more desirable for heavy laboring). If the individual was too poor to redeem his or her vow according to the above assessment, a priest was to determine an appropriate redemption amount based on what he or she could pay (v. 8).

If an animal had been vowed (i.e., promised as a gift) to the Lord, the following criterion was applied:

- Clean animals which were suitable for sacrifice could not be redeemed; these must be offered to the Lord (Num. 18:17).
- One animal could not be exchanged for another; if a switch was attempted, both creatures would be the Lord's (vv. 10, 13).
- An unclean animal could be redeemed; its assessed worth plus twenty percent more was to be paid (vv. 11-13).

If someone dedicated a house to the Lord, but later changed his or her mind, it could be returned to the donor if he or she paid the priest its calculated value plus twenty percent (vv. 14-15). Assessing the redemption price for land that had been dedicated to the Lord was more complicated (vv. 16-25). F. Duane Lindsey summarizes the general process for evaluating the redemption value of a plot of land:

> The system of evaluating land began with the cost of the amount of seed required to plant if for 49 years, and then was discounted according to the number of harvests left until the next Year of Jubilee (vv. 17-18). Redemption required payment of the adjusted evaluation plus 20 percent (v. 19). Failure to redeem the land by the Year of Jubilee resulted in permanently forfeiting its title to the priests (vv. 20-21).

> However, lease land (i.e., not part of one's family land) would automatically revert to the original owner in the Year of Jubilee, so if a lease was dedicated to the Lord...its value had to be established and paid to the priest on the day it was dedicated. Verse 25 clarifies the standard weight of the silver in the sanctuary shekel.[1]

In setting the redemption value of the land, the priest had to consider whether or not the individual who made the vow was the actual owner or someone who had leased the land from the owner. He also had to correlate the land's value in reference to how many years it was to the year of Jubilee (25:23-38). As stated in Leviticus 25, all land returned to its original owners in the year of Jubilee to ensure tribal and clan inheritances were not lost over time (including the lands that were given to God through vows).

The Lord's Things

Directives are given in verses 1-25 to govern the dedication of people and things to the Lord, as well as the appropriate manner of evaluating the price of redemption (in silver shekels), if applicable. The final verses of Leviticus identify three things which could not be dedicated or redeemed in this fashion because they were already the Lord's. These included: the firstborn of a sacrificially clean animal (vv. 26-27), anything sentenced to death or destruction (vv. 28-29), and the tithe of a harvest (vv. 30-31).

Although no firstborn of an animal suitable for sacrifice could be vowed as a gift to God, an allowance is provided for firstborn unclean animals in verse 27; because these could not be sacrificed, the priests would set the value of the animal and an individual could redeem it back for its value plus twenty percent.

Animals or things designated for destruction were referred to as "devoted things" and could not be redeemed because they were already the Lord's. A Jew could dedicate to the Lord anything the Lord did not lay claim to, but no Israelite could dedicate to the Lord what was already His – "the devoted things." Should anyone take or keep what was devoted to the Lord, this was, in fact, stealing from Him.

Perhaps the best example to illustrate this occurred shortly after the Israelites entered Canaan some forty years later. The first Israeli attack of the campaign targeted the city of Jericho; it was a complete success, without any Jewish fatalities. The only blemish on this great victory is that one Jew named Achan disobeyed the Lord's prohibition against taking spoil from Jericho. All the spoil was the Lord's and He requested that it all be burned, except the metals of value which were to be put in the Lord's treasury. Jericho pictures the world and the Israelites were to be consecrated to the Lord, and not the world. They were to be solely dependent on Him for direction and provision and were not to venture into the world for satisfaction or assistance.

Achan disobeyed the Lord. The Lord informed Joshua of the secret offense; someone has taken *"of the accursed thing, and have also stolen"* (Josh. 7:11). Achan succumbed to lusting and secretly stole what was the Lord's. The Hebrew word *cherem*, translated "accursed" (the supplied word "things" is implied), literally means "dedicated to be utterly destroyed." It is translated twice as "devoted" in Leviticus 27:28: *"Nevertheless no **devoted** offering that a man may devote to the Lord of all that he has, both man and beast, or the field of his possession, shall be sold or redeemed; every **devoted** offering is most holy to the Lord"* (emphasis added). The *cherem* things were solely the Lord's and were destined for destruction by fire; even the metals would later be melted, refined, and reformed by fire. In this sense the spoil of Jericho was "devoted" to the Lord; it was not for personal benefit, and thus, it could not be redeemed. Achan and those associated with him in the crime, his family, were put to death for the offense.

It is important to understand the biblical distinction between "devoted things," which are already the Lord's, and "dedicated things," which is what man can freely give to the Lord. In one sense, as condemned sinners we all were of the devoted things destined to destruction, which means only the Lord can change that designation. Thankfully, He chose to do so by the offering of His Son who shed His blood that what was accursed could be redeemed:

> *For you were bought at a price; therefore glorify God in your body and in your spirit, which are God's* (1 Cor. 6:20).

> *Knowing that you were not redeemed with corruptible things, like silver or gold, from your aimless conduct received by tradition from your fathers, but with the precious blood of Christ, as of a lamb without blemish and without spot* (1 Pet. 1:18-19).

God chose to redeem that which was already His and devoted (i.e., dedicated) for destruction – condemned sinners who trust Christ receive salvation. As the redeemed, we have the stupendous privilege of being dedicated to Him. He owns us and our sole objective in life should be to honor Him in all that we do (1 Cor. 10:31). All that we have and all that we are (spirit, soul, and body) is His and is thus to be dedicated for the cause of Christ. We are not our own. In a positional sense, believers were formerly children of the devil, vessels of wrath fit for destruction; but now, we are redeemed children of God, vessels of mercy committed to bring God glory (Rom. 9:22-23; Eph. 2:1-3, 5:6-8). Hence, it is appropriate for the redeemed to return an ample gesture of thanksgiving and appreciation back to the Lord. This matter is the final topic of this chapter and the book of Leviticus.

The firstfruits of the harvest were to be waved before the Lord as an offering of thankfulness to the One who had granted the increase. Thus, the Lord laid claim to one-tenth of the entire harvest; this would be a provision for sustaining the Levities and their ministry. Likewise, one-tenth of the clean animals in a herd or flock were also His. Every tenth animal that passed under the shepherd's rod (the common method of counting sheep or goats) was the Lord's. A Jew was not to attempt to contrive which ones were dedicated to the Lord; whatever order the animals passed by while being counted determined this. The selected animals would provide the Levites with meat and would also be used in Levitical sacrifices (e.g., two lambs were to be offered each day on the Bronze altar, and even more animals were offered each Sabbath day). Given all the Lord had accomplished for His people, Leviticus 27 is a fitting final chapter to the book – the redeemed are gladly bestowing back to the Lord that which He had graciously provided them.

Conclusion

The last verse of Leviticus informs us that all the contents of the book were commandments Moses had received from the Lord while the nation was camped near Mount Sinai. The Israelites lived undisturbed at this location for about a year. While we have seen the practical and spiritual aspects of all the blood sacrifices, laws of holiness and cleanliness, and purification rituals pertinent to God's covenant people, we have also been amazed to see how these foreshadow and typify the future accomplishments of God in Christ.

God had prescribed a specific way that Israel could approach Him in worship, this being through explicit atoning blood sacrifices as offered by the priests. In the Church Age we also are to be occupied with the way we can approach God in worship, only for us it is through Christ and in the power of the Holy Spirit. Each Christian is a believer-priest and is called on to be a continual living sacrifice. This is accomplished through a variety of ways, such as: offering up praise to God (Heb. 13:15), yielding to God's Word to avoid non-conformity to the world (Rom. 12:1-2), supporting the Lord's work through gifts (1 Cor. 16:2), and by frequently remembering the Lord Jesus by observing the Lord's Supper (1 Cor. 11:22-33).

Application

One of the ways that believers worship the Lord is to reject the world's philosophies and attractions by renewing our minds on what is true and spiritual. Paul writes:

> *I beseech you therefore, brethren, by the mercies of God, that you present your bodies a living sacrifice, holy, acceptable to God, which is your reasonable service. And do not be conformed to this world, but be transformed by the renewing of your mind, that you may prove what is that good and acceptable and perfect will of God* (Rom. 12:1-2).

Scripture speaks of two complementary means that call the believer's heart out of the world. The first is to set one's mind on things above (Col. 3:1-2), and the second is to come to realize that the things of the earth are temporary and shakable. As the writer of Hebrews reminds us, in a coming day, all that is not of the Lord will be removed: *"... removing of those things that are shaken, as of things that are made, that those things which cannot be shaken may remain. Wherefore, we receiving a kingdom which cannot be moved, let us have grace, whereby we may serve God acceptably with reverence and godly fear; for our God is a consuming fire"* (Heb. 12:27-29). The world is nasty and temporal, but heaven is wonderful and eternal. This is why believers should devote not just ourselves to the Lord, but all our resources also. All that is not dedicated to Him will ultimately burn up, without securing for us any eternal benefit.

This miserable reality is what prompted the Lord's rebuke of the Church at Laodicea: *"You are wretched, miserable, poor, blind, and naked – I counsel you to buy from Me gold refined in the fire, that you may be rich; and white garments, that you may be clothed, that the shame of your nakedness may not be revealed; and anoint your eyes with eye salve, that you may see"* (Rev. 3:17-18). Those in the Church at

Laodicea were not living for Christ; consequently, God's righteousness was not displayed in their lives. Thus, from the Lord's perspective, they were naked! While it is true that all the redeemed in heaven will be wearing white robes and have human form (Rev. 4:4, 19:14), some will be shining brighter than others in their spiritual appearance.

In heaven, the bride of Christ must have righteous attire; she is *"arrayed in fine linen, clean and bright, for the fine linen is the righteous acts of the saints"* (Rev. 19:8). While all believers in the Church have been positionally declared righteous in Christ, each believer has the opportunity to labor in righteousness for Christ. Those things which are done in accordance with revealed truth and in the power of the Holy Spirit have eternal value; these righteous acts are what the believer is adorned with throughout eternity.

Paul explains in 1 Corinthians 15:40-42 that, after the resurrection, some saints will shine forth the glory of God more brightly than others, just as some stars in the nighttime sky are brighter than other stars. This acquired glory directly reflects the righteous acts (good works) that are done for Christ by His strength in this present life (Rev. 19:8). Eternal glory, evidently, has a weight to it; in other words, its quality is measurable (2 Cor. 4:17) and can be earned by believers through selfless service for Christ now. Thus, to be appropriately dressed for eternity, believers should secure for themselves a covering of eternal glory, which consists of righteous acts. Such personal acts of righteousness on earth provide believers with varying reflections of God's glory in heaven (Rev. 3:18; 1 Cor. 15:41-42; 2 Cor. 4:17). Without being justified in Christ, no one can enter into heaven, and only by doing righteous acts for Him and by His power do believers contribute to their eternal attire of glory. This means that believers will be reflecting the glory of God throughout eternity in varying degrees of brilliance.

What is delightful and precious about heaven is everyone will shine forth the glory of God and desire to worship and to honor Him in everything they do. The same motivation pervades the entire framework of Leviticus, which was committed to the priests in order to enable and inspire the Jews to worship and honor God in all aspects of their lives. God extended them a great privilege by abiding with them and permitting them to come near to Him to worship. But flesh is flesh, and their failures would be ours as well if we lived under the same economy of truth.

Today, the Church has much more than a rigid manual focusing on physical offerings and purification ceremonies – we have received the substance of what these only foretold. As believer-priests we have the revealed counsel of God that we may know His will for our daily lives, we have the indwelling Spirit of God to enlighten our understanding of revealed truth and to empower us to live it, and a resurrected Savior who has proven His love for us and who continually intercedes on our behalf. With careless ease we might peer down our long religious noses and criticize the Jews for their repeated spiritual fiascoes, but then again, what excuses do we have, who have experienced much more in Christ than they ever did? So, the observance of the stringent accountability the Levitical Law held over the Jews should prompt our exceptional care as to not disappoint the Lord. Our God is a consuming fire and all that is not for Him will be consumed at His presence – what excuses will we have then?

Mediation

When I survey the wondrous cross
On which the Prince of glory died,
My richest gain I count but loss,
And pour contempt on all my pride.

Forbid it, Lord, that I should boast,
Save in the death of Christ my God!
All the vain things that charm me most,
I sacrifice them to His blood.

See from His head, His hands, His feet,
Sorrow and love flow mingled down!
Did ever such love and sorrow meet,
Or thorns compose so rich a crown?

Were the whole realm of nature mine,
That were a present far too small;
Love so amazing, so divine,
Demands my soul, my life, my all.

— Isaac Watts

Endnotes

Understanding the Levitical Types
1. F. Duane Lindsey & Dallas Theological Seminary, *The Bible Knowledge Commentary: An Exposition of the Scriptures* (Victor Books, Wheaton, IL; 1983-1985), p. 172
2. Ibid., p. 172
3. F. W. Grant, *Genesis – In the Light, The Serious Christian Series* (Loizeaux Brothers, Inc., Neptune, NJ), pp. 6-7
4. Andrew Jukes, *Four Views of Christ* (Kregel Publications, Grand Rapids, MI; 1966), p. 15

Overview of the Levitical Offerings
1. C. H. Mackintosh, *Genesis to Deuteronomy* (Loizeaux Brothers, Inc., Neptune, NJ; 1972), pp. 236-237
2. C. H. Mackintosh, op. cit. p. 275
3. F. B. Hole, http://stempublishing.com/authors/hole/Pent/LEVITICUS.html

The Burnt Offering
1. Harry Ironside, http://www.moodymedia.org/articles/psalm-burnt-offering/
2. C. I. Scofield, *The New Scofield Study Bible* (KJV) (Oxford University Press, NY; 1967), p. 127
3. Arthur W. Pink, *Gleanings in Exodus* (Moody Press, Chicago, IL; no date), p. 280
4. F. C. Cook, *Barnes Notes: The Bible Commentary – Exodus to Ruth* (Baker Book House, Grand Rapids, MI; reprinted from 1879 edition), p. 109
5. C. H. Mackintosh, op. cit., p. 288

The Meal Offering
1. Ibid., pp. 301-302
2. L. M. Grant, http://stempublishing.com/authors/grantlm/LEVITICU.html
3. Ibid.
4. John Darby, *Synopsis of the Books of the Bible Vol. 1* (Stow Hill Bible and Tract Depot, Kingston, ON: 1948), p. 121
5 Edward Dennett; http://stempublishing.com/authors/dennett/EXODUS1.html
6. Henry M. Morris, *The Genesis Record* (Baker Book House, Grand Rapids: 1976), p. 347

Be Holy and Come Near

The Peace Offering
1. William Kelly, Lev. 3, http://stempublishing.com/authors/kelly/1Oldtest/leviticu.html
2. F. C. Cook, op. cit., p. 125
3. J. N. Darby, op. cit., p. 135
4. L. M. Grant, op. cit., chp. 3

The Sin Offering
1. William MacDonald, *Believer's Bible Commentary* (Thomas Nelson Publishers, Nashville: 1989); C. H. Mackintosh, *Genesis to Deuteronomy* (Loizeaux Brothers, Inc., Neptune, NJ; 1972), p. 140
2. J. N. Darby, op. cit., p. 145
3. L. M. Grant, op. cit., chp. 5
4. J. N. Darby, op. cit., p. 138

The Trespass Offering
1. William Kelly, op. cit., Lev. 5
2. Matthew Henry, *Matthew Henry's Commentary on the Whole Bible: New Modern Edition* (Electronic Database by Hendrickson Publishers Inc.; 1991) Lev. 5
3. C. H. Mackintosh, op. cit., p. 329
4. Ibid., p. 335

Consecration and Service
1. L. M. Grant, op. cit., chp. 8

Strange Fire
1. C. H. Mackintosh, op. cit., p. 343
2. F. B. Hole, http://stempublishing.com/authors/hole/Pent/LEVITICUS.html
3. F. Duane Lindsey, op. cit., pp. 189-190
4. F. B. Hole, op. cit., chp. 10

Clean and Unclean Food
1. F. Duane Lindsey, op. cit., p. 190

The Law of Motherhood
1. S.I. McMillen, M.D., *None of These Diseases* (Fleming H Revell Co., Grand Rapids, MI; 1984), p. 93
2. Edythe Draper, *Draper's Book of Quotations for the Christian World* (Tyndale House Publishers, Inc. Wheaton, Il.)
3. Ibid.

Endnotes

Inspection and Diagnosis of Leprosy
1. Kenneth J. Ryan, C. George Ray, *Sherris Medical Microbiology,* 4th ed. (McGraw Hill; 2004), pp. 451–453
2. F. B. Hole, op. cit., chp. 13
3. C. H. Mackintosh, op. cit., p. 361
4. William Kelly, op. cit., Lev. 12

The Cleansing of a Leper
1. William Kelly, op. cit., Lev. 14

A Needy People
1. F. B. Hole, http://stempublishing.com/authors/hole/Pent/LEVITICUS.html
2. F. Duane Lindsey, op. cit., pp. 194-195
3. William Newell, *Hebrews Verse by Verse* (Moody Press, Chicago, IL; 1947), p. 148
4. F. W. Bruce, *The Serious Christian, Notes on Hebrews* (Books for Christians, Charlotte, NC; no date), p. 26

The Day of Atonement
1. Alfred Edersheim, *The Temple - Its Ministry and Services As They Were at the Time of Jesus Christ* (Hendrickson Pub.; 1995: Originally published in 1874), chp. 16
2. Ibid.
3. C. H. Mackintosh, op. cit., p. 381
4. Alfred Edersheim, op. cit.

The Place of Worship
1. C. H. Mackintosh, op. cit., p. 388
2. http://www.tentmaker.org/Quotes/atheismquotes.html

The Life of the Flesh
1. C. H. Mackintosh, op. cit., p. 389

I Am the Lord Your God
1. F. B. Hole, op. cit., chp. 18
2. F. Duane Lindsey, op. cit., p. 200
3. http://www.betterhealth.vic.gov.au/bhcv2/bhcarticles.nsf/pages/Genes_and_genetics?open
4. http://www.cousincouples.com/?page=facts
5. William MacDonald, op. cit., p. 155

Be Holy
1. F. Duane Lindsey, op. cit., p. 201

Condemned Behavior
1. C. H. Mackintosh, op. cit., pp. 390-291
2. Charles Spurgeon, *Spurgeon's Morning and Evening Devotions* (Electronic Edition STEP Files, Parsons Technology, Inc; 1999), Feb. 8 – Morning

Priestly Regulations
1. L. M. Grant, op. cit., chp. 22
2. C. H. Mackintosh, op. cit., p. 395

The Spring Feasts of Jehovah
1. F. Duane Lindsey, op. cit., p. 207
2. L. M. Grant, op. cit., chp. 23
3. C. H. Mackintosh, op. cit., p. 403

The Fall Feasts of Jehovah
1. William Kelly, op. cit., Lev. 23

The Oil and the Bread
1. George Rodgers, *The Gospel According to Moses: The Tabernacle and Its Services* (Morgan and Scott, London, England; 1880), p. 67

Blasphemy
1. Warren Wiersbe, *Be Holy: An Old Testament Study—Leviticus* (Victor Books, Wheaton, IL; 1994 – electronic copy)
2. Charles Hodge, *Systematic Theology* (Logos Research Systems, Inc., Oak Harbor, WA; 1997 – electronic copy)
3. William MacDonald, op. cit., p. 2080

The Law of the Land
1. F. Duane Lindsey, op. cit., p. 210

Blessing or Chastening
1. Arthur W. Pink, *Gleanings in Exodus* (Moody Press, Chicago, IL; no date), p. 122

Dedicated to the Lord
1. F. Duane Lindsey, op. cit., pp. 213-214

HALLOWED BE THY NAME

Revering CHRIST in a casual World

Is scriptural terminology important? Does wrong terminology tend to lead to erroneous Church practices? Do I ignorantly show disdain for the Lord's name by the way in which I address Him or speak of Him to others? What is the sin of blasphemy? Can a Christian blaspheme God today? These are some of the questions *Hallowed Be Thy Name* examines in detail. Our speech and behaviour reflect our heart's adoration for the Lord Jesus and, thus, directly affect our testimony of Him to the world. May God bestow us grace to *"buy the truth, and sell it not"* (Prov. 23:23), and may each one be subject to the *"good, and acceptable, and perfect, will of God"* (Rom. 12:2).

Binding: Paper
Size: 5.5" X 8.5"
Page Count: 160 pages
Item #: B-7450
ISBN : 1-897117-45-0
Genre: Christian Living

Warren Henderson

An aerospace engineer, who now serves the Lord with his wife Brenda in "full time" ministry. They are commended by Believers Bible Chapel in Rockford, Illinois. Warren is an itinerant Bible teacher and is involved in writing, evangelism, and church planting.

 GOSPEL FOLIO PRESS
I WILL PUBLISH THE NAME OF THE LORD

304 Killaly St. West | Port Colborne | ON | L3K 6A6 | Canada | 1 800 952 2382 | E-mail: info@gospelfolio.com | www.gospelfolio.com

BEHOLD THE SAVIOUR

CONTEMPLATING THE VAST WORTH OF THE SAVIOUR

It was refreshing and encouraging to read a book, that did not focus on man's needs or a "how to" method for success. *Behold the Saviour* focuses on the Lord Jesus: His Godhood, human goodness and glories as revealed in the multi-faceted presentation of Holy Scriptures. For when we behold Him in His glory we are *"changed into the same image from glory to glory, even as by the Spirit of the Lord"* (2 Cor. 3:18).
—Anonymous Pre-Publication Reviewer
(to Christ be the glory!)

Charles Haddon Spurgeon once said, "The more you know about Christ, the less you will be satisfied with superficial views of Him." The more we know of Christ, the more we will love and experience Him. This study has refreshed my soul. In the long hours of contemplating the vast worth that the Father attaches to every aspect of the Saviour's life, I have been encouraged to love Him more. If you're feeling a bit dry or spiritually despondent, *Behold the Saviour* afresh – and may the Holy Spirit ignite your passion for Christ and invigorate your ministry for Him. —Warren Henderson

Binding: Paper
Size: 5.5" X 8.5"
Page Count: 208 pages
Item #: B-7272
ISBN : 1-897117-27-2
Genre: Devotional

Warren Henderson
An aerospace engineer, who now serves the Lord with his wife Brenda in "full time" ministry. They are commended by Believers Bible Chapel in Rockford, Illinois. Warren is an itinerant Bible teacher and is involved in writing, evangelism, and church planting.

GOSPEL FOLIO PRESS
I WILL PUBLISH THE NAME OF THE LORD

304 Killaly St. West | Port Colborne | ON | L3K 6A6 | Canada | 1 800 952 2382 | E-mail: info@gospelfolio.com | www.gospelfolio.com

Overcoming Your Bully

Warren Henderson

"The flesh" describes the natural man. God has no program to change the flesh. Rather He brings in something new: *"and that which is born of the Spirit is spirit"* (John 3:6). A new struggle is brought to our attention. It is no longer the new nature or the believer striving for mastery over sin in the body; it is the Holy Spirit striving against the old nature. The little boy coming home from school was beaten up by a big bully. He was on the bottom, and the big bully was pounding him very heavily. Then he looked up from his defeated position on the bottom, and saw his big brother coming. The big brother took care of the bully while the little fellow crawled up on a stump and rubbed his bruises. The believer has the Holy Spirit to deal with the flesh, that big bully. I learned along time ago that I can't overcome it. So I have to turn it over to Somebody who can. The Holy Spirit indwells believers. He wants to do that for us, and He can!
—from the Preface by James Vernon McGee

A timely book, in a day when many believer's lives, marriages and ministries are being destroyed by being too easy on the flesh. Here is a call to give no quarter to the flesh but to be like Phinehas of old, and Ram the javelin home! Read it, meditate on it, and most of all apply it! —Mike Attwood

ISBN: 9781926765358 ✦ US: $11.99 ✦ CDN: $12.99 ✦ Pages: 136

Hiding God

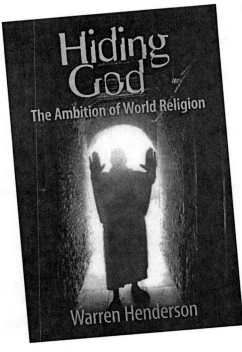

The Ambition of World Religion

World religion is an exhaustive system of doings apart from God's truth and enablement. Ask yourself...
* How does world religion obscure divine truth and prevent man from knowing God?
* What general trends are consistently found in humanized religion?
* What advantage does biblical Christianity have over the religions of the world?
* Why should I trust Jesus Christ alone to secure eternal life? Examine the evidence and determine for yourself if biblical Christianity is a logical choice.

PB | X-8711 | Retail $9.99
(Shipping & Handling Extra)

Warren Henderson was an aerospace engineer, he now serves the Lord with his wife Brenda in "full time" ministry. They are commended by Believers Bible Chapel in Rockford, Illinois. Warren is an itinerant Bible teacher and is involved in writing, evangelism, and church planting. He is the author of *Be Angry and Sin Not, Behold The Saviour, The Fruitful Vine, The Olive Plants, Glories Seen and Unseen, Hallowed Be Thy Name, Mind Frames, Seeds of Destiny,* and *Your Home: A Birthing Place of Heaven.*

GOSPEL FOLIO PRESS

To Order: Call 1-800-952-2382 | Email: orders@gospelfolio.com | www.gospelfolio.com

CPSIA information can be obtained
at www.ICGtesting.com
Printed in the USA
FFOW02n1041020215
10740FF